Pı
THE POF

"In a turbulent world, this is a guide to leading a balanced life. Drawing on her background as a serial entrepreneur, Christina offers actionable advice to help you anticipate—and navigate—disruption."
—**Adam Grant, #1** *New York Times* **bestselling author of** *Think Again* **and host of the TED podcast** *Re:Thinking*

"*The Portfolio Life* is the rare book that gives you both theory and practice. I hope you have the courage to read and apply Christina's timely advice!"
—**Chris Guillebeau, author of** *The $100 Startup* **and** *The Money Tree*

"Masterful. *The Portfolio Life* challenges the traditional notion that work and life must be kept separate and provides a new model for leading a fulfilling life."
—**Greg McKeown, CEO of McKeown Inc. and** *New York Times* **bestselling author of** *Essentialism* **and** *Effortless*

"*The Portfolio Life* is a manual for pursuing a prismatic, polyvalent life. Christina Wallace masterfully illustrates that you don't have to abandon your creative pursuits to advance professionally, and planning for one's financial future shouldn't be reduced to just drinking fewer lattes or whatever. *The Portfolio Life* is an urgent, insurgent guide that empowers readers to live their lives—and manifest their careers—on their own extraordinary terms." —**Sydney Skybetter, Dean at Brown University**

"Your life is your enterprise. In *The Portfolio Life*, Christina Wallace masterfully shows you how to treat it as such, pursuing your personal and professional dreams to find happiness and success."
—**Arthur C. Brooks, Professor, Harvard Kennedy School and Harvard Business School, and #1** *New York Times* **bestselling author**

"Christina Wallace—and this book—are gifts to Gen Z. In a world that's never changed faster, but will never change this slowly again, Christina has written an essential playbook for how emerging adults can build big, brave, and beautiful lives. She's the human Venn diagram she writes about, living and working at the intersection of head, heart, and humor. And while her own story is outrageously inspiring, she writes with humanity and humility that make her delightfully relatable. This book is the antidote to hustle culture, and a compelling case that durable success comes not from working harder and faster, but better and smarter. If you are ready to get in the driver's seat of your career—and life—but not sure how to start, this book is your roadmap!"

—Abby Falik, Founder and CEO of
Global Citizen Year

"*The Portfolio Life* is the book I wish I had twenty years ago, when I was just starting out and thought I had to hide the creative parts of myself to be taken seriously in tech and business. Christina Wallace makes the brilliant case in this book that embracing your various skills, interests, and communities will actually de-risk your career, make you stand out from the pack, and offer you a life as unique as you are."

—Randi Zuckerberg, tech entrepreneur, author,
and Tony Award-winning Broadway producer

"Whether you are just starting out in your career or you are considering a new chapter, put aside a day and read *The Portfolio Life*. Christina Wallace wrote a playbook that is equal parts inspirational and tactical, offering the mindsets and tools to craft a life that is gratifying, flexible, and sustainable."

—Kathryn Minshew, Founder and CEO of The Muse,
author of *The New Rules of Work*

"An indispensable companion for anyone eager to shape their life based on who they are rather than some predefined linear path."

—Hubert Joly, author of *The Heart of Business*,
former Best Buy CEO

THE
PORTFOLIO
LIFE

THE PORTFOLIO LIFE

HOW TO FUTURE-PROOF YOUR CAREER, AVOID BURNOUT, AND BUILD A LIFE BIGGER THAN YOUR BUSINESS CARD

Christina Wallace

balance

NEW YORK BOSTON

Copyright © 2023 by Christina Wallace

Cover design by Kishan Rajani. Cover infographic by Giovanna Castro.
Cover copyright © 2024 by Hachette Book Group, Inc.

Balance
Hachette Book Group
1290 Avenue of the Americas
New York, NY 10104
GCP-Balance.com
@GCPBalance

Originally published in hardcover and ebook by Grand Central Publishing in April 2023
First Trade Paperback Edition: April 2024

Balance is an imprint of Grand Central Publishing. The Balance name and logo are registered trademarks of Hachette Book Group, Inc.

The publisher is not responsible for websites (or their content) that are not owned by the publisher.

The Hachette Speakers Bureau provides a wide range of authors for speaking events. To find out more, go to hachettespeakersbureau.com or email HachetteSpeakers@hbgusa.com.

Balance books may be purchased in bulk for business, educational, or promotional use. For information, please contact your local bookseller or the Hachette Book Group Special Markets Department at special.markets@hbgusa.com.

Illustrations by Giovanna Castro

Image on page 22 used with permission of WaitButWhy

Library of Congress Cataloging-in-Publication Data
Names: Wallace, Christina, author.
Title: The portfolio life : how to future-proof your career, avoid burnout, and build a life bigger than your business card / Christina Wallace.
Description: First edition. | New York : Balance, 2023.
Identifiers: LCCN 2022053136 | ISBN 9781538710470 (hardcover) |
ISBN 9781538710494 (ebook)
Subjects: LCSH: Work-life balance. | Industries—Social aspects. |
Social responsibility of business.
Classification: LCC HD4904.6 .W35 2023 | DDC 306.3/6—dc23/eng/20221109
LC record available at https://lccn.loc.gov/2022053136

ISBNs: 9781538710487 (trade paperback), 9781538710494 (ebook)

Printed in the United States of America

LSC-C

Printing 3, 2024

For Arden and Sebastian

All the world's a stage,
And all the men and women merely players;
They have their exits and their entrances,
And one man in his time plays many parts.

—William Shakespeare,
As You Like It (Act II, Scene 7)

Contents

Introduction: Life, Disrupted   xv

PART I: WHY

Chapter 1: The New Normal   3

Chapter 2: The Four Pillars of a Portfolio Life   15

Chapter 3: A Caveat: Failure   40

PART II: WHAT

Chapter 4: What's in Your Venn Diagram?   59

Chapter 5: Design the Business Model for Your Life   75

Chapter 6: Craft Your Portfolio   92

PART III: HOW

Chapter 7: Define Your Personal Balanced Scorecard   111

Chapter 8: Build Your Team   125

Chapter 9: Tell Your Story   143

Chapter 10: Manage Your Time   161

Chapter 11: Crunch the Numbers   186

Chapter 12: Forecast the Future   208

Conclusion: Build a Life Worthy of You   221

Acknowledgments   225

Notes   227

About the Author   235

Life, Disrupted

My grandfather built cars on the assembly line for General Motors for over forty years. He spent a couple of years in the army during WWII plus one year of college when he got home and landed a union job welding chassis, which allowed him to send all three of his kids to college while my grandmother worked as a homemaker. His pension made retirement possible and almost comfortable. My mom earned her degree in secretarial studies and has been a full-time, salaried-with-benefits administrative assistant for nearly four decades. As a single mother, she couldn't pay for college for my sister and me, but she earned enough to make our life work with a little assistance from her parents.

Today, neither of those jobs exist at a pay scale that would support a family. The stability and security of long-term employment at livable wages that my parents' and grandparents' generations enjoyed is long gone. Instead I am of the generation that has been preached at about the value of hard work and frugality, as though our occasional Sunday brunch of avocado toast is the reason we don't have a down payment for a house, rather than a combination of astronomical student loan debt, restrictive housing policies that limit supply in many of the biggest employment markets, and the aforementioned disappearance of well-paid, salaried jobs for all but the most elite white-collar professions.[1]

You've all seen the headlines. "Why Millennials Are Facing the Scariest Financial Future of Any Generation Since the Great Depression," the Huffington Post cried out.[2] "My rent consumes nearly half my income, I haven't had a steady job since Pluto was a planet and my savings are dwindling faster than the ice caps the baby boomers melted," Michael Hobbes wrote, three years before a global pandemic set in. He goes on to note: millennials have taken on 300% more student debt than their parents,[3] are half as likely to own a home as young adults were in 1975,[4] and based on current trends, many of us won't be able to retire until we're seventy-five.[5]

Meanwhile, over at Medium, Clio Chang declared us the "Generation Shaped by Layoffs."[6] Chang profiled the layoff-riddled career path of San Francisco–based aspiring teacher Jayme Brown, who offered a sobering perspective: "My relationship with my work is one of mistrust," she said. With five different jobs in less than seven years across tech startups and the nonprofit museum sector, Brown still hadn't come any closer to the work she had wanted to do as a teacher. "I have very little trust for the system and for people running systems."

And at BuzzFeed, Anne Helen Petersen had an equally dire assessment of the situation, granting millennials the title of the "Burnout Generation."[7] "Burnout and the behaviors and weight that accompany it aren't, in fact, something we can cure by going on vacation. It's not limited to workers in acutely high-stress environments. And it's not a temporary affliction: It's the millennial condition. It's our base temperature. It's our background music. It's the way things are. It's our lives," she wrote.

Despite being better educated than our parents, millennials are the first generation in American history to be worse off economically.[8] Why? Because earnings have stagnated, industries have cratered, the cost of housing, health care, and education have ballooned, and "innovations" in capitalism like moving employees off the balance sheet and turning them into permalancers, gig workers, or contract hires without benefits or future prospects rippled beyond Jack Welch's much-lauded tenure at GE to become the norm for many of the biggest companies looking to boost their quarterly reports to Wall Street.[9]

But that's not the only bad news here. Unfortunately, there's a second trend we have to consider: Change is the new normal. The pace of innovation continues to accelerate, triggering changes both large and small, from the way we stay in touch with friends and family to the way new business models and technological capabilities shake and transform entire industries. Then there are disasters billed as "once-in-a-lifetime" that have somehow already made three appearances in my adult life (and probably yours too): 9/11 (my third week of college), the 2008 financial crisis (my third week of business school), and the COVID-19 global pandemic (just a few months after I became a mother). Add in the ongoing threat of global climate change and you have a recipe for a world that experiences a tectonic shift every decade or so with the aftershocks driving a state of nearly continuous disruption that touches every part of our lives.

So what's a person to do? A pint of Ben & Jerry's and a few affirmations aren't going to solve this. And if we're waiting for political or business leaders to save us, we're going to be waiting a very long time. Instead, we need a new playbook to build a life that can withstand disruption and volatility, while providing for our needs and fueling the pursuit of our personal and professional dreams. It's a tall order, but it's not impossible. In fact, that playbook already exists in other contexts. It just requires a bit of creativity to adapt it for our purposes. Enter: The Portfolio Life.

I stumbled upon the idea for a Portfolio Life early on in my career, though I didn't have the language for it until much later. At seventeen, I was a scholarship kid at an expensive college, where I took out loans and worked three jobs to cover my family's financial contribution. While my interests were so varied that I wouldn't have wanted to focus on just one thing, my economic situation made it clear that I couldn't: I needed to put all of my skills to work if I was going to make it through school with decent job prospects on the other side. And given how hard I was working, I wanted to get my money's worth. Since tuition was a flat rate whether I took 12 or 23 credits each semester, I graduated four years later with two majors, three minors, and more than 50 credits beyond what was required. Without a network or financial safety net from my family, I knew I had to be scrappy and create my own.

When I graduated, I opted to start my career in the nonprofit arts world, first as a regional theater director, then as an arts administrator for a national opera company. But as much as I loved the work, I soon discovered that these were not jobs that would cover my expenses. In a recent shift to run nonprofits more like businesses, philanthropists have begun to measure how much of an organization's funding goes directly to their mission, which means the overhead needed to actually run things is usually underfunded. Instead, nonprofit employees are expected to take note of the warm, fuzzy feelings they get from doing work they care about, even though feelings cannot pay rent or be invested in a retirement fund. So I dug deep into my skill sets yet again to surface opportunities to supplement and diversify my income, lining up work as a set carpenter, taking on clients for standardized test tutoring, teaching piano lessons, and freelancing in content marketing. But when it finally became clear that working-class kids without other sources of support were unlikely to last very long in the arts, I decided to pivot to the business world and got my MBA before jumping into entrepreneurship and technology.

Like the arts, tech startups are a place where uncertainty, creativity, and opportunity go hand in hand. Building something from nothing can be terrifying, but it also can give you the space to think beyond the status quo and imagine something bigger, something better. Also like the arts, startups require you to wear many hats, making use of every skill, connection, and toolkit you can find because there is no surplus of resources.

The similarities between these seemingly disparate worlds—performing arts and tech startups—didn't really surprise me. After all, I'd been a math and computer science geek as long as I had been a musician and theater nerd. And when I met a fellow math and theater multi-hyphenate through a mutual friend, I knew there had to be more than two of us. So we set out to discover and connect with our fellow multidisciplinary weirdos because we had a hunch that, collectively, they might hold the key to building a life of joy, growth, and fulfillment amid the seas of constant change.

My partner in podcasting was Cate Scott Campbell, an actor, director, and writer based in Los Angeles who also tutors math, consults on branding, and has the most impressive collection of wigs you've seen this side of *RuPaul's Drag Race*. In early 2016, we teamed up with Forbes to create *The Limit Does Not Exist* to interview multihyphenates who were crafting custom lives by coloring outside the lines. We wanted to find the common threads, the hacks, and the best practices of people building the vivid, multidimensional lives they dreamed of rather than the linear ones they had permission to build.

In episode after episode, we heard the same story: These folks crafted a collection of activities to satisfy their multifaceted identities, afford them financial stability, help them withstand unexpected disruptions, and offer more flexibility than a linear life could. In the middle of one early interview, a lightbulb switched on. We were talking with tech executive, angel investor, and Tony Award–winning Broadway producer Randi Zuckerberg when I noticed the similarities between investing in startups and investing in commercial theater productions. They both relied on portfolio strategy, which in a sense, was what all of our guests were using as they pieced together their lives.

I suddenly recalled a conversation I had had with an MBA classmate in 2010. "I don't want a linear career," I told Julie as we walked over the Charles River footbridge a few days before graduation. "I don't even want a portfolio career. I want a *portfolio life*." My MBA finance classes had taught me equations to calculate the risk, reward, diversification, and volatility of a portfolio of financial assets. Surely those same ideas could be applied to our lives. Yes, this includes paid work, but it also includes hobbies, family, community, personal development, health, and relationships.

After more than a decade of speaking, writing, coaching, and noodling on this idea, I finally sat down and put pen to paper. Drawing on academic research, case studies of individuals already building portfolios, and my experiences, I wrote this book to help you get your own game plan in order. This isn't just about education or inspiration; this is about action. By the end of this book—if you put in the work—you'll have a concrete sense of who you are, where you are now, where you want to be, and how to connect the dots to live a life you only dreamed was possible.

I also intend for you to share it far and wide. Maybe you'll use it to explain to your parents why your diverse interests are your superpower, not a sign of flakiness. Or you can show it to your boss to help them understand the value of your life outside of work. Perhaps you'll return to it from time to time for reassurance as you fight against the indignities of late-stage capitalism to sculpt a life that combines work, relationships, personal interests, and rest in equal measure.

This book is written in three parts. Part I focuses on understanding how we got here (spoiler alert: this is about both systemic failures of leadership and unsustainable greed) and how we can fight back using a portfolio to cultivate identity, optionality, diversification, and flexibility in our lives. In Part II we get to roll up our sleeves: It's an opportunity to uncover the full breadth of your identity, define the business model that fits you best, and sketch out a strategy to meet your needs while pursuing your wildest wishes. And, finally, Part III gets into the nitty-gritty of it all, with the tools and tactics to operationalize that strategy. We'll look at your portfolio through the eyes of a chief executive officer, chief marketing officer, chief operations officer, chief financial officer, and chief strategy officer to see what mindsets and resources each of those leaders would bring to the table as you build your team, tell your story, make use of your time, manage your money, and keep one eye on the future.

After a decade as a serial entrepreneur, I recently returned to Harvard Business School, my alma mater, as a senior lecturer of entrepreneurship and marketing. While I still love the thrill of building new companies, I needed to "rebalance" my own portfolio to have more flexibility for my young family. My ambitions have not changed, but my needs have, and I wanted to adjust my responsibilities and the investment of my time and talents accordingly. This is the power of a portfolio: It is as dynamic as you are, ensuring you have what you need for each season of life without taking your eyes off your goals. Because the point of all of this is to design a life that serves you, not the other way around. Disruption may have gotten us here, but we get to decide how to go forward. A Portfolio Life puts you back in the driver's seat. So, let's get going.

PART I

WHY

CHAPTER 1

The New Normal

How did you get to be here? / What was the moment?
—Stephen Sondheim, *Merrily We Roll Along*

I've often described myself as fluent in three languages: English, math, and music. I started all three around the same age, and I can't really remember my life without any one of them. In high school, I attended a school for the performing arts, where in addition to studying piano and cello, I learned calculus and physics through the lens of the arts. I understood torque through arabesques, studied sound waves by building an African finger piano, and first experienced permutation groups through chord inversions in figured bass. Despite the obvious-to-me interdisciplinary connections, the pressure to focus was always there: "What are you going to do when you grow up?" my teachers would ask. "Which will you choose?"

I chose not to choose.

In college, I double-majored in math and theater with minors in music, physics, and political science. I used trigonometry to build scenery; learned entrepreneurship by producing plays; and split my days between cryptography, stage combat, chamber music, and colloidal particles: researching, telling stories, and creating something from nothing. And then, as graduation came nearer, the questions came back once again: "What kind of career are you going to build with all of those interests? Isn't it time to get serious and focus?"

But why did I have to focus? Leonardo da Vinci never had to focus.

In the fifteenth century, the ideal of the polymath Renaissance man came into being, defined as one with "unquenchable curiosity."[1] No one embodied this ideal better than da Vinci; he was an artist who was also an inventor, botanist, architect, poet, mathematician, cartographer, and a whole bunch of other things. This polymath ideal grew out of the notion of universal education, which, sadly, did not mean education for all, but rather education across a broad array of subjects, including science, philosophy, languages, and theology, rather than specializing in just one area. It's the basis of what we call a liberal arts education today.

So how did we get from there—the ideal of the well-rounded, interdisciplinary, universal education that supports the development of polymaths—to here, a world in which teenagers are pressured to choose a specialty and decide what path they will follow for the next sixty years?

Well, for one thing, the Industrial Revolution happened.

A BRIEF HISTORY OF CAPITALISM

A quick aside: If you don't want to dwell on how this all came about and would rather get straight to some solutions, I give you permission to skip this section. I get it. Some of us have been knee-deep in this for so long we don't need more evidence. We need a plan. If that's you, jump ahead to the section called "Writing a New Playbook" on page 10 and pick up reading from there. I won't take it personally. I want to talk about this, though, because I think it's important for folks to understand that this is a *systemic* problem, not your personal failure to figure it all out. (Translation: Feel free to share this chapter with your parents.)

Okay, here's the short(ish) version of how we got here: Just before the Industrial Revolution, most Western people who were not enslaved lived and worked in a world that valued diversity of expertise. Education across multiple subjects was still something that only wealthy people could access, but the working class did master multiple skill sets. They transformed their talents into marketable skills and swapped goods and services with people who possessed the expertise that they lacked. Those who could handcraft leather shoes or turn raw clay into kitchen wares, for example, were valued for their abilities and became indispensable members of local communities, and in the years before the cotton gin, artisans with specialized skills produced the majority of Europe's manufactured goods.[2]

But no one lived off a single talent or task. Most families grew their own food, tended their land, and divided all of the labor required to keep the homestead running. An artisan who wove textiles for cash might also be an expert at repairing leaky roofs, keeping pests off crops, or helping livestock give birth. Even shopkeepers and craftspeople typically had to juggle multiple chores and household duties when they were home with their families. It was a hybrid artisan-agrarian economy that forced people to master multiple disciplines to meet their basic needs.

Then in the mid-1700s—when labor began to move from family farms and close-knit villages to factories and sprawling cities—our understanding of work and specialization began to transform. Assembly lines, mechanized operations, and mass production led to division of labor and forced specialization. Factory owners and supervisors divided their workers into groups, and assigned each group a task. Strong workers transported raw materials to and from the site, mechanically inclined workers fixed broken machinery, and dexterous workers tended the line. A single skill became the nexus of an individual's working life,[3] and since that work was rewarded with cash wages, any essential needs that fell outside of that nexus were purchased. Urban life supported this by transplanting goods and services once handled at home to shops; instead of growing their own vegetables or making their own soap, people grew dependent on wages to buy what they could not produce.[4]

Divided labor was efficient, factory-made goods were cheap, and cities were booming. Polymaths and masters of multiple trades began receding from the spotlight. And then professional management became a thing, which accelerated the shift even further.

The first factories in Europe and the United States were controlled by the families who built them. Factory owners and supervisors were inevitably related to each other, usually father to son. Back then, single families often dominated entire industries: the Rockefellers ran oil, the Carnegies ran steel, the Morgans ran the banks. People working the factory floors were hired off the streets, but for nearly a century all industrial leadership was kept in the family.

When the 1930s rolled around, however, economists began to make noise about all that nepotism. They believed that separating the oversight of an organization from its ownership helped create stability. They argued that it was better to entrust some of that high-level decision-making to dispassionate professionals, trained to manage both people and systems.[5] So a new type of professional leader was created, paving the way for even more specialization within the ranks of business leadership.

The role of the manager was to make decisions about how work was to be done, and the role of the employee was to execute the work. This power dynamic eclipsed the previous working culture of artisans and experts, casting employees as minor participants in a large-scale labor process. Cogs in a machine, as the saying goes.* Narrowly focused jobs became the norm, both within factories and in newly minted office settings where clerical and communications work took place.[6] The service sector emerged in the late 1950s, encompassing jobs ranging from restaurant waitstaff to janitors and truck drivers,[7] further encouraging specialization.

By the middle of the century, there were hundreds of types of jobs available, and very few of them required deep knowledge of more than one subject or skill. The economy flourished and the middle class was born. What was the secret sauce for making the whole system work? Companies actually took care of their employees.

I know, it's a strange concept. But during this "golden age" of American capitalism, many corporations were raking in profits so robust that they never had to choose who to please; there was enough to go around, so both shareholders and employees were handsomely paid.[8] In return, workers were loyal to the companies who hired them, acknowledging that

---

* The vast power differential between management and employees gave rise to the labor movement, as a way of collectively fighting back against long hours, horrific working conditions, and unlivable wages. It is no surprise, then, that union membership, after declining in the back half of the twentieth century, is once again growing in the twenty-first.

sustained care at that level merited fidelity. This was the near-mythical era when people dedicated their entire careers to a single organization, received holiday bonuses every year, and were gifted gold watches upon retirement.[9] It was a brief, shining moment in economic history, and one that influenced ideas of "success" for millions of people. Possibly including your grandparents and maybe even your parents. If they came of age during that "shining moment," they may be mentally stuck in that narrative of success, back when white men could come home from war, afford a college education, and be guaranteed a great job, steady promotions, and a pension at retirement.* But then the world changed.

THE REAL COST OF TODAY'S ECONOMY

When international travel and shipping became easier and cheaper in the 1970s and 1980s, companies started to expand across the globe. Corporate competition became fiercer, and business leaders realized they needed to satisfy shareholders to drive ongoing success. This brought a newfound focus on "efficiency" in the workplace characterized by Six Sigma,† repeated rounds of layoffs, and seemingly endless restructuring. In this new shareholder-centric economy, companies could no longer afford to be so generous with their employees.[10] So they slashed benefits and handed out pink slips, whittling down overhead by shifting full-time headcount to part-time employees and automating work via technology.

Then came a string of economic recessions, six in total since the late 1970s, including the Great Recession that stretched on for two painful

---

* In the postwar workplace, the story wasn't so rosy for white women, who earned around 60% on average of what white men did and were typically fired or forced to quit once they had children. And Black and brown women and men were largely excluded from the prosperity of the 1950s and continued to face de facto segregation in the workplace, in housing, and in education for the next few decades. As a result, the Black–white wage gap was as large in 2020 as it was in 1950.

† Six Sigma is a set of techniques and tools for manufacturing and business process improvement, first introduced by Motorola engineer Bill Smith in 1986.

years after the subprime mortgage crisis in 2008. These were paired with stagnant pay rates: average weekly wages increased only 17.2% *in total* over the four decades from 1979 to 2019 (an average annual increase of about 0.43%), while the productivity of American workers increased by 72.2% over the same period.[11] For many Americans, the only way to make ends meet in the face of stagnant wages was to turn to consumer debt.

And then we pile on the cost of a college education. According to the US Department of Education, the average annual cost of tuition, fees, room, and board at a four-year postsecondary institution was $2,809 in 1980 (or around $9,500 in today's dollars); by 2021, it was closer to $26,000.[12] As the cost of higher education has steadily increased, most borrowers are stuck paying burdensome student loan debt well into middle age. Millions of Americans are collectively carrying more than $1.75 trillion in student debt—more than triple the amount in 2005. I was one of those borrowers with loans from undergrad and graduate school topping six figures. Chances are, you are too.

Unlike household debt, student loans can't be discharged in bankruptcy, making them utterly inescapable. Plus, don't forget the ballooning cost of housing, health care, and childcare. The median house price increased by 40% in inflation-adjusted dollars between 1970 and 2017 while the median household income effectively stayed flat.[13] By 2019, Americans spent twice as much on health care as they did in the 1980s.[14] And prices for childcare were over *one thousand percent* higher in 2021 versus 1977, an average growth rate of 6.10% per year (nearly twice the rate of inflation over the same period).[15]

I'm not trying to paint a bleak picture here,* but I am trying to help you understand why the economic model we inherited isn't working for you or probably anyone you know. To put it simply, your failure to achieve the milestones of a successful middle-class American adult—a stable career, a house, a partner, and a couple of kids and/or mildly expensive hobbies, decent health insurance, the beginnings of a retirement nest egg, plus a little free time for relaxation, volunteering, or travel—is not, actually, *your* failure. A systemic shift has made reaching each of those

---

* Though I recognize it might feel pretty bleak!

milestones significantly harder than it used to be, and checking off all of the boxes is virtually impossible for anyone not starting off with the cushion of generational wealth.

These shifts over the last two to three decades have fundamentally changed how we think about our careers and lives, which means that all of the well-intentioned guidance our parents and grandparents offer just won't work for us. And despite what countless news stories would have us believe, *This is not our fault*. The challenges we face are the result of a systemic collapse. There are many arguments for fixing the system, and I am all there for that. (Universal healthcare untethered from employment would be a great place to start.) But while we work on long-term systemic solutions, let's also acknowledge and embrace the options we have at the individual level to survive and thrive in the current situation.

IT'S NOT ALL BAD NEWS

Another considerable change was already in motion before the COVID-19 pandemic hit, but the dramatic disruption of lockdown and the mass shift to working from home for many industries and long periods of unemployment for others accelerated the realization that the rat race isn't worth it. Working unsustainable hours for a precarious life that could be turned inside out at any moment just doesn't seem like a great deal to a lot of people anymore. "We've seen now a sea change in people really re-evaluating their relationship to their work," Hayden Brown, CEO of freelancing website Upwork, told the *New York Times*. "They're saying: 'Wait a minute. I need some different things. I want to draw boundaries in different ways. I want to have a different relationship to my work than I did in the past, where I am much more in control.'"[16]

In June 2021, the US Department of Labor reported that an unprecedented four million Americans had quit their jobs in April alone—the beginning of a phenomenon that news outlets called "the Great Resignation." While we can't ascribe a singular motivation to these resignations, for many workers—particularly those in the knowledge economy—this was an opportunity to reset and reframe their relationship with work. "These people are...leaving their jobs not because the pandemic created obstacles to their employment but, at least in part, because it nudged them to rethink the role of work in their lives altogether. Many are embracing career downsizing, voluntarily reducing their work hours to emphasize other aspects of life," wrote Cal Newport in the *New Yorker*.[17]

Some mocked these choices as a YOLO move,[18] but even if they were, the impulse wasn't entirely wrong. You *do* only live once. And after surviving a global pandemic, many younger and mid-career workers came to the same realization all at once: As much as you might love your work, work won't love you back. Or, as writer Maris Kreizman put it, "the idea of meritocracy is a lie and the only thing hard work guarantees is unpaid overtime, not success."[19]

But believe it or not, there's an upside to this collective collapse: It frees us from the straitjacket of narrow specialization and linear career paths many of our parents felt stifled by, and instead offers the opportunity to build vibrant lives that fit us better. We cannot make the same choices our parents made because we are not living in the same world. So we are making different choices. Ones that align with our *actual* needs and values, not the ones we're expected to maintain. And with the prospect of working until we die—or at the very least, a solid decade or two beyond what our parents are planning—the mirage of retirement makes it feel even more urgent to find a model that is fulfilling and sustainable for the long haul.

This is an opportunity to redefine what "success" looks like using our own variables, and eschew the cult of ambition that has made so many folks miserable. The good news amid all of this disruption is that we get to toss out the status quo and design a new approach to career, relationships, and life that actually makes us happy.

WRITING A NEW PLAYBOOK

The old playbook doesn't work: Trothing your long-term commitment to a company in exchange for an identity, some financial stability, and a chance to climb the corporate ladder is no longer a lucrative trade. So what does an alternative model look like?

First, it disentangles your identity from your current job. To put it bluntly, you are more than your work. Derek Thompson, a staff writer for the *Atlantic*, argues that the decline of traditional religious affiliation in America has coincided with a plethora of "new atheisms," including what he calls "workism."[20] That is, the idea that your work is the crux of your identity and life's purpose. More disturbingly, defining your identity solely by your work means that "anything short of finding one's vocational soul mate means a wasted life." Your work can absolutely offer meaning to your life, but it should not be *the* meaning *of* your life. Instead, consider your identity through a wider aperture, taking your personal, professional, and relationship goals all into account to define your purpose. Otherwise, Derek cautions, "to be a workist is to worship a god with firing power." Whew. Write that on a sticky note and keep it handy. Don't leave your identity in someone else's hands.

Second, an alternative model is one that redefines your future opportunities (and even your present ones) as a broad set of potential paths rather than a narrow, singular trajectory. As engineer and creative writer Jai Chakrabarti wrote in *Fast Company*, "There is no linear life, at least I haven't found one I'd wish to live. Rather there are the meandering paths, all the pursuits of beauty that reward us with their own vistas of the world underneath."[21] He pushed back on the pressure he felt to continue his fast-rising engineering career and decided to take a break to earn his MFA in fiction, knowing he would return to computer programming at some point. "Growing up in Kolkata, India, I knew that my favorite Bengali writers all had day jobs. Bankim Chandra Chatterjee, who helped bridge Sanskrit influences with Victorian ones, wrote fourteen novels and collections of poems. He also wrote a series of essays on science and worked for most of his life as a tax collector." Chakrabarti recognizes that there is space in his present and his future for all of his passions, and the ability to pursue them all, over time and in creative combination, gives him both fulfillment and optionality.

Third, this new model offers the option to meet your needs (financial, developmental, social, and professional) through a combination of sources, rather than depending on one job, company, or industry to provide everything in one offering. It is unlikely that companies are going to reverse their cost-cutting trends and suddenly offer the generous benefits of yesteryear. A more likely possibility would be lobbying for dramatic policy changes around benefits: separating health insurance, life insurance, short- and long-term disability, retirement accounts, and flexible spending accounts from the workplace and making them available—at accessible prices—to individuals. But even that is a medium- to long-term dream, and largely out of our control. In the short-term, this new model allows you to assess what you need and diversify how you address those needs to ensure you can take care of yourself (and, should you wish to have one, your family), now and into the future.

And fourth, this model provides flexibility when it comes to time management, transitions, and rebalancing your commitments. Forget about a parochial definition of work-life balance based on an equal split of your time between personal and professional. Instead, this is about the ability to make time for important things, however and whenever they show up. Rather than the stark binary of on or off, working full-time or taking a break to attend to other commitments in your life, a model that encourages a mix of activity streams—including the uncompensated labor you might be providing to your family or community—offers a more nuanced and inclusive definition of work-life balance.

Identity. Optionality. Diversification. Flexibility. These are the four pillars of the Portfolio Life.

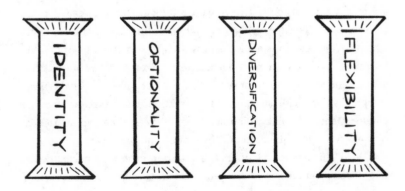

THE PORTFOLIO LIFE

So what exactly do I mean by a "portfolio"? The simplest definition of a portfolio is a curated collection of items that meet a specific aim or objective. You've likely seen it in a number of contexts: An artist's portfolio might include selected pieces that best represent their abilities and interests. A student's portfolio might contain key projects and papers that demonstrate the range of their learning. A financial portfolio is a collection of instruments like stocks, bonds, cash, real estate, and other places to put your money to work that, together, aim to maximize the return on the investment for a given level of risk.

It is this last example, the financial portfolio, that is the most applicable when we are talking about a Portfolio Life. Roughly, it acknowledges that you shouldn't put all of your eggs in one basket, and it knows that success comes from crafting a diverse mix of opportunities to address your current needs, while building in opportunity to adjust that mix when (yes, *when*, not *if*) your needs change. The Portfolio Life is built on the same ideas:

1. You are more than any one role or opportunity.
2. Diversification will help you navigate change and mitigate uncertainty.
3. When your needs change, you can and should rebalance your portfolio.

The term *portfolio life* was first coined in 1989 by Charles Handy in his book *The Age of Unreason*. He bristled at the notion that your life's work should be one narrowly defined job and instead argued it could be a collection of passions, interests, and hobbies. While his definition was still work-focused, I expand the definition of a Portfolio Life more broadly to include relationships, community, personal growth, and impact. After all, you are more than your economic output, and the imprint of your life is far bigger than your business card.

Make no mistake: The Portfolio Life isn't about the future of work;

this is the *present* of work. And it offers the freedom to pursue what fits us and what fills us. It grants us permission to step back from the cult of ambition and define our lives outside of our paid labor. It is the chance to write a new story where we can be happy not in the future, after we've tap-danced our way around one world-altering event after another in hopes of keeping our heads above water,* but one where we can be happy now. After all, you only live once.

---

* Please forgive the mixed metaphors, but in a world that can literally be both on fire and underwater from simultaneous crises, I feel like I could use an entire library of metaphors and still not express the precarity we all feel.

CHAPTER 2

The Four Pillars of a Portfolio Life

This model of separating work from identity, embracing optionality, de-risking through diversification, and gaining flexibility is one that anyone from any generation can adopt. It simply gained momentum and greater acceptance over the last decade or two because the old model is no longer viable for (nor wanted by) millennials. In the face of stagnant wages and limited upward trajectories, measuring success only by professional traction isn't working. So we need a more holistic definition, one that includes factors like health, relationships, and (gasp!) free time.

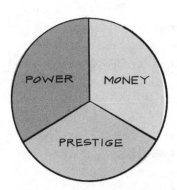

HOW WE'RE TAUGHT TO MEASURE SUCCESS

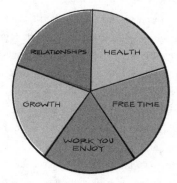

HOW WE SHOULD MEASURE

In expanding our idea of success, we see the strength of the four pillars of the Portfolio Life: *identity* insulated from the unpredictability of the market; *optionality* to pursue opportunities without the constraint of linearity; *diversification* of resources to mitigate both individual and systemic risk; and *flexibility* to accommodate work and life in whatever proportion is needed from one day to the next. Let's dive into these pillars in more detail.

PILLAR 1: IDENTITY

> You are not your job, and I am not mine. Take your eyes off the distorted reflection, and have the courage to experience your full life and true self.
>
> —Arthur C. Brooks

Since I was a child, I have struggled to describe who I am—the theater/musical/math nerd who chose to create at the intersection of those worlds rather than pursuing one linear path. It was hard enough as a college graduate, but as I finished business school and set out as an entrepreneur, I felt a real urgency to find a way to capture the complete picture of who I am, what I care about, and what I want to create. I was founding a startup and spent a great number of evenings at dinners and hackathons and pitch nights where I had sixty seconds (at best) to introduce myself before people moved on to the next entrepreneur. When I tried to explain my experience and interests in that setting, I felt like a dilettante rather than a driven, multitalented, three-dimensional human. Finally, late one night at a venture capital event in 2011, after a glass of wine and a dozen handshakes, I offered a droll one-liner: "I'm a human Venn diagram, building a life at the intersection of business, technology, and the arts."

The investor smiled. "Huh. I love that description. Clearly you have interdisciplinary experiences. Tell me more."

Oh! Maybe this concept might work!

A quick recap on Venn diagrams: Popularized by mathematician John Venn in the late 1800s, these diagrams are simple ways to visualize the logical relationship between sets of things, people, ideas, and so on. They are widely used in probability, logic, statistics, computer science, and linguistics, but these days you're equally likely to come across them in viral memes.

Here's the Venn diagram I use to describe myself and my unique set of interests:

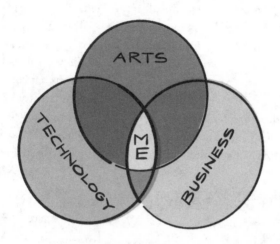

The power of using a Venn diagram here to describe a person is twofold: First, it acknowledges that there are natural overlaps between different fields—after all, there really are no silos when medicine and comedy can intersect to turn an ophthalmologist into a viral TikTok star.* Second, it helps visualize how a person's work can span multiple fields and yet be integrated and intentional by sitting at the natural intersection of those interests.

In my Venn diagram, the intersection between arts and business is the field of arts management, where I started my career at the Metropolitan Opera. The intersection between business and technology is the world of tech startups, where I spent the decade after business school. The intersection of technology and the arts contains tech-enabled and

---

* Yes, I am referring to Dr. Will Flanary, or Dr. Glaucomflecken, as he is known on the internet.

tech-informed theater, opera, dance, and visual art, including works I've had the privilege to co-create, contribute to, and advise. And now I choose to build a life at the center of all three worlds, searching for and inventing collaborations between my various interests. Some are paid, while others are personal projects; some are professionally executed, and others are new skills I'm developing or hobbies that I'm happy to be a part of at an amateur level. Yet all of them reflect my sense of self.

I started using this phrase more widely—through my podcast, in my professional bio, via introductions when giving talks—and saw how strongly it resonated with so many people. As I suspected, I am not the only person with diverse personal and professional interests, and many people felt relief at finally having a way to express all of the different sides of themselves rather than feeling constrained to a simplistic, one-dimensional identity. Or, as author and futurist Amy Webb put it on Twitter, it's a way to see the focus that multidisciplinary people bring to their careers.

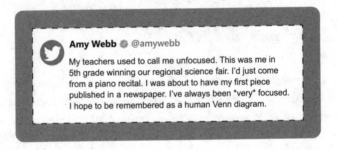

Amy Webb @amywebb

My teachers used to call me unfocused. This was me in 5th grade winning our regional science fair. I'd just come from a piano recital. I was about to have my first piece published in a newspaper. I've always been *very* focused. I hope to be remembered as a human Venn diagram.

The Myth of Left and Right Brains

Here's one example of how we like to reduce people to a singular dimension: Do you consider yourself "left-brained" or "right-brained"? Whether you first stumbled on this idea via a BuzzFeed quiz or had a teacher or parent introduce it, most people have an inkling that they are either an analytical, language-driven thinker (left-brained) or a creative, big-picture thinker (right-brained).

This theory is based on the lateralization of brain functions—that is, the brain contains two hemispheres, each performing specific roles.

The left hemisphere is said to drive logic and language comprehension while the right drives visual and spatial reasoning. This left/right dichotomy is so well known that it's often used as a shorthand for categorizing people, from young children who show an early predisposition for math or art to employees taking a personality assessment as part of new-hire onboarding.

Except, like many "facts" of pop psychology, it's not true.[1] You can be no more left-brained than you can be left-lunged or left-kidneyed. Our organs function together! So where did this frustratingly persistent idea come from? From the misinterpretation of real science.

In the 1960s, a doctoral student named Michael Gazzaniga worked with famed neurobiologist Roger W. Sperry on a Caltech study of patients with epilepsy whose corpus callosum—a wide, thick nerve tract that connects the two hemispheres—was severed to prevent seizures from spreading across the brain. Without that bundle of nerve fibers connecting the two sides of the patients' brains, the scientists were able to devise a way to show images to only one side of the brain or the other. One patient who had a square shown to his left hemisphere said he could see a box. But when the image was shown only to his right hemisphere, even though he could still see the image and point to it, he was unable to name it. As a result, Gazzaniga theorized that both hemispheres are involved in processing an image, though only the left hemisphere could articulate what it was since, as in this patient's case, without communication from the left side, the right side couldn't find the word for "box."[2]

While the main result of Gazzaniga's research was to show how much the two sides needed to work together to carry out simple tasks, a 1973 *New York Times Magazine* article titled "We Are Left-Brained or Right-Brained" misinterpreted the results as "two very different persons inhabiting our heads...One of them is verbal, analytic, dominant. The other is artistic..."[3] *TIME* magazine featured the story a few years later, followed quickly by articles in *Harvard Business Review* and *Psychology Today*, and the myth of right-brained and left-brained people took hold of our cultural consciousness. Neuroscientists have been trying to debunk this idea for more than fifty years, but the misleading framework persists.

You see, humans like to categorize the world into neat little groups.

For one, it's cognitively efficient: Once you have assigned something a category, you no longer need to consider information about each individual member of the group. Yet a limitation of this natural compulsion to categorize is that, by definition, those categories are often rigidly defined, mutually exclusive, and collectively exhaustive.* The quickest way to assess and categorize people is to reduce them to a singular dimension: short or tall; dark hair or light hair or no hair; like cilantro or don't like cilantro. That's fine when all you want to know is whether you can put cilantro in the guacamole for your party, or whether someone is tall enough to ride a roller coaster, because the nuances of *how much* someone dislikes cilantro or exactly how tall someone is beyond "this tall to ride" doesn't make much difference. But that simplistic categorization doesn't work when multiple dimensions come into play.

As an example, nearly anyone can tell you that racial, ethnic, gender, and socioeconomic identities are intersectional. The neat little boxes on census forms and college applications don't work for many people because their identities exist at the intersection of many factors from cultural and ethnic heritage to the physical attributes that may be associated with one or several races to the resources, access, and safety net they did or did not experience while growing up. A Black woman born in Japan to mixed-race parents who immigrated to the United States as a young child would have very different experiences, biases, and cultural references than a Black man descended from enslaved Africans who grew up in the rural American South or a Black nonbinary person born into an affluent family in the Pacific Northwest. Lumping them together and ascribing to each individual all of the assumptions and attributes you associate with "Black Americans" does nothing to help you understand the vibrant humanity of anyone in that category.

But even knowing that our biases don't serve us, our brains happily default to MECE categories for all aspects of our lives. We're introverts or extroverts. Fitness fanatics or couch potatoes. Baby boomers or Gen X or millennials or Gen Z. (Yup, I'm guilty of this too. Generational divisions

---

* "Mutually exclusive and collectively exhaustive" (or MECE) means everything you are categorizing fits into one, and only one, category.

are flawed since they often lead to sweeping generalizations that may be roughly true for the group but may not apply at the individual level.) And, of course, we have a propensity to categorize people into narrowly defined career paths or professional identities. It's cognitively efficient to reduce a complex human being down to a single label like "engineer" or "therapist" or "librarian," but confining yourself or other people into these one-dimensional personas is incredibly limiting.

Former Baltimore Ravens offensive lineman John Urschel left the NFL in 2017 and earned his PhD in mathematics from MIT in 2022. He knows how hard it is to disassociate his identity from his job. "One of the things that makes it really hard for people to make a switch...is that, when you have a job, you start to think that your job is who you are. Your job is something that defines you in some way to family, friends, and other people. I think that actually limits a lot of people because they have a hard time imagining themselves outside of a certain thing."[4]

We all have a collection of interests, skills, and relationships that are greater than the job title currently on our LinkedIn. But some of us have been advised to shrink them or hide them away for fear of not looking "serious" about our careers. While that may have been true in previous generations, I would argue that advice is out of date. Instead, embracing the full multidimensionality of your human Venn diagram will give you two incredible things: First, it will ensure you feel like yourself, in all of your weirdly-shaped-puzzle-piece glory. And second, it will equip you with a diverse network and skill set to lean on when your worlds intersect or when you may need to zig or zag between them to stay on your feet.

There's no contradiction in being a complex, multidimensional human. When it comes to your identity, think "and" not "or."

PILLAR 2: OPTIONALITY

Henry: Pick one.
Danielle: I could no sooner choose a favorite star in the heavens.

—Ever After

The misconception starts in early childhood. The question "What are you going to be when you grow up?" plants the idea that we each have a single, correct future ahead of us, and it's incumbent upon us to choose wisely. Somehow the college major we choose at eighteen and the first job we accept in our early twenties should set our path forward until the day we retire (or die). Yet anyone who has been in the workforce for more than a few years should know that this hyper-focused worldview does not reflect reality.

In truth, there are many paths we can take at any given time, and even if some close off, new paths emerge at just about every juncture. Some may feel like they are once-in-a-lifetime opportunities, but more often than not you'll find there are many on-ramps to creating the life you want to live.

I stumbled across this illustration by Tim Urban on Instagram who regularly blogs and posts on social media under the handle @waitbutwhy. It stopped me in my tracks because it was the first time I was able to visualize the incredible optionality that is available to us if we are open to it.

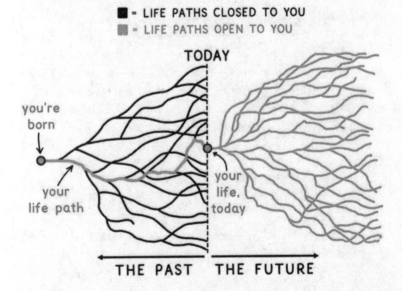

■ = LIFE PATHS CLOSED TO YOU
■ = LIFE PATHS OPEN TO YOU

TODAY

you're born

your life path

your life, today

THE PAST   THE FUTURE

This image packs a punch with two important messages: First, there are many available paths at any given juncture if you open your eyes to the possibilities, and second, rather than looking backward, mourning the paths you didn't choose, look ahead to all of the opportunities still to come. Pillar 1, identity, reminds us that we are more than one thing, and Pillar 2, optionality, reveals that we have more than one path to choose from.

Case Study: Star Power

Dr. Aomawa Shields is one of my favorite examples of this optionality pillar. As a child, her love of acting had developed alongside her love of the stars, and she had no problem pursuing both in high school, where she starred in their production of *Steel Magnolias* and served as a proctor in the observatory. But when she chose to focus on astronomy for college and graduate school, she felt she needed to pare back her theatrical aspirations to be taken seriously. Cutting off such a meaningful part of her life worked for a while. Until it didn't. When she found her grades and interest in science slipping in the first year of her PhD program, she knew it was time for a change. So she dropped out and headed to Los Angeles to focus on acting instead.

In her MFA program at UCLA, she found she needed to use less of the analytical part of her brain for a while and reengage the emotional part. "I had to turn my head off and my heart on," she told me. But even as she thrived as an actor, she hadn't lost the science bug entirely. "I missed being part of the community that was trying to learn more about the universe. I didn't want to learn about discoveries on the news with everyone else. I wanted to be a part of those discoveries."

So while working as a professional actor, she took a day job at Caltech supporting the Spitzer Space Telescope. Then, to her great delight, she landed a job as the host of *Wired Science*, a TV show produced by PBS, and *Wired* magazine. She loved it, but wondered if she needed to circle back to her roots in astronomy. "I had been put in touch with Neil deGrasse Tyson, who had seen the pilot for that show, and he said, 'You know, without a PhD, you're just another person who wants to be on television. A PhD will give you the street cred.'" At the same time, on a whim, she applied to NASA's astronaut candidate program. "I had gotten laser eye surgery, but I barely met the qualifications because I didn't have a PhD. It seemed like all roads were saying go back and get that PhD."

Sixteen years after dropping out from her first graduate program, she earned her doctorate in astronomy and astrobiology from the University of Washington and is now an astronomer, astrobiologist, and associate professor in the Department of Physics and Astronomy at the University of California at Irvine. In addition to her robust research agenda in exoplanets,* she continues to invest in science communication work as a TED fellow, via her memoir *Life on Other Planets*, and through a program she founded called Rising Stargirls, which leverages science, theater, and creative writing to inspire middle school girls to explore the universe.

Like Jai Chakrabarti, the software engineer and novelist we met in Chapter 1, Aomawa embraced her desire to make a change and took an unexpected on-ramp to acting (and then another back to astronomy) on a nontraditional timeline. Rather than getting mired in a "it's too late" mindset, she selected the right path at the right time for her journey and found ways to integrate her many interests into a life that serves her.

It's Not Too Late

The general attitude in acting and academia alike is that it's a young person's game. In Hollywood, age is usually seen as a liability (especially for women), which can spur aspiring artists to go all-in on a highly

---

* Planets outside our solar system.

speculative career when they have the fewest resources and weakest safety nets. Similarly, more and more evidence is emerging of academic hiring committees with a bias against older candidates,[5] leading many aspiring researchers and professors to charge ahead, single-mindedly, from undergraduate studies through a multiyear doctoral program without stopping to gain any other work or life experiences. Yet Aomawa's story shows how her nonlinear path offered her advantages in both acting and astronomy by granting her a completely different perspective of the world.

It's no secret that American culture is obsessed with youth. From the proliferation of "30 Under 30" lists to the not-even-subtle (and completely illegal) job postings looking for someone "young and hungry" to the "anti-aging" of all the things, we consistently hear that someday we will age out of opportunity. As a result, there is an ever-present message that people who want to be successful need to pick something, get moving, and achieve as much as we can before we hit our expiration date. Anything that might distract from that achievement is often considered a waste of time.

Yet research shows time and time again that age and experience can be a catalyst for new ideas, fast-growing ventures, and extraordinary creative success. Despite the near-deification of tech startup founders in their early twenties, MIT professor Pierre Azoulay and his colleagues found the average age of the founder of a successful, high-growth company is forty-five.[6] "Super talented people are going to do great things even when they're young," Azoulay told Bloomberg News.[7] "That doesn't mean they're not going to do even better things when they're older." Similarly, Dutch economist Philip Hans Franses studied the peak creativity of 90 Nobel literature laureates, 100 of the most popular classical composers, and 221 artists who painted the most-valued works in the world, and found that these luminaries had lived, on average, two-thirds of their lives before they created their best work.[8]

How, then, do we reconcile perception with reality when it comes to age and achievement? Canadian journalist and author Malcolm Gladwell summed it up well in an essay for the *New Yorker*: "Genius, in the popular conception, is inextricably tied up with precocity—doing something truly creative, we're inclined to think, requires the freshness and exuberance and energy of youth." But this is where optionality grants Portfolio Lifers an advantage: A fresh perspective can come from entering a new discipline as much as it can come from youth. It's less about age and more about seeing the world through a different lens and connecting the dots that no one else sees. Or, as Proust is often paraphrased, "The real voyage of discovery consists not in seeking new landscapes, but in seeing with new eyes."[9]

In the early 2000s, business school professors Jeffrey Dyer, Hal Gregerson, and Clay Christensen undertook a six-year study to uncover the origins of creativity, particularly in innovative companies. They studied the habits of 25 innovative entrepreneurs and surveyed more than 3,000 executives and 500 individuals who had started companies or invented products.[10] What they found were five "discovery skills" that distinguish creatives in business: associating, questioning, observing, experimenting, and networking. The core skill—the "backbone"—is associating, anchoring the other four skills in place like the double helix of DNA.

"Associating, or the ability to successfully connect seemingly unrelated questions, problems, or ideas from different fields, is central to the innovator's DNA," they wrote in a 2009 article in *Harvard Business Review*. One entrepreneur they spoke with, Frans Johansson, called this the "Medici effect," pointing to the creative explosion that fueled the Renaissance when the Medici family convened artists, poets, philosophers, architects, scientists, and more to connect and collaborate in fifteenth-century Florence. "The more diverse our experience and knowledge," the professors wrote, "the more connections the brain can make. Fresh inputs trigger new associations; for some, these lead to novel ideas. As Steve Jobs frequently observed, 'Creativity is connecting things.'"[11] Thus, Pillar 2, optionality, is not just a benefit to you, highlighting the plethora of paths you can pursue, but is also a boon to society, fueling creativity and innovation by granting Portfolio Lifers a fresh perspective on the status quo.

PILLAR 3: DIVERSIFICATION

> It is the part of a wise man to keep himself today for
> tomorrow, and not venture all his eggs in one basket.
> —Miguel de Cervantes

Let's get this out of the way: Doing just one thing is the riskiest career move you can make. Yes, you heard me right. The classic advice to secure a single full-time job with benefits at a stable company means putting your income, health care, and retirement savings all in the hands of a leader who may or may not know how to steer the company through the unpredictable future ahead. And when they decide to "restructure" to be more "agile," you may be surprised to learn that you're a liability, not an asset. "Employment can be riskier than self-employment,"[12] counseled Charles Handy in *The Age of Unreason*, "even for the whizz kids of the money world, for they can be fired at ten minutes' notice, not allowed to even return to their desks. A high salary or a good wage guarantees neither security nor freedom."

According to a 2019 survey conducted by the Harris Poll, more than 40% of American adults have been laid off at some point, and nearly 50% suffer from layoff anxiety.[13] "The [2008] recession was kind of the key point of change. From that point onwards, the working experiences of young workers, and millennials, in particular, has been marked by precarity," Dr. Arif Jetha told *GEN* magazine, a now-shuttered publication on Medium.[14] He's a scientist at the Institute for Work & Health, where his research focuses on young and vulnerable workers. It left a long-term scarring effect for workers who graduated right into the recession.

Given these dual tensions—a shortage of jobs that give us the opportunities we want and the ever-present anxiety that the jobs we do have could be taken away at any point—it is clear that we need a way to combat that uncertainty. Enter: diversification.

Portfolio Theory and Diversification

One of the biggest "aha!" moments in my MBA education was when I learned that you could actually quantify how risky a particular asset was.* Financial analysts look at how much the value of an asset (like a stock) varies compared to the overall market—they call that variance *beta*—and it is one way to measure volatility or systemic risk. When an asset follows the market (i.e., rises when the overall market rises; falls when the market falls), it has a positive beta. When it is in opposition to the market, it has a negative beta. To build a balanced portfolio, you can offset your risk by choosing assets with negatively correlated betas.

What does that mean in plain English? Here's an example: Let's say you buy some equipment for your small landscaping business. You pay a lot of money up front and expect to earn revenue over time that will pay back that initial investment (and hopefully a lot more). But what happens if the equipment gets damaged or stolen? To mitigate that risk, you also invest in an insurance policy. In good times, the equipment is just fine and you make money by providing expert landscaping services while the money you spend on your insurance premiums doesn't pay off. In bad times, when something happens to the equipment, your business income disappears but the insurance policy pays out and takes care of the loss. Because the revenue and the insurance payments occur in opposite scenarios, they balance each other out. In either case you are covered.

A Portfolio Life can offer that same diversification across income streams, industry volatility, emotional roller coasters, and personal fulfillment. Building a portfolio could mean leveraging a hobby into a promotion or career pivot. It could also mean developing a new skill set and connecting with a community through a volunteer opportunity while serving as a caregiver for your family. (We'll look at three common business models for your portfolio in Part II.) Plus, when circumstances

---

* There's an entire branch of economics dedicated to portfolio theory and mean-variance analysis. If you're interested in learning more, I'd recommend starting with Harry Markowitz's paper "Portfolio Selection" published in the *Journal of Finance* in 1952. (It earned him a Nobel prize four decades later.)

throw a curveball at an entire industry or function, you have more of a chance of riding out the disruption.

For a brief period of time, American workers had the upper hand with negotiating roles, salaries, and working conditions as employers faced a painful pandemic-related worker shortage. But by the end of 2022 the winds changed again, and employers began to regain their leverage to call the shots. The longer you've been in one role, at one company, or in one industry, the more you are at risk. So the best way to future-proof your career is to diversify. This isn't just about building multiple income streams (though that's always helpful), it's also about diversifying your network, skill sets, even industry experiences. This, in turn, can help you de-risk your life. Let's take a look at how.

The Extreme Users of Portfolios

One of my favorite customer research techniques from the startup world is called "extreme user research." When looking to understand a new problem or behavior, product designers and researchers go talk to the most extreme segments of that new need or behavior. Some designers refer to these users as those who can either "break your product or make it bulletproof"[15] because they can help you surface unmet needs and solution hacks or work-arounds. For example, I worked with one company that was focused on making more sustainable clothing. The team conducted extreme user research by talking with Amish families, since they make and mend their own garments to have a long life span and fit many wearers.

So, who are the extreme users of a Portfolio Life? Who not only *don't*, but also *can't* rely on one full-time day job to meet all of their professional needs? Who have been compelled to combine various pursuits to ensure they have income, insurance, flexibility, and fulfillment?

Artists.

From actors to dancers, to novelists to sculptors, to musicians to filmmakers, creators have long relied on portfolios of work to fuel their lives. They work in industries that are heavily weighted toward project-based work rather than open-ended employment; there is a fair amount of subjectivity in how they land those projects, which means they have limited control over outcomes;* projects are not always clearly defined in length or scope at the outset; and each project may engage only part of the artist's skill set or creative interests at one time. Thus, they not only need, but also want, a diversity of endeavors to mitigate the risk or uncertainty of any one project. This is why many of the case studies you'll read in this book feature people who have some kind of creative pursuit as one part of their portfolio—by definition, they have had to adopt this business model early on and can offer us clues on how to do so successfully in our own lives. But these concepts apply to everyone, even if you're not the "creative type."

Case Study: Surviving a Pandemic

After nearly fifteen years as a Broadway actor, Carla Stickler was ready for a change. Her first love had been acting and singing, and she had enjoyed her experiences touring the country, headlining cruise ships, and performing on the Great White Way. But now in her late-thirties, Carla wanted more than this profession was giving her. She wanted steady health insurance, a new intellectual challenge, and the ability to see friends on nights and weekends; plus she was ready to start a family with her longtime partner. So, while she subbed in as a swing in the Broadway production of *Wicked* and taught voice lessons to her private studio of students,† she completed a coding bootcamp at the Flatiron School. Learning how to code made her feel rejuvenated by the creativity she had been missing. "Suddenly there was something that I had created from scratch. I ran around to all of my friends, beaming with pride, saying, 'Look at this thing I just built!'" Carla admits that she wasn't quite ready

---

* Ever been to an open-call audition with dozens of performers who look and sound exactly like you?

† Performing plus teaching lessons on the side is a classic portfolio for many actors, singers, and musicians.

to leave acting and singing entirely, but she was building the skills and the network for when that day came.

When the COVID-19 pandemic forced her new show to close after just one performance, Carla realized the decision of how and when to change careers was on her doorstep. While her Broadway friends and colleagues faced what turned out to be more than a year of unemployment in the theater world,* Carla secured a job at a tech company in a role that bridged the engineers and product managers building a new technology platform and the customers who were learning how to use it. She was able to combine her technical skills as a software engineer with her incredible communication skills as an actor and voice teacher to excel in a dramatically different world than the one she had always known.

Building a Portfolio Life means stepping into the driver's seat and navigating the unexpected twists and turns of life, rather than climbing up a predictable career ladder that someone else built (and that someone else can tear down, move, or force you to wait your turn to climb if there are too many folks above you). You could say it's like becoming the CEO of your life. Yes, it's a role that requires more responsibility and active management than following a preset path, but it also grants you autonomy, visibility, and intentionality in creating the life you want to live.

Now, a caution: A Portfolio Life is not about "hustle porn."† If you're already exhausted, the thought of doing even more is likely terrifying. Trust me, this *isn't* about glorifying nonstop work. A successful Portfolio Life means making time for your priorities and putting everything that doesn't make the cut on the back burner, knowing you can always reprioritize when your needs or resources change. This is about building a life that is both fulfilling and sustainable. We'll dig into how to balance the

---

* And, unfortunately, the restaurant industry, which is the typical sector for actors and performers to find temporary jobs as waitstaff and bartenders between gigs.

† The fetishization of long work hours and glorification of workaholism, often with mantras like "rise and grind."

moving pieces in Part III, but for now just know that taking time for rest and investing in relationships are key elements of your diversification strategy.

I also want to acknowledge that there are meaningful differences in circumstance and choice between those who are crafting a diverse portfolio of income streams and experiences and those who have to juggle multiple jobs to make ends meet. The same economic factors that trigger precarity among knowledge workers also undermine the security and stability of working-class folks. Whether it's the unpredictability of hourly shift work, the growth of childcare deserts, or the laughable federal minimum wage that hasn't increased since 2009, there are many who are piecing together multiple income streams just to survive. And while that approach does offer some diversification, I don't want to pretend that they should spin their survival into a glossy Cinderella story. When working full-time hours at a minimum wage cannot cover the most basic cost of housing in 93% of counties in the United States,[16] you cannot help but admit that American capitalism has failed the working class. So, if you can, consider building in some time and energy to fight these systems, or donating your money and talents to organizations that work to bridge the gap. Until we change the system that got us here, all of our livelihoods are at risk.

PILLAR 4: FLEXIBILITY

Better to bend than break.
—An ancient proverb, according to the internet

When I first moved to New York right after college, I was determined to make the most of living at the epicenter of performing arts in America. I was not much of a dancer, but I bravely took classes at Joffrey Ballet School, Broadway Dance Center, and Alvin Ailey American Dance Theater alongside aspiring and professional artists. I considered it a cross between exercise, creative church, and a regular dose of humility. One day, in a Horton technique class at Ailey, the teacher stopped mid-class to give a sermon on the relationship between flexibility and strength. "Strength gives us stability. It's about ensuring you have the roots to support movement without getting hurt. Flexibility gives us that movement, allowing us to respond to stimuli and adapt to new circumstances. You must have both to survive as a dancer." Arguably you also must have both to survive as a human.

Together, the first three pillars of the Portfolio Life give us strength, providing stability in the face of constant change. The fourth pillar is flexibility, allowing us to adapt and respond when work and life make conflicting demands. The power of this pillar is most obvious at the moment when people need to take on extensive and unpredictable responsibilities outside of their careers or make major, unexpected changes to accommodate the realities of life.

This is a common inflection point for new parents of young children, as you'll see in a moment, but it is just as relevant for those who need to support aging parents, a life partner needing to relocate for a job, a close friend or family member experiencing an emergency, or any number of other curveballs that life throws our way. It can show up at other moments too: when you're facing burnout and need a sabbatical, when you want to step up for a community in crisis, or when your values or priorities suddenly change. It is at these moments that the flexibility of your portfolio can really shine, allowing you to dial up or dial back your commitments, rebalancing the weight of your paid work, unpaid work, hobbies, family responsibilities, and community to fit the new circumstances.

When I got pregnant with my first child in 2019, I knew I needed to make some meaningful changes. At that point, I had been a founder of or an executive in early-stage companies for nearly a decade across a wide variety of industries and business models, and the one thing that had been consistent throughout was the nonstop intensity of the work. I regularly logged seventy to eighty hours of work a week, sleeping with my phone inches from my head, checking Slack at all hours of the day, and responding to emails during significant life moments ranging from my grandmother's funeral to my own honeymoon. Sometimes these choices were made out of fear, succumbing to the always-on culture that company leaders had set. But many times, they were driven by my own priorities: I was creating something that didn't yet exist and that process didn't fall neatly between the hours of 9:00 a.m. and 6:00 p.m., Monday through Friday. Still, I didn't mind the hard work as long as I had some degree of visibility and control over my calendar. I could slot in the other things I cared about—my podcast, writing, choral singing, mentoring, travel, exercise, and friends—into the downtime of my primary commitment: my full-time job.

But when my husband and I started discussing the reality of young children, I realized I would need to significantly alter my portfolio in order to be the kind of parent I wanted to be. My primary commitment was changing. I didn't want to fly 100,000 miles a year while attempting to breastfeed nor miss bath time more nights than not, and we didn't have a large tribe of extended family nearby to provide extra bandwidth or emergency coverage. So I spent the majority of my pregnancy researching other roles and professional opportunities that might be a better fit for the next chapter of my life. (It wasn't a moment too soon: by the time I was wrapping up my maternity leave, the company I had been with went through a round of layoffs and it wasn't clear I would have a job to return to.) In January 2020, I gave my notice and increased my writing, freelance consulting, and paid speaking work to fund some time to investigate what to do next.

After my first startup shut down in 2013, my entrepreneurship professor at Harvard Business School (and angel investor in the company), Tom Eisenmann, had asked if my co-founder and I would allow him to write a case study about our failure.* That case took on a life of its own and opened the door to developing a deeper relationship with HBS, as it was taught year after year to all 900 first-year MBA students. It also made the rounds to other colleges and business schools and gave me the opportunity to guest lecture at more than a dozen universities. So when I went back to Tom for advice on my next career move after becoming

---

* Given that I had complained as a student about not studying any failures in the entrepreneurship course, despite the majority of startups failing, I felt an obligation to say yes.

a mother, it shouldn't have been a surprise that he suggested I join the faculty at HBS teaching entrepreneurship and marketing.

The pieces of my portfolio were already in place, ready to be rebalanced in order to offer the flexibility I needed to be there for my family: I upgraded my volunteer teaching and mentoring work to become a full-time senior lecturer at Harvard. Meanwhile, I dialed back my startup and corporate innovation work from being an executive to serving as an advisor and occasional guest speaker for leadership trainings or company off-sites. As a result, I gained the incredible privilege of being able to work from home and reschedule many of my commitments when my children are sick or childcare falls through. I also have complete control over my travel schedule, and bath time remains a highlight of almost every day.

There are yet other elements of my portfolio that I've put on the back burner for now to create flexibility for my family at this new life stage: I decided to wrap up my podcast after the third season; I don't have the time or energy to make theater or write personal essays right now; and I put singing in a choir on hold for a little while. But none of them are gone entirely. They're just simmering for now, with an occasional stir to sneak a whiff of what will return to the forefront someday soon.

The Privilege of Flexibility

It's true that flexible full-time roles like mine in academia are scarce, and only accessible by a privileged few. The reality for many women starting families requires stepping away from paid work entirely. We've all read the statistics on the cost of women leaving the workforce when they can't find the flexibility to accommodate the outside demands on their time, most often as unpaid caregivers. Before the pandemic, it cost the US economy $650 billion a year, according to the National Partnership for Women & Families;[17] the hit from women leaving the workforce during the COVID-19 crisis added an extra $97 billion. In some cases, these workers really do prefer to opt out of paid labor and focus on their family full-time. But for many, this is a sacrifice made necessary by employers who cannot fathom that the talented people who work for them can also manage real lives.

This is where a portfolio can be most powerful. Anyone who sees their career as a singular job or professional path must face the binary choice of "work" or "don't work" at these moments. But folks with a collection of skills, interests, and networks can craft a combination of activities that can be reshuffled or restarted when necessary. Full-time careers could shape-shift into freelancing; hobbies could step up to become small businesses; professional certifications could become meaningful volunteer work to keep you engaged in the sector; frustrations with major frictions could spur an insight into an innovative venture. If you allow your identity to be greater than your job title, and take advantage of your optionality and diversification, you'll find flexibility when you need it the most.

Case Study: A Hobby, Some Grit, and a Whole Lot of Luck

It's not just artists, parents of young children, and the "sandwich generation" supporting aging parents who are affected. There's another "extreme user" of portfolios driven by the need for flexibility: anyone with a partner whose career requires frequent relocation with little control over the whereabouts. Military spouses, partners of untenured academics, and anyone who has made a life with a leader who works in the international arena all come to mind as those who often struggle to build momentum and security in their careers due to the demands of their significant other's work.

Joseph Solosky experienced this firsthand when his wife was stationed in Germany. He was no stranger to military life, with a degree from the US Naval Academy and a year as a naval officer under his belt. But when a back injury caused him to leave the service unexpectedly, he had to scramble to figure out what came next. A lifelong love of baseball* (and the Yankees in particular) led him to

---

* Joe is quick to note that he was not a great baseball player himself. But his grandfather loved the Yankees and it was an important affinity they shared.

hop on a plane to Florida to watch spring training, where he decided to shoot his shot and tell one of the team executives he had Google-stalked how much he wanted to work for them. The exec looked him up and down in his navy whites, sweating in the Tampa sun, and asked him to start that evening. He did.

For the next year he had his dream internship, but the reality of life soon set in, and he missed public service, so when the gig wrapped up, he headed back to DC, determined to get a job at the FBI. His résumé was thin, with eight months with the navy and a year with the Yankees, so he started waiting tables at the restaurant next door to the Hoover building, where the FBI is headquartered. The bet paid off when a fellow Naval Academy grad—and CIO of the FBI—spotted his alumni ring and struck up a conversation. Weeks later he started a role as an analyst in the bureau. Not long after, he fell in love with a law student who was in the District visiting her sister.

For three years, Joe and his girlfriend did the long-distance thing; while he worked his way up to qualifying as an FBI agent, she finished law school in Kentucky and was commissioned to the US Army JAG Corps. When they got engaged, they decided they were done with long-distance and agreed that whoever made it through the final steps of their process and was given an assignment first would determine where they moved. So when she got a posting in Germany, he followed her abroad, which meant walking away from the FBI and heading back to square one with his career.

He applied to every job he could find on the army post, looking into roles as varied as at the post office and Subway sandwich shop. But he wasn't getting any bites. So he returned to his love of baseball and started writing (for free) for a sports tech blog. Four months later, with a string of clips to point to, he applied to sports betting firms in Europe. Note: He didn't actually know anything about sports betting. But he found a CEO who was willing to take a bet (pun intended) on him, the Naval Academy grad from the FBI who, for some reason, wanted to work in sports betting in Germany. Joe was able to get his feet wet in a sales and account management role, which is how he found himself on the cutting edge of sports betting in Europe at a time when the industry was still illegal in the United States.

Three years later, his wife's tour was wrapping up and they were preparing to head back to the States when Joe caught a lucky break: Sports betting was on the cusp of legalization in the States and instead of having to start a new job search, the European firm asked him to stay on to help set up US operations. With three years of experience in the field, he was, comparatively speaking, an expert. He stuck around for three more years, but by then was itching to move from the tech platform side to the league side of the industry. He and his wife were also ready to start a family. So as she wrapped up her commitment to the army, Joe cold-LinkedIn-messaged the chief digital officer of NASCAR on Christmas Eve 2020 and told him he would love to lead sports betting for the iconic company. By the spring of 2021, they had moved to Charlotte, North Carolina, for him to start at NASCAR and in the summer, they welcomed their first child.

Joe never expected his hobby to become a significant part of his professional path. The plan had always been a career in public service. But when he was faced with disruptions to that plan and needed to move to support his wife's career, he had to get creative and see what else he could leverage from his Venn diagram. The result gave him and his family the flexibility he needed, and it helped him be in the right place at the right time to drive the growth of a new industry from the ground up.

While I'm extolling the benefits of flexibility on an individual level, this is my chance to make a direct plea to employers and hiring managers who may be reading this book: It is far past time for you to embrace a broader definition of experience and hire based on capabilities more than credentials. Look past the gap in the résumé or what seems to be a series of unrelated roles without real momentum behind them, and evaluate lived experiences alongside paid ones. Anyone with a robust Portfolio

Life will bring with them a host of skills, expertise, and judgment that cannot be captured by an automated hiring system, and it is incumbent upon you to uncover and assess those talents and experiences.

The more that companies insist on a rigid definition of work as all-in or none-at-all, the more that workers will have to walk away entirely when the realities of life hit. But those who can see the benefit of a portfolio, of encouraging meaningful part-time or remote work that is complemented by personal commitments and side projects will gain an edge in attracting and retaining incredible human beings.

The rise of the Portfolio Life may have been born out of necessity, a creative response to sustained fractures in the economic model previous generations could reasonably rely on. But the silver lining to this burgeoning movement is the freedom it offers. It unshackles our identity from our profession (or worse, one specific job). It erases the myth of a singular career path and shines a light on the many options we have at any given moment. It de-risks our income through diversification. And it provides the flexibility to protect our priorities and respond to life as it happens. As frustrated as I am by the circumstances that got us here, I am infinitely grateful to have the freedom to build this life.

By this point I'm sure you're eager to start building your own portfolio, but there's a Big Important Topic to discuss before we go much further: To successfully build a Portfolio Life, you will need to get comfortable with failure. Let me explain why.

CHAPTER 3

A Caveat: Failure

Ever tried. Ever failed. No matter. Try again. Fail again.
Fail better.

—Samuel Beckett, *Worstward Ho*

The classic graph of success is a straight line that goes up and to the right. But as we saw in Chapter 2, life is not linear, and I promise that that is a good thing. In reality, it is probably going to have a lot of twists and turns.

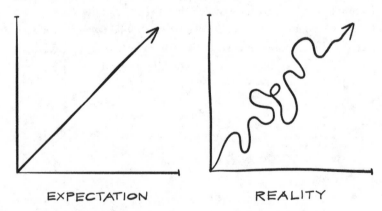

EXPECTATION   REALITY

And along the way, if you are building a Portfolio Life, some of those twists and turns are going to be failures. Why? Because the very premise of a portfolio is that some things won't work out but those that do will offset the losses. Still! The F-word. I'll let you sit with it for a minute. It's uncomfortable, right? I know. No really, I *know*.

I was a Type A overachiever who never failed at anything until the very day that my first startup, Quincy Apparel, shut down. My co-founder, Alex Nelson, and I were bright, eager twentysomethings fresh out of Harvard Business School, riding a wave of venture-backed e-commerce startups in the New York tech scene. We raised around $1 million in angel and venture capital and had a big, splashy launch, hot on the heels of Bonobos, Rent the Runway, and Warby Parker. We were set on building a brand for professional women with work clothes that actually fit and also weren't hideous (a bold value proposition at the time), and our business was predicated on some pretty innovative changes to the design and production process of women's clothes.* As outsiders to the fashion industry, we thought we could see opportunities for improvement where lifers saw "the way things are" and assumed we could hire a great team to make up for our lack of expertise. But the specific product and operational innovations we were championing were more complex and costly than we realized and we ran out of runway† before we had perfected the business model.‡

It was a humbling moment for me. I failed, and not only did my employees lose their jobs as the tech press touted our failure with glee, but I also had to face where I fell short and how much I still needed to learn. And yet, it was a defining moment in my career. Because not only did future employers and business partners not hold that failure against me, but they also saw those experiences as really valuable. They didn't ask "What did you do that caused you to fail?" Rather, the questions they asked were "What did you learn?" and "Under what conditions would you try again?" When I was given the opportunity to launch the New York

---

* That is, we acknowledged that breasts were a thing and created suiting sizes that took bra size and height into account. Truly: it was revolutionary. And also, extraordinarily difficult to execute.

† *Runway* is startup jargon for "money," which buys you time.

‡ There was also some drama, but you don't get that story without buying me a drink first.

campus of Startup Institute as my next endeavor, the board of directors saw my entrepreneurial journey—including my failure—as a considerable qualification for the role, rather than a drawback.

IT'S NO SURPRISE WE FEAR FAILURE

Most millennials were raised to avoid failure. It wasn't necessarily an intentional strategy for most parents, but it was certainly the outcome of the messages we heard over and over again. The empowerment mantra of "you can be anything!" got internalized as "it's your fault if you aren't something amazing" and the prevalence of helicopter parenting told us even small mistakes would be devastating to our future. While the outside world mocked our generation for requiring participation trophies, we would like to point out that it was *our parents* who both insisted upon and gave out those trophies. The message was received loud and clear: Even in the context of sports where, by definition, there is a winner and a loser, walking away empty-handed was a fate to be avoided at all costs.

As a result, we "often arrive[d] at the threshold of higher education without the benefit of experiencing much failure in [our] lives, and when faced with failure, or the risk of failure, often [did] not know how to respond."[1] Then we graduated into the Great Recession and found that even our academic success was not enough to ensure we'd get a foothold into the working world at an income substantial and dependable enough to both live on and build a future with. Combine that friction with the rise of social media, where all we saw were others' successes, and every year we didn't hit Forbes' 30 Under 30 list felt humiliating. Then we turned thirty, and we *still* hadn't changed the world (far from it, we were probably hitting our first early-life crisis) and the anxiety just snowballed from there.

While entrepreneurship obviously isn't the only path, it is one way to measure changes in generational risk profiles. According to the 2013 Federal Reserve's Survey of Consumer Finances, the share of people under thirty who owned private businesses fell between 1989 and 2013, from 10.6% to 3.6%, a twenty-four-year-low, and a survey by Babson College in 2015 found that 41% of twenty-five to thirty-four-year-olds say the "fear of failure" was their biggest roadblock to starting a business.

Research into elite young athletes[2] and students marked as "gifted and talented"[3] alike tell the same story: that a fear of failure leads to "anxiety, perception of low control, unstable self-esteem, pessimism, and self-handicapping."[4] Overall, it can serve as a barrier to participation in settings where success is uncertain. As in, "If I'm not sure I'll be amazing at it, I won't even try."*

FAILURE IS OFTEN OUT OF YOUR CONTROL

Yet here's the terrifying truth: While you can try your best to avoid failure by taking the predictable, straightforward path, there are so many variables outside of your control that can still trip you up. You might get fired from that "safe" job because you were a low performer; or it could be because the company is cutting costs under pressure from Wall Street investors, or the economy is contracting, or internal politics left you on the chopping block. Or maybe you had a significant health concern that required special accommodations, or you needed flexibility to care for an aging parent, or any number of other outside forces.

Similarly, you could decide to launch a business right as a global pandemic comes along and mucks up worldwide supply chains, cratering your cost structure and sinking your business model before you really had a shot at success. Or you could save your pennies for a down payment and do the "responsible" thing and buy a home for your growing family, only to enter at the top of the market just before a housing crash.

---

* I got a B- in Differential Geometry in college and tried to drop my math major. I know what it means to be socialized to succeed above all else. (Thank goodness my advisor refused to sign the form.)

Sure, you still have a house, but you now owe more than it's worth, which means you can't move or do much of anything with this asset until the market recovers. Or you could work hard and finally catch a break in an industry you've always dreamed of working in, only to discover it is constantly roiled by acquisitions, downsizing, and unreliable income streams, which means an annual layoff may very well be in your future.*

I hope you're starting to get the picture: Failure, like death, taxes, and running into your ex when you are in your rattiest sweats, is virtually guaranteed in life. So instead of hiding from it, let's learn how to get comfortable with it.

THE MATH OF RISK AND REWARD

Here's the mathematical argument: It all comes down to the relationship between risk and reward. The general rule of thumb in investing is "low risk, low reward; high risk, high reward." This usually means that things that are sure bets tend to offer more modest payoffs while really risky bets might have sky-high payoffs but a very low probability of that ever happening.

So, for example, if you have a very low-risk financial portfolio, like keeping all of your money in cash and certificates of deposit, then you'll have a dependable but low return from modest interest rates. Putting your money in high-risk investments like buying equity in startups or taking big positions in speculative opportunities like NFTs and cryptocurrencies means you *could* make a gazillion dollars, but you could also lose your investment altogether, and that outcome is much more likely. The probability of the outcome times the value of the outcome gives you the expected value. Mathematically speaking, as long as the expected value is higher than the cost of trying, it's worth giving it a shot (as long as you can afford to lose your full investment).

For our parents and grandparents, having one steady, full-time job and rising through the ranks at one company or within one industry was considered a pretty low-risk income strategy. It was akin to the risk of

---

* Yes, I'm talking about journalism.

keeping your money in a traditional savings account. But with the financial, geopolitical, and climate disruptions that keep coming every five to ten years, combined with the pace of technological innovation and the resultant changes to most industries, this is no longer a low-risk strategy. It's the worst kind of investment: medium or high risk, low reward.

To offset this risk, you need to diversify. That could be a medium-risk, medium- or high-reward bet like starting a small business on the side while still working your day job. It could also be a high-risk, high-reward project that you only allocate a small amount of your portfolio to, limiting your downside if it fails. (Think: doing stand-up comedy on nights and weekends in small venues around town to see if you have what it takes. The only real downside if you totally bomb is the hit to your ego, which is definitely a hit, but not one that knocks you off your feet.)

By definition, some of the activities in your portfolio *will* fail, because you aren't filling it up with safe bets. You have to add risk in order to have a shot at higher returns. The goal is to diversify that risk across several opportunities so the failure in any one activity doesn't crater the whole portfolio.

RESILIENCE, ADAPTABILITY, AND POST-TRAUMATIC GROWTH

Did the math not sway you? That's okay. I have another argument that you may find even more compelling. Novelist Mary Renault once wrote, "There is only one kind of shock worse than the totally unexpected: the expected for which one has refused to prepare."* Given everything you know about the world, it is wise to expect the unexpected to occur at some point in your career (and, unfortunately, your personal life as well). Leaning into disruption and failure, rather than shying away, builds two

---

* From her moving postwar novel *The Charioteer*, which is worth the read if you like historical fiction. Incidentally, Renault's first novels were written while she worked full-time as a nurse. It wasn't until her forties that she had built enough of a name that she could make a living solely as a novelist.

important psychological muscles: resilience and adaptability.[5] For those truly open to it, it can even lead to meaningful growth.

Resilience is the capacity to bounce back from setbacks. Put another way, it is the ability to brush yourself off, get back up, and continue making progress toward your goals given the resources you've already gathered. *Adaptability* is the skill of revising your goals or tactics to accommodate new information or a new reality. It's the art of the pivot. Rather than assuming there is nothing they can do about their setbacks, people who have developed the capacity for adaptability see failures as *temporary*, *local*, and *changeable*.[6]

Dr. Martin E.P. Seligman, the so-called father of positive psychology, dedicated his career to research on failure, helplessness, and optimism. He learned that the way people respond to extreme adversity is normally distributed: some struggle with depression or PTSD; many bounce back after initial negative reactions; and some show considerable growth, eventually ending up better off than they were before the trauma. His work has been incorporated by organizations ranging from Fortune 100 companies to the US Army as more and more leaders recognize that how folks respond to failure is more valuable than avoiding failure in the first place. Dr. Seligman outlined five behaviors known to contribute to post-traumatic growth:

1. Accept that your response to failure—including shattered beliefs about yourself, others, and your future—is totally normal and not some indication that you are flawed.
2. Reduce anxiety by controlling intrusive thoughts, including by recognizing when negative emotions are out of proportion to the reality of the threat you are facing.
3. Be open and honest about your failure. Bottling up or obfuscating failure can lead to feeling even worse.
4. Engage in constructive storytelling in which failure is seen as a fork in the road, providing an opportunity to lean on strengths, improve relationships, and try new doors.
5. Articulate your personal principles and be explicit and intentional about where you go from here.

Do you know why lifting weights causes your body to build muscle? Because the stress creates tiny tears in the muscle fibers, which the body repairs to be even stronger. Pushing yourself out of your comfort zone and into the realm of potential failure is like lifting mental and emotional weights. Take advantage of your failures to build strength so that next time you can meet the moment and succeed.

THE COSTS OF FAILURE

Now, I acknowledge that failure is a complex subject; it's not as simple as saying, "Go try things and who cares if you fail!" I don't want to gloss over the real costs of failure that can vary pretty dramatically depending on an individual's privilege. To be blunt, the consequences of failure are more extreme for some people than others. And the opportunities to rebound from failure are more accessible for some people than others. So any discussion of failure must acknowledge this inequality and address it head-on.

I like to break down the costs of failure into three buckets:

1. Financial costs—direct losses and indirect opportunity costs
2. Social costs—damage to relationships and reputational costs
3. Psychological costs—damage to self-perception, grief, and the stress of financial and social costs

Individuals with safety nets in any or all of these areas will find they can mitigate and absorb these costs more easily. Some safety nets can be built; others are ingrained. In either case, a realistic view of the costs of failure will help you manage your risk appropriately. Let's look at each bucket in more detail.

Financial Costs

The financial costs of failure are generally pretty transparent: loss of income if you lose a job; loss of capital and potentially the personal assumption of debt if you shut down an entrepreneurial venture; legal costs if you dissolve a partnership, personal or professional; and if you really want to pile on, play the "what if?" game to enumerate the opportunity costs you missed out on by not doing something else. Some people are better set up to mitigate these financial costs, whether through personal savings, a partner who can shoulder the financial responsibility for the entire family, or generational wealth that can be tapped into, like a trust fund or moving back in with parents and relying on them for a while. For those without any of these forms of a safety net, the financial costs of failure can loom large. They did for me when I was paying my rent with my credit card and staring down a negative bank balance as we shut down Quincy.

But there are creative ways to think about mitigating financial risk that you should not forget about: the strength of your professional and personal network to help you land on your feet; the full breadth of your Venn diagram that you could put to use for future employment opportunities; even your personal rebound rate and track record for moving through feelings of failure rather than sitting in and dwelling upon them.

While I didn't have any financial safety net to speak of, I knew I had what one therapist called a "fast emotional metabolism": I dig down deep into my feelings, feel them all in Technicolor, untangle the narratives that don't serve me, and get to the other side with a bias toward action, all on a pretty speedy timetable. I also knew that I had faced an anemic bank account before, like when I first moved to New York at twenty-two with five suitcases, a cello, and about six hundred bucks after paying first, last, and deposit on an illegal sublet in Brooklyn. I had a few job leads at that point but no actual offer. But a combination of grit and luck made that bet pay off; two weeks later I landed a full-time role at the Metropolitan Opera. My greatest financial safety net is that I tell myself the story that "I may not know what is going to happen, but I am smart enough and strong enough to figure it out."

Take a minute and consider what your financial safety net looks like. What resources, skills, networks, or relationships could you rely on to soften the blow of any potential financial costs of your failure? If your financial safety net currently looks pretty skimpy, is there a way you can begin to strengthen it to better support you in the future?

Social Costs

The social costs of failure include both the relationships that may be fractured by the failure (e.g., broken business partnerships) and the reputational hit you might experience. Those in the startup world who proclaim that failure isn't a big deal are often the same people who are given the benefit of the doubt as to their potential, even in the wake of evidence to the contrary. If you are white, male, Ivy League educated, attractive, able-bodied, well-networked, and/or from a trusted pedigree (whether that's a prior job at a blue-chip firm or a family name that everyone recognizes), you will be given a second chance more readily than folks who do not possess those descriptors.

"In a lot of organizations, the people who are allowed to fail and fail up, the people who are allowed to learn from those mistakes and still be given an opportunity to get back up again, are overwhelmingly male and overwhelmingly white," says Ruchika Tulshyan, founder of the Seattle-based inclusion strategy firm Candour.[7] Conversely, research from Utah State University in 2020 reported that "women and BIPOC employees in elite leadership roles who make even minor missteps at work, whether violating the dress code or displaying unacceptable emotions,* can be judged much more harshly than white men."[8]

I've experienced both sides of those biases. While my entrepreneurial failure was public and painful, I had a business degree from Harvard in my back pocket, which meant I was absolutely given the benefit of the doubt that my potential was greater than this one specific performance. I am also tall, white, able-bodied, outgoing, a confident public speaker, and conventionally attractive, which means I literally look the

---

* As opposed to acceptable emotions, like anger, which are more often seen as masculine and powerful.

part of what we've decided a leader looks like (except for the fact that I'm a woman). On the flip side, I have absolutely been penalized in jobs where my passion for the work was interpreted as combative rather than inspirational, and my Technicolor feelings have been reprimanded more times than I can count for being unprofessional and unproductive (one time, quite memorably, while my male boss threw a tantrum in an adjoining conference room that was loud enough for the entire company to hear).

The social costs of failure are not borne equally, and it is important I call that out as I encourage you to take (appropriate) risks. There is work to be done to change this at a societal level, but in the meantime, it is absolutely rational to weigh the social risks of failure as you construct your portfolio. That might mean teeing up a softball so you can hit a single or double, establishing a track record of success before attempting the home run you really have your eyes on. It might also mean building an informal team of cheerleaders with in-group privilege who can lend you some of that privilege through endorsements, references, and introductions. And it can mean ignoring the advice, no matter how well-meaning, of those who don't face the same social costs when evaluating opportunities. How strong is your social safety net and what actions can you take to shore it up before you need it?

Psychological Costs

One of the hardest parts of trying and failing is the ego-crushing realization that you are flawed. For high achievers this can be the most painful cost of all, even if it seems fairly obvious when you look at it in black and white. Even for those who have a more nuanced view of their fallibility, bombing a project, losing a job, or shutting down a company can trigger a sense of lost self. This is especially true for folks who define themselves by their job title over all else.

"As it is, work sits at the heart of Americans' vision of human flourishing," wrote Jonathan Malesic in an op-ed for the *New York Times*. "It's much more than how we earn a living. It's how we earn dignity: the right to count in society and enjoy its benefits."[9] Yet equating our identity and our dignity with our work is dangerous in more ways than one, as we saw in Chapter 2. So how do we mitigate these psychological risks? First and foremost, we can define our self-worth beyond our work. (Human Venn diagram, check!) Second, we can use the five tools Dr. Seligman outlined to focus on the opportunities for growth in the wake of failure. In particular, I'd emphasize the mental practices of not catastrophizing the situation and effective storytelling of how failure will catalyze productive, forward action.

Lastly, we can lean on our portfolio. All three costs of failure are mitigated by a portfolio of income streams, track records of success, and opportunities to define meaning and self-worth. And you don't have to take my word for it. Research published in the *Journal of Management* in 2013 about life after business failure points out this very reality: The emotional costs of failure are "diluted" for portfolio entrepreneurs because they have at least one other opportunity to fall back on, which allows them to better learn and recover from that failure. On the other hand, serial entrepreneurs who put all of their energy and resources into one opportunity experience the effects of failure to be "more emotionally challenging," thus obstructing their ability to rebound.[10]

HOW TO PRACTICE FAILING

Okay, you're warming to the idea that you should grow familiar with failure. But how do you actually do it? Simple: fail in small ways on a regular basis. "The more that you can embrace all the little failures you have, and treat them as ways of improving the system, the less likely that the entire system will collapse," says Shikhar Ghosh, my colleague in the entrepreneurship unit at HBS.[11]

Some people have had opportunities to build their failure and resilience muscle in childhood or their early career. Playing team sports is one way to grow accustomed to losing. Folks who thrive in sales careers learn pretty quickly how to shake off rejection and keep trying until they close a deal. Artists who can develop a thick skin toward auditioning and submissions processes don't let failure hold them back (though many do end up leaving their profession over rejection burnout—it's hard to remain creative and vulnerable yet grow a thick skin at the same time). There's even some research that points to how boys are socialized earlier than girls to bounce back from failure since the traditional expectation in heterosexual relationships is for boys to ask girls out.[12] As a result, they get used to being told no and keep trying anyway, while girls are trained to wait for an attractive offer or to opt out entirely if none comes along.

Maybe you are super comfortable with failure and don't need any more practice. In that case, congrats! (Also, please tell me your secret.) But for the rest of us, the opportunity here is to get good at failing small to avoid failing big. Building your failure muscle is one of the best ways to construct your own safety net.

Case Study: Well-Documented Failure

Jason Haaheim is an expert at failing. Growing up, he studied piano and percussion while tinkering and cultivating a growing fascination with science. In college he double-majored in music and physics, playing timpani in the orchestra while delving into research in nanotechnology. After college he chose to pursue the science path professionally, earning a master's degree in electrical engineering and landing a job as a research and development engineer at a nanotech company in Chicago. But he kept up his amateur musical pursuits, playing timpani in the Chicago Civic Orchestra, a training ensemble for emerging early-career musicians.

While he enjoyed his work as a scientist, over the next decade he realized he'd prefer to pursue a career as an orchestral musician. But instead of heading to conservatory to make the switch, he took a scientific approach to his practicing and started on the audition circuit. "Most of science is well-documented failure. And most of orchestra auditioning is failure. So, I just figured I needed to document it well and with the same rigor," he told me. What does that mean? Taking incredibly detailed, meticulously organized notes

documenting his process, a method developed by Swedish psy-
chologist K. Anders Ericsson called "deliberate practice." After each
failure, looking through those notes to map out what didn't work
and forming a hypothesis about what *might* work next time. And
when things did go well, being skeptical of how he influenced that
success and then trying to repeat it.*

The steadiness of his day job gave him the runway to learn
and develop as a musician, and to fail over and over again, taking
twenty-seven auditions for other orchestras before finally winning
an audition to become the principal timpanist in the Metropolitan
Opera Orchestra.

As a scientist, he defined failure as anything that didn't turn
out as he had hoped/expected/hypothesized. Which means that
his work was mostly trying to tease apart *why*. Rather than beat-
ing himself up for falling short, Jason exhibited the quintessential
growth mindset: assuming that just because his ability was inad-
equate at present didn't mean he couldn't develop it eventually. (Dr.
Carol Dweck would be so proud.)

Unlike his fellow auditioners who felt every failure as another
nail in the coffin of their professional musical career, Jason low-
ered the cost of his failed auditions by having a thriving career outside of music. It gave him the money, time, and mental fortitude
to build his musical muscles, so to speak, until he was ready to go
all-in.

After Quincy shut down, I decided I needed to get better at failing,
so I took up long-distance running. To be clear: I am not a gifted athlete. I was the only student ever asked to leave my high school basketball
team because I was so bad the coach knew I would spend all of fresh-
man year on the bench. I also cheated on the mile run in junior high gym

* Jason writes a fantastic blog about the idea of deliberate practice and well-
documented failure that is worth checking out: https://jasonhaaheim.com/well
-documented-failure/

class. We didn't have a gym and instead ran four laps of the parking lot to complete the Presidential Physical Fitness Test, so I hid behind a tree for three laps, spritzed myself with water to appear sweaty, and then trotted out for the final lap (being smart enough to finish next to last so as not to arouse suspicions). I wasn't a total slouch, but I had mostly sedentary hobbies: I spent my adolescent years practicing piano and cello, competing on the math team, and leading the student council. Exercise in general—and running in particular—was my kryptonite.

Which is why, after I picked myself up and got my first post-failed-startup job building Startup Institute New York, I decided to run thirteen half-marathons in a year. It was 2013, after all, and half-marathons are 13.1 miles, so it felt like a good banner for my efforts: 13x13.1 in 2013. (The fact that I had run maybe a total of 20 miles in my entire life up to that point did not seem to be relevant.) I wasn't doing this to cheer myself up in the wake of my startup implosion. I was doing it because I knew it would be hard, I would be bad at it, and each race would be long enough that I couldn't ignore how bad I was at it, but rather, face it over and over again as I took each step to the finish line. I had avoided so many things in my life because I was afraid of being bad at them, and I wanted to shake that mentality.

Over the next six months, I ran twelve half-marathons and finished the year with the New York City Marathon after my thirteenth race through a national park got canceled in the wake of a federal government shutdown. Even if I never set the goal of winning a race (obviously that was out of the question), I often set goals for a personal record or tried to hit a certain split time, and I didn't always succeed. Sure, my finish times improved over the season, though I still ran nearly a six-hour marathon. And my body started to recover quicker after each race. Plus, I got a series of great selfies and a handful of medals out of it (yes, more participation trophies). But none of that was the point. I was learning to do things I was bad at.

Now, you might point out that being bad at something is not the same as failing. But as an overachiever, I must respectfully disagree. Until my midtwenties, I would actively avoid literally anything that I wasn't assured I would excel at. My internal narrative was one of success. I didn't want to put that at risk, so I refused to even try things that seemed uncertain. For me, while my financial and social safety nets felt relatively strong, the psychological costs of failure felt potentially devastating. I needed to rewrite that narrative.

It's true, the stakes of not finishing a recreational run are not the same as shutting down a company. But that's the point: We want to build our failure muscles in small ways rather than try our hand at big, painful, expensive failures on our very first try. By allowing myself to be bad at running, I was able to shift my self-perception from my track record of "success" to focus instead on my ability to show up, be brave, push through when things got hard, and get back up when I fell down. Sometimes, quite literally, like when I wiped out in the first mile of a predawn trail run.

FAILURE SHOULDN'T BE A WAY OF LIFE, BUT IT SHOULD BE A WAY OF LEARNING

Do I want you to fail? Yes. At something. Maybe several things. Not all the things, obviously; overall, I want you to succeed beyond your wildest dreams. But if you don't fail at *anything*, it means you aren't pushing yourself beyond your comfort zone. You aren't testing the limits of your abilities so you can learn and build new muscles. You aren't taking on enough risk to earn a return that will support and sustain you through the virtually guaranteed disruptions ahead. I promise that once you have experienced a failure or two, you'll realize it's not nearly as life-threatening as it may seem right now. And, rather than hiding those failures, they can play a meaningful part in your story, as Quincy has mine.

As we wrap up Part I, I want to emphasize that the struggle you're feeling is real. The economic equation we're trying to solve is substantially harder than the one previous generations had to wrangle. But it's not unsolvable; it just requires a different approach, one rooted in port-folios of options rather than singular answers. And we're prepared to face some failures along the way in the name of our future success.

Now it's time to get our hands dirty in Part II as we uncover the elements of our portfolio and piece them together in a way that feels fulfilling and sustainable. And may Mother Earth forgive us for the number of sticky notes we're about to plow through. (You may want to plant a tree when you're done.) Ready? Let's go.

PART II

WHAT

CHAPTER 4

What's in Your Venn Diagram?

Do I contradict myself? Very well then, I contradict
myself. (I am large, I contain multitudes.)
                                —Walt Whitman, *Song of Myself*, 51

We have an ambitious goal ahead of us in Part II: To define a fully
visioned strategy for how we want to shape our lives. To kick
things off, I want to start by focusing on you. Who are you? And what's
in your Venn diagram?

In Chapter 2, we talked about how important it is to define your identity beyond your profession or current job title. But we didn't talk about
how to actually do that...until now. The first step for seeing yourself
beyond your job is to actually *see* yourself. You are so much more than
the economic value of your labor; you are a three-dimensional human with
dreams, talents, and relationships, and you're worth more than your work.

For example, imagine you are employed as a flight attendant but
the people who know you best see someone who loves to travel, kills at
karaoke night, solves any logistical problem without breaking a sweat,
and finds humor in even the most stressful moments. You shine in the
spotlight, and when you're in charge, everyone around you relaxes their
shoulders just a bit more. If a friend were describing you to a stranger,
they might say a half dozen other things before mentioning that you get
paid to crisscross the globe wearing a jaunty neckerchief. In this scenario,
being a flight attendant is *what you currently do*, but it's not *who you are*.

The goal in this chapter is to finally see yourself like others see you.

I want you to ignore that narrow job title you've been trying to fit into and instead take a fresh look at what you can offer the world and what makes you feel most fulfilled. Broadly speaking, we're going to find the fields of your Venn diagram.

If you've been in the workforce for a few years (or a few decades), it's likely that you may have carved off, hidden away, or shut down aspects of yourself that didn't fit the mold of the path you were setting out on. It may not be your instinct to claim such a variety of identities anymore, and I'd like to remind you that (a) that's not your fault and (b) it's okay if this feels uncomfortable at first. On the other end of the spectrum, those of you who are just starting out may feel like you're in touch with the things that interest you, but struggle to define what makes you stand out in a crowded room. Maybe you don't yet see how your unique combination of skills and experiences can contribute something truly special to the world (or help pay the bills).

In either case you may not be able to draw a complete picture of your Venn diagram simply by being introspective. Which is why we're going to start not with self-reflection and navel-gazing, but by asking others who they see when they look at you.

William E. Ketchum III ✔ @WEKetchum

Recently told a friend how it confuses me when people think more highly of me than I do of myself. She said "they see who you really are instead of what you've lied to yourself about." It's stuck with me ever since. Fellow imposter syndrome sufferers, keep that in mind.

START WITH A CUP OF COFFEE

I know how powerful this process is because I've used it myself. When my startup Quincy failed, I faced a debilitating crisis of confidence. At that moment I felt like I had no idea who I was. My résumé touted a few years' experience in arts management, three summers as a set carpenter, one year of management consulting, an MBA, and a defunct fashion company where, as a startup CEO, I did a little bit of everything (whether I was good at it or not). My Venn diagram had some clear fields—business, technology, the arts—but I didn't know what that actually *meant* when it came to what I had to offer the world.

So, at first I ignored the question altogether and instead crawled into bed and watched all seven seasons of *The West Wing* from top to bottom. (It takes about three weeks, by the way.) I didn't talk to anyone or leave my apartment except to get food at the corner bodega and take out the trash. In short, I wallowed.

It felt good to rest for a minute after a year and a half of the nonstop roller coaster of building a venture-backed startup. Yet after the credits rolled on the end of the Bartlett administration, I realized I didn't have any more answers than when I started. Neither solitude nor escapism was solving my identity crisis. So I decided to talk to the people who knew me best and ask for help. I took a shower, ate some vegetables, and emailed everyone in my network, asking them to meet me for coffee (and also to buy the coffee, since I was flat-out broke). I reached out to folks who had known me since high school and fellow startup community members who I had only known a few months. I contacted business school professors, former bosses, colleagues across various jobs, and former collaborators.

I sent almost a hundred emails, which, in retrospect, was overkill. But I asked for so many meetings first, because I wanted to make sure I was getting a perspective that reflected all sides of me. If I had met with folks who only knew my startup days, they wouldn't have any insight into how I shined—and where I struggled—when I directed and produced plays or when I did research on colloidal particles in a physics lab.

But it was also largely because I didn't think that many people would say yes. People are busy and this was an ask that would really only benefit me. And yet, my network showed up for me and was more generous than I could have imagined. As one former coworker put it, "You've paid into the bank account of our relationship so many times over the years. It was an easy 'yes' when you said you needed to make a withdrawal this time."

In the end, more than seventy people responded, and I set out on a whirlwind month of coffee chats,* asking my friends and professional contacts the same three questions:

1. When have you seen me happiest?
2. What do you come to me for?
3. Where do I stand out against my peers?

I landed on these questions because I was struggling to see myself the way others saw me. My internal monologue was like a broken record and I didn't feel like I could trust it at the time. So I wanted to know what was the exact moment that made my friends and colleagues think of me. What was the problem they faced where they said, "You know what, I should see if Christina can help here"?

Somewhat surprisingly, the answers I got to those three questions were fairly consistent across people who had known me for over a decade and those who had known me only a few months. Also notably, they didn't mention specific industry expertise, but instead identified the mindsets, skills, and settings where they had seen me thrive.

They saw me happiest when I was in charge of my calendar and able to incorporate all of my interests alongside my work—from performing with musical ensembles to mentoring recent grads to taking writing workshops. I wasn't afraid of working hard; I just wanted to do it on my terms. This meant I needed a substantial level of autonomy in roles and made certain business models like client services not a great fit.

They came to me for help with storytelling—for positioning a new product or connecting the arc in their résumé or just pulling up one level to see the forest through the trees. This skill is most closely aligned

---

* If you're not familiar with this concept, it generally means a thirty- to forty-five-minute meeting that is unrelated to the other person's business interests. It could be an informational interview about their industry or a chance to introduce yourself for future opportunities, or, in my case, a way to catch up and ask for feedback. And it doesn't have to include coffee, by the way. I did several of these as walking meetings where we strolled through a nearby park or I joined them for after-work errands. Since these are often one-way asks, it's best to make it as easy as possible for the other person.

with marketing and communications jobs, though it is also essential for founders and chief executives or anyone in a role that requires articulating big ideas and attracting the resources to build them. It also is something I could easily put to use on the side, through freelance work like coaching, content creation, or public speaking.

And I stood out against my peers in my ability to create something out of nothing. I thrived in the 0–2 stage of things and could recruit talented folks who believed in my vision and wanted to work with me. This was an insight on both my mindset and the stage where I fit best, pointing out that going from nothing to something was more interesting to me than going from something to something a little bit better. While I could apply this mindset in a wide variety of worlds, from the performing arts to startups, I needed to be clear on when I could deliver the most impact and when I should transition out and hand things over to a more operationally focused leader.

Throughout this process, I tried to keep track of the patterns I was hearing. Those conversations helped me understand what kind of roles I might enjoy, what kind of workplace culture I would excel in, and that my multidisciplinary life was a superpower and something I should continue to invest in. I now had better parameters for my job search, looking for leadership roles in early-stage tech startups that were either focused on brand marketing and communications or would give me the opportunity to build something from the ground up, like launching a new product or expanding into a new region for the business. More importantly, I could see myself beyond my current job title and realized how many opportunities I had to make my contribution to the world.

To be honest, the insights were all kind of obvious the more I thought about it. But sometimes it really does take seventy cups of coffee to see things clearly.

WHY GET A SECOND OPINION?

I recently called up my friend Kathleen Stetson, a professional coach, to ask why getting an outside perspective from friends is so valuable. A former opera singer and acoustical engineer, Kathleen started her career bringing people together at the intersection of arts, science, and business. She founded an arts/tech startup while getting her MBA at the Massachusetts Institute of Technology and co-founded MIT's Hacking Arts—the world's first arts+tech festival and hackathon—before consulting for startups and arts institutions, including the Los Angeles Philharmonic. In her midthirties, she pivoted again. Depression, sparked by the challenges of startup life, plus a chronic years-long migraine, spurred her extensive research into wellness, meditation, and mindfulness. Using this knowledge and her deep desire to help entrepreneurs, she became a personal and executive coach for "many-hats-wearing" folks.

"The goal at this stage is not about finding the 'right' answers. It's about gathering information and then processing it in a way that helps you make sense of the many possibilities that are open to you," she told me. Internal information is an important piece of the puzzle: You can uncover a great deal about yourself from meditation, journaling, mindfulness practices, and so on. But external information—how others see you—can provide missing pieces. Don't think of it as necessarily asking for feedback; think of it simply as gaining perspective. Hearing how others perceive you might teach you about a communication gap as much as about your skills or interests.

 ## Seek That Second Opinion

Asking friends and colleagues to tell you about yourself is a powerful way to see a three-dimensional portrait of you that you may not (yet) be able to see. Do you need to talk with seventy people to pull this off? Absolutely not. But you'd be surprised by how valuable it is to ask for help from a wide range of folks. Get out of your head and seek that second opinion.

Draw up a list of friends, colleagues, managers, and professional contacts that you'd like to ask for coffee (or a walk or a Zoom chat). The goal is to talk to enough folks that you start seeing some patterns in their feedback. (In the startup world, when we're doing discovery for product development, we generally say five to seven interviews per customer segment is the sweet spot.[1] Other studies suggest you can identify more than 90% of the key insights from qualitative research after about a dozen conversations.[2]) When you can start predicting what they'll say before they've said it, you know you've done enough.

Keep your list of questions short so you can leave space to discover something new. I recommend these three, but feel free to riff off them to craft your own:

1. **When have you seen me happiest?**
2. **What do you come to me for?**
3. **Where do I stand out against my peers?**

Take a notebook with you and jot down their answers, along with anything surprising or novel. If you hear something that you truly have not heard before, ask your next few coffee chats about that insight. Don't get hung up on something you only hear from one conversation, but if others corroborate it, it's worth digging in to learn more. The goal here is to spot trends and gather intel to help you form a complete picture of yourself.

By the end of your coffee chats, you should have one or two answers for each of your questions that the majority of your friends and colleagues would agree with. Keep them handy; they'll be important inputs to drawing up your Venn diagram.

BE WELL-LOPSIDED

Sometimes that second opinion reveals that we have a superpower. Maybe it's a skill or a mindset we take for granted because it just comes naturally to us. As such, we may not realize how rare and valuable it actually is. In this case, that outside perspective can help us understand how it might pay off to lean into that superpower to make our impact. Rather than trying to be well-rounded, this is an opportunity to be well-lopsided.

Lanette* was surprised by how powerful it was to see herself through someone else's eyes. A recent MBA grad in her early thirties, she had already had one career in the entertainment industry before deciding to pivot into management consulting. She joined a top-tier consulting firm's Atlanta office after graduation and kept her head down to learn the skills required of her new job: research, data analysis, slide writing, client management, and presentation skills. The firm had a rigorous training program for new hires and Lanette enjoyed the opportunities for structured learning and feedback throughout her first year, along with learning on the job with her team.

"That first year is hard for nearly everyone," she reflected, "because the hours are long, the expectations are high, and the culture is up-or-out." Like many elite professional service firms, Lanette's consulting firm had a policy that you were either promoted or "counseled out" (i.e., fired) every two years or so. "But for folks like me coming in from a previous career in a very different industry, it can also be painful when we feel like underperformers because we're being measured along a very different yardstick than in our last role. We're learning new skills, new jargon, new office politics, and in many ways, I felt like my superpowers weren't useful while the things I kept stumbling over were make-it-or-break-it competencies."

Lanette decided to spend time one-on-one with a professional development coach the firm offered all first-year consultants. In her third session, they focused on her presentation skills. The coach asked her to bring some slides from a recent project, and he had her present to imaginary clients sitting around the boardroom table. He set up a camera to film the session so they could review the tape together afterward, and grabbed a notebook to take notes in real time as well. But instead of jotting down opportunities for improvement, he sat perfectly still for fifteen minutes while Lanette walked her "clients" through the team's

---

* At her request, some identifying details have been changed.

recent analysis and insights and outlined their work plan for the next phase of the project. When she finished, he turned off the camera and sat down opposite her at the long oak table.

"I think you should leave this company," he said quietly but firmly. Lanette was taken aback. She didn't think her presentation was that bad. In fact, she kind of thought she had rocked it. What was happening here? "Don't misunderstand me," he said. "It's not because you did poorly. It's because that was the single best presentation I've seen in more than twenty years of coaching new consultants across dozens of offices for this firm. You are a natural communicator. You have a stunning presence. And you will not get to use that gift to its full potential until you are a partner here in six or seven years. In the meantime, you will get dinged for struggling with other skills that they see as dealbreakers and you may never make it to partner at all. Go find a job that puts you in a presentation role at least fifty percent of your time. That is what you were meant to do."

Lanette sat in silence as she absorbed his feedback. She had always loved public speaking. While others battled nerves and struggled with notecards or carefully scripted comments, she felt comfortable with all eyes on her and had a knack for speaking off the cuff while staying on message. She was eloquent, magnetic, and felt like the best version of herself on days she got to give a presentation. This was a far cry from the feelings she had on days she spent building Excel models, fighting with formulas, or searching bleary-eyed for the tiny errors that made her analysis not line up. On those days she felt small, uncertain, and, sometimes, stupid.

"I have just one question," she finally replied. "Shouldn't I be looking for opportunities to improve my areas for development* rather than just double down on the things I know I can do well?" As a high achiever, she felt uncomfortable knowing there were things she wasn't good at.

The coach laughed a little. "This isn't school anymore. Being forgettably well-rounded isn't rewarded in the real world. Be memorably

---

* The business world has jargon for seemingly everything, including this delightful argot. "Areas for development" is a fake nice way of saying "you suck at this."

well-lopsided. If you are this good at something, run full speed ahead to build your career on its foundation."

There's some solid neuroscience research to back up the coach's advice to lean into your lopsidedness. During infancy, the brain experiences an explosion of synapse formation between neurons. This intense period of brain development plays a key role in learning, memory formation, and adaptation early on. Around two to three years old, your synapses hit a peak level. But shortly after this growth spurt, the brain starts to remove synapses it no longer needs.

The process follows the "use it or lose it" principle: Active synapses are strengthened, while inactive ones are pruned. Early synaptic pruning is mostly influenced by our genes. Later on, it's based on our experiences. Recent research indicates this process goes on much longer than initially thought—until your midtwenties rather than finishing in your teenage years.[3]

But after this intense period of pruning, your unique network of synaptic connections does not significantly change. This means a person's recurring patterns of thoughts, feelings, and behaviors generally do not shift without a notable life disruption. If you are detail-oriented, you will stay detail-oriented. If you are competitive, you will continue to be competitive. If you are a curious tinkerer, you will remain a curious tinkerer. Rather than spend four or five decades of your career trying to improve upon the things you are not, neuroscience tells us that we will learn the most, grow the most, and improve the most in the areas of our brain where we already have the strongest synaptic connections—that is, we should identify where our talents lie and then seek out skills, knowledge, and experiences that build on those talents to do consistently excellent work.

High achievers tend to spot their weaknesses more easily than they do their strengths.[4] Sometimes their strengths go unnoticed because they are things that seem easy to them, like Lanette and public speaking. However, most high-achieving folks rarely miss spotting their weaknesses because they generally put them in the category of things they should change. Here's the thing: By all means, be open to general self-improvement, but your long-term growth will be the most dramatic when you invest in your strengths and build on existing synaptic connections.

I like to describe the result of this work as discovering and embracing your weirdly shaped puzzle piece. Once you have identified and revealed the contours of where you excel and what you have to offer, you will figure out *really quickly* if your puzzle piece is what someone else is looking for. Rather than trying to reshape yourself to fit in more places, embrace your jagged edges and ruthlessly select opportunities where you'll thrive.* As Lanette's coach put it, be memorably well-lopsided, not forgettably well-rounded.

 Circle Up

You may be reading this and thinking, "Sure, Christina, this all makes sense, but what if I don't have superpowers? What if I might just be an average puzzle piece after all?" I hear you. The fear is real. But I promise there's a lot more to you than that. (And I never make promises, so you know I'm serious.) So let's take what you learned from your coffee chats and expand on it to flesh out your full Venn diagram.

Before you can put the many dimensions of your life into conversation in a portfolio, you need to get a clear picture of the "circles"

---

* I feel compelled to add that this is true in your search for a romantic partner as well. Be open to growth, yes, but don't take every piece of negative feedback from someone only half interested in you as evidence of what you need to fix about yourself. Rather, spend your time identifying your weirdly shaped puzzle piece and then search for someone who *fits you*.

in your Venn diagram and understand where they intersect. These circles could be industries (law, media, education, health care, etc.), functions (writing, teaching, selling, coordinating, etc.), hobbies or interests (playing music, baking elaborate cakes, decluttering all the things, saving the whales, etc.), or even specific skills (being an Excel whiz, having a photographic memory, bench pressing more than you weigh, taking legitimately excellent selfies, etc.). By the end of this exercise, you'll have a draft of the Venn diagram that will power your portfolio.

STEP 1: WHAT'S IN YOUR CIRCLES?

You've already gotten started by seeking an outside perspective on what makes you happy, when you stand out, and where you might be delightfully lopsided. Those insights are a great first data set for crafting your Venn diagram. Grab a pen and a stash of sticky notes or index cards and write each insight from those chats on a separate piece of paper.

Now you're going to add to that pile by thinking through four questions:

1. What do you currently do?

Let's start with the easiest piece: What are you doing right now? Don't just jot down the job title—think about what you actually *do* in your role. Do you plan events? Write marketing copy? Design the overall framework for the code base? Interview sources? Make cold calls? Coordinate all of the people and moving pieces to get a project over the finish line? Plot out complex logistics and persuade folks to make it happen? (Hint: These are some of the bullet points that should be on your résumé if they aren't already...) Don't evaluate or edit your answers just yet—write down *everything* (even the stuff you don't love doing!) and we'll pare it down a little later.

And don't just think about work; consider all the parts of your life. Do you write the community newsletter for the PTA? Take headshots for your friends when they need new photos for LinkedIn? Do you not-so-secretly think you should apply for *The Great British Baking Show* because of your impressive laminating and piping skills? Get it all down on paper. Look at all of the things you are already doing! But we're not stopping there...

2. What else have you done?

Now, think back to roles before this one, including any gigs that you don't consider "real jobs" that you might have done just for the summer or part-time while in school. Again, jot down the actual things you did (took elaborate customer orders, triaged nonstop phone calls for a demanding boss, taught swimming lessons to tantruming toddlers without losing your cool).

3. What do you nerd out about?

Next, consider what you do for fun. Or, perhaps, what you did for fun back when you had time for fun. What clubs did you join in school? What activity or invite do you always say yes to? What section of the newspaper do you read first? Who do you follow on Twitter? What corner of TikTok has the algorithm taken you to? Is there a Reddit community or Discord server you are a regular on? Give each one a sticky note.

4. What are/were you known for?

Lastly, think about when your friends seek you out. Do they come to you when they need a podcast recommendation or relationship advice or to fine-tune a new recipe? This is your chance to mine that second opinion beyond the "professional" insights, taking note of what other people have noticed about you.

Another way to think of this is where you've stood out against your peers, even if it didn't mean much to you at the time. I'm talking about that creative writing contest you won in middle school or the superlative you were given in your high school yearbook. Maybe you had a killer free throw even though your team never had a shot at the championship and you were too short to play basketball in college or beyond. (While you can probably rule out the NBA from your set of future paths, you might consider coaching a kid's team or joining a community league to make new friends and stay active.) Add these moments where you shine to your pile of Post-its.

STEP 2: FIND THE COMMONALITIES AND CATEGORIZE INTO SETS

Now grab your sticky notes and let's start making sense of them. Take a look through your stack and triage anything you don't like doing into a separate pile. Of the stickies that remain in your "like to do" pile, add a star in the corner for ones that you would love to do more of.

Now start to look for patterns and overlaps. Your goal is to arrange these seemingly distinct facets of your life into clear themes. For example, if you have sticky notes like student body president, *Pod Save America* superfan, volunteered as an election pollster, and CNN is your home page, "Politics" might be a good category to establish. Maybe another grouping describes a job function: You have stickies about your killer spreadsheets, how you are always the one to take point organizing trips for your friend group, and that innovator award you won for optimizing your company's payroll process, pointing to your superpowers as an "Operations Whiz." Or perhaps you notice a throughline emerging around a skill set or attribute: You are a people person who others come to for advice and you always bring out the best in everyone around you. You might pull those stickies into a category called "Coaching."

An ideal category is broad enough for ten-plus stickies, but narrow enough that you have at least three to four categories (and more likely five to seven) once you're all done.

Once you've categorized all your "like to do" stickies, take another look at your "don't like to do" stickies. Some of these you can absolutely ignore if you truly are not a fan of that kind of work or that particular field (maybe you thought you liked it until you tried and now it's an easy no). Or maybe you are great at it, and everyone keeps putting it on your plate, but you sincerely don't like to do it. (After all, there are plenty of things you could be good at that aren't good for you.) But some might be more situational: Maybe you would like to do that work in a different environment or with more resources. Maybe the company culture didn't make you feel supported to take risks or there was some interpersonal drama that ruined a leadership experience, but in another setting, under different circumstances, you would be game to try again. If that's the case, add a question mark in the corner of those stickies and then place them in their respective grouping. Then throw the remaining "never again" stickies out (or burn them while blasting your favorite breakup song if that's more cathartic for you).

STEP 3: ARRANGE THE SETS AND LOOK FOR INTERSECTIONS

On a table or large whiteboard, draw the biggest Venn diagram that will fit, with as many circles as you have categories. Label the circles with your categories and spread out the respective sticky notes in each. If some stickies seem like they could go in multiple groups, that's great! Those are the overlaps between the sets in your Venn diagram. For example, maybe you have a circle for finance and another for coaching, and they overlap with stickies that show you are the person your friends come to for 401(k) advice; you like to help colleagues negotiate raises or new job offers; and in your free time you've been writing a blog for tweens and teens on the basics of personal finance.

It may take a few tries to figure out where your interests intersect, but I suspect you'll find at least three of your circles will overlap in some way. However, if every circle feels distinct with no overlap, don't panic. Perhaps you haven't had the opportunity or prompting to look for the places where your interests collide just yet. This might give you a jumping-off point for brainstorming new projects or professional opportunities when we start looking at constructing your portfolio. When all of your stickies have been placed, give yourself a high five and take a breather.

Et voilà! You have a rough draft of your Venn diagram! Snap a photo and look at it over the next few days to try it on for size. How do you feel when you look at it? Is something missing? Just right? Does it feel like *you*? (Feel free to gut check it with two or three folks from your coffee chats if that's helpful!)

This will be refined over time as you learn more about yourself, and it will change as your life and career progresses and your interests evolve. Nothing is set in stone here; your Venn diagram is as dynamic as you are and will necessarily change with you over the course of your life as you add more experiences and cull others that no longer suit you. When it feels right, I hope you can breathe into that broader definition of who you are, what you care about, and what you can contribute to the world.

Knowing who you are is the first step to connecting the dots between where you are and where you want to be. Next, you need to figure out how all of those pieces fit together: Which circles become an income stream and which are hobbies or volunteer efforts? What proportion of your week does each take up? How do you prioritize, resource, and protect the things that matter to you? These questions—and more—will help you choose the right business model for your life. After all, there's more than one way to build a portfolio.

CHAPTER 5

Design the Business Model for Your Life

You will have many lives within this one life. Some may end badly. But every place you've been, every person you've loved or let love you, every life you've lived already adds up to who you are. You make yourself as you go. Keep moving.

—Maggie Smith (the poet)

My family didn't have much money when I was growing up. My mom was a single mother with two kids and retired parents who pitched in where they could thanks to my grandfather's pension and their modest Social Security benefits. We all lived together in a split-level house that was carpeted wall-to-wall in red shag from the 1970s. (Note: I did not grow up in the 1970s.) It was...a look.

Because we didn't have much money, I didn't get many opportunities to learn about personal finance or the many different instruments for debt and investments. I knew about credit cards, checking and savings accounts, and cash. As each month came to a close, they moved money around between them to ensure we didn't go hungry and then when payday hit, they tried to get things back in a bit of order. You could say that those tools made up my family's financial portfolio and it mostly worked for us (until the financial crisis hit in 2008 and then everything fell apart. But that's a story for another time).

So when I started my first job out of college, I did what I knew: I put a bit of money into a savings account at the same bank that held my checking account, and any spare cash in my budget went toward paying down my student loans. I tried to avoid using my credit card unless there was a big, unexpected disaster like an expensive car repair. It never occurred to me to look into opportunities to invest my money in mutual funds or to open a retirement account. I was twenty-one, and I didn't know what I didn't know about money. It wasn't until business school that I really had my eyes opened to the possibilities for my financial portfolio.

This isn't an uncommon story. Many of us learn about money and career paths in the same way: by observing our parents, our friends' families, and those in our community. So whether nearly everyone you knew had a single, steady job, or they all did unpredictable shift work, or they were ambitious and working nonstop to climb the corporate ladder, that's going to be your default understanding of what a career looks like. And yet, it's likely that both of your baselines—personal financial management and career planning—are as outdated as the red shag carpet in my childhood home.

So in this chapter we're going to examine three common portfolio business models—moonlighters, zigzaggers, and multihyphenates—and dig into the opportunities and trade-offs of each. (And later, in Part III, we'll unpack that dated financial advice you may still be clinging to.)

While the Portfolio Life is about more than just what you monetize (and how, and when), you do have to pay the bills. And the decisions you make about the business model for your career will impact how much time, flexibility, and money you have to direct to the other parts of your portfolio like hobbies, relationships, community service, and self-care.

BUT FIRST, WHAT IS A BUSINESS MODEL?

A business model is the overall design for the successful operation of a business, identifying how you will make money (products, revenue sources, costs, logistics) and what resources you will need to assemble to pull it off (team, capital, and partnerships). There are many ways to create a business model, but the core details remain the same: What are you offering, to whom, how much will they pay you for it, can you turn a profit at that price, and what resources or help do you need in order to be successful?

You might be cringing at the idea of analyzing your life as a business, chalking this suggestion up to the crass capitalistic mindset of a business school professor, but hear me out. Understanding who is willing to pay for what you want to offer the world, how much they are willing to pay, and whether that value is greater than the effort and cost of the work is vital analysis that will help you build a life that is fulfilling and *sustainable*. When we don't talk about money, or we don't think creatively about the ways we can affect different levers of the business model, we end up settling for a life someone else defined.

For example, there are many ways to approach the business of being a writer. On one end of the spectrum is being a full-time author, which means being self-employed and selling a manuscript or book proposal every year or so. This business model means being paid either via an advance or royalties (or both), income streams that are sporadic and highly variable from one book to the next. On the other end of that spectrum is taking a job where writing is central to the role, offering a more predictable revenue source, though even then there is a wide range of possibilities: from journalism to content marketing to nonprofit grant writing to academic research, the context and "customers" for your writing offer very different pay scales, work environments, autonomy, and opportunities for growth. And sitting somewhere in between those extremes are models where writing is part of your work, or a key side project, but not exclusively how you make a living.

Each of these models offers benefits and drawbacks, meeting different needs along the way. Which model you choose depends on what you want at a given point in time. Let's take a look at three common models for a Portfolio Life and see them in practice.

🌙 MODEL 1: MOONLIGHTERS

The first model is one you are likely most familiar with: moonlighting. Moonlighters have a primary, often full-time, responsibility and one or more secondary projects that they make work during down periods like nights and weekends. Your more traditional "day job" likely provides financial stability while your projects on the side might offer creativity, community, growth, and/or income diversification. For some, moonlighting is a model they stick with throughout their career. For others, it's an on-ramp to a zigzag or multihyphen model. In either case, it's an opportunity to try something new, bring in another source of income, maintain an interest and community that is outside your main line of work, or all of the above.

MOONLIGHTING VS. SIDE HUSTLES

How is moonlighting different from a side hustle? I think of moonlighting as a choice, an opportunity to spend significant time and energy on a side project that you may or may not monetize. It could be a small entrepreneurial endeavor, a serious hobby, or a meaningful volunteer gig. It brings you fulfillment in a way that your day job may not, and you are in control of your commitments. The term *side hustle*, on the other hand, is often used to reference a second (or third) job that is needed just to stay afloat, co-opting a term from Black culture that for more than a century was used to describe the work of surviving in a rigged system.[1] Modern capitalism has rebranded "hustle culture" as a virtue, masking subsistence wages and an economic model that doesn't net out for many Americans as something to aspire to. But as Howard University professor Niambi M. Carter put it, "the hustle hits different when you choose it rather than your circumstances doing the choosing for you."[2]

When does it make sense to choose the moonlighting model? It is often employed by folks who have an interest in a line of work that is volatile, not well-compensated, or has a long on-ramp to success. (Unsurprisingly, the creative fields frequently fall into this bucket, from filmmaking to playing in a band.) Choosing a "good enough" job to provide financial stability and a predictable schedule allows moonlighters to feel supported in pursuing their side projects.

Bethany Baptiste grew up in Jacksonville, Florida, where she thrived on Southern food and stories.[3] At sixteen, she dropped out of high school due to chronic illness and enrolled in a nighttime GED program while writing science fiction and fantasy during the day. Over the years, as she completed associate's and bachelor's degrees in early childhood education, writing grew from a hobby to a career dream. But she knew the business of being an author was a bumpy one, and she needed more stability than it alone could provide.

So she began a career as an educator and quickly saw an opportunity for her storytelling: "My fourth-grade students weren't fond of reading because they didn't see characters that looked like them." So, she started writing a story about a Black boy, secret government agencies, a subterranean society of aliens, and a dog named Teeth. As she finished each chapter, she read it to her students the next day and got real-time feedback from her audience. Soon her first middle-grade science fiction book was finished, and ideas for the second started to percolate. But a combination of personal and world events kept throwing wrenches into her plans of being published. Bethany kept on teaching and honing her craft while other pieces of her life fell into place: She got engaged, bought a house, and adopted three dogs. Four years later, she landed a literary agent and is now working toward a publishing deal while she works with families and teachers of preschoolers with special needs and disabilities.

Moonlighting is also a useful model during career transitions, when folks may want to ease the shift by turning their former full-time work into a side gig while they ramp up in their new field. Whether it provides some income during the transition or simply keeps you connected to a community during a time of great change, this model can offer stability and flexibility when you need it the most.

Jennifer-Ruth Green leveraged a different flavor of moonlighting: Rather than pursuing a volatile line of work on the side, she used it as an off-ramp from a first career in the air force, keeping a key part of her identity in place. A third-generation combat veteran, she had originally imagined she would spend her entire career in the service. From junior ROTC in high school, to attending the US Air Force Academy, to being commissioned as a second lieutenant and starting her career as a pilot upon graduation, she was on a linear path to military leadership. But her training as a pilot made her realize she wasn't a perfect fit as an aircraft commander, and perhaps her interest in investigative journalism and lifelong love of languages might be put to use in an intelligence role instead. So she transitioned to the Office of Special Investigations and was deployed as a federal agent to Baghdad to help the Iraqi government take over security of the region.

Then 2012 hit, the air force began a reduction in forces as part of their drawdown out of Iraq, and Jennifer-Ruth found herself facing an unplanned transition out of full-time service. But instead of walking away entirely to pursue an unrelated second career, she opted to join the California Air National Guard as a guardsman while enrolling in grad school to earn a master's degree in church ministry. When she graduated and moved to Indiana to serve in a church, she continued her service with the Indiana Air National Guard. Then suddenly her moonlighting work became incredibly relevant to her day job: On a mission trip to Brazil, she discovered a lack of pilots was preventing volunteers from distributing supplies and aid in remote parts of the Amazon. So she renewed her pilot's license and set out to train other mission-minded students and young adults with aviation skills, founding MissionAero Pipeline, a nonprofit dedicated to aviation, character, and career training for youth.

The most visible tension in the moonlighters model is time management. Because you have a full-time job, after you factor in other responsibilities like friends and family, it's easy to see how side projects can fill every moment without opportunity to rest (let alone afford any buffer time for things to go wrong). This is where modern "hustle culture" can seep into your mindset if you don't watch out. Rest is an important part of your Portfolio Life and will always be in tension with moonlighters' other projects.

For this reason, many who successfully moonlight choose a day job that tends to be more predictable, from a set working schedule to clear expectations of when you're off duty. Sometimes they look to that day job to fulfill needs that their side projects can't, like a steady income and good health insurance, and don't mind so much if the work is less creative or has fewer opportunities for growth. (After all, Albert Einstein loved his day job in the Swiss patent office because it was highly paid and intellectually *un*demanding.[4]) Plus there's research to support the idea that side projects actually make you better at your day job: The psychological empowerment of moonlighting can make people feel more positively about their full-time role (where they may have much less autonomy or fulfillment).[5] In other words, people following this model appreciate their "good enough" job because it enables them to pursue the many other things they want and love to do.

The trade-off in this model is that your side projects may have periods when they have to take a back seat or be deprioritized, like when Bethany had to put aside her hopes of being published while working through unexpected curveballs in her personal life. This model requires flexibility, planning, and self-discipline to pull off without burning out. So it's important to develop some operational systems to keep track of everything (we'll go into those in detail in Part III) and also to give yourself grace when you drop a ball or three. Self-discipline is only truly effective when coupled with self-compassion.

The other consideration in the Moonlighting model is whether your "day job" has rules that might prohibit earning outside income or that might claim ownership over any intellectual property you develop while you are employed there. Read your employment contract carefully and don't be afraid to consult with a lawyer to ensure you don't run afoul of your obligations. If there are contractual issues, be proactive about communicating with HR and see if they will grant you an exception (in writing!). This is one place that is much better to ask for permission than forgiveness.

MOONLIGHTING MIGHT BE RIGHT FOR YOU IF...

- You want to pursue a field that is risky, volatile, or not well-compensated and you don't have a safety net like generational wealth to support you.
- You enjoy having a "good enough" job that frees up time and energy to devote to side projects while providing stability and/or other benefits.
- You are interested in learning a new skill or developing a serious new hobby without the pressure of monetizing it.

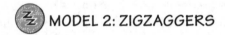 MODEL 2: ZIGZAGGERS

Zigzags are a model of interdisciplinary jumps and diagonal moves between seemingly unrelated industries and functions. Sometimes unfairly judged as being "flighty," zigzaggers pursue their various interests (mostly) one at a time, even when the connections between their choices don't make sense to the outside world.

Zigzagging can feel harder than just picking up a side project like moonlighters do; we invest a lot of time, effort, and money into pursuing a career path and to make a zig or zag into something else completely unrelated requires both the courage to quit the first path and an investment in a new one. (This is why zigzaggers often start getting up to speed in their new field via moonlighting before going all in, like Jason Haaheim did with his transition from nanotechnology to classical timpani.) But there's a huge upside to this model: Zigzaggers bring interdisciplinary connections and associative thinking to both worlds, which can help them stand out and make them more successful in the long run.

Catherine Jennings zigged and zagged when she decided to leave her first career as a middle school science teacher and become a doctor. Growing up in Knoxville, Tennessee, she had long been attracted to biology and dance, and split her time between the rehearsal studio, the lab, and the barn where she rode horses. She started college with a double major in dance and biology, but a back injury put her dancing on hiatus and a summer of teaching swimming made her realize how much she enjoyed working with kids. So she decided instead to focus on education like her mother had and ended up earning a bachelor's and a master's degree from the University of Tennessee along with her teaching certificate.

Catherine got a job teaching seventh-grade science in her hometown school district, but became frustrated that many of the levers for delivering high-quality education were out of her control. They ranged from the decisions made at the school board or state level about funding to the social and emotional factors in the kids' lives that prevented them from being fully present and able to focus on the lesson at hand. After seven years of giving it her all in public schools, she decided to make the leap to an independent school in Brooklyn. Perhaps a different setting with different constraints might make her feel like she was doing the work she was meant to do.

She thrived in Brooklyn and enjoyed the resources and development opportunities of teaching in a private school, but something still nagged at her. After months of reflection, she finally realized what was missing: She loved teaching, but she felt she had sold herself short. "My decision to become a teacher had been multifaceted, but it was largely influenced by the societal expectations for a young woman in my conservative Southern community," she told me. "I wanted both a family and a career, and the majority of women I knew in that same position were educators, so I pushed my aspirations for medicine aside because I saw teaching as a more 'appropriate' choice." Still, after a decade of teaching, she dreamed of being a doctor.

So Catherine decided to make it happen. After talking it through with her girlfriend, her parents, and her best friend (that would be me), she quit her job, and at age thirty-four she enrolled in a postbaccalaureate program at Columbia University for folks interested in medicine who didn't have the prerequisite undergrad courses. The two-year program to prepare her for medical school was a lower-cost way of validating this new trajectory (though obviously not no-cost, since she had to quit her job and take out loans to cover tuition and living expenses for those two years). Still, it gave her a way to test her skills and interests before investing in four years of medical school and three to seven years of residency, depending on her specialty.

Catherine was a star in her program (yes, I am biased, but also, they asked her to give the graduation speech, so clearly I'm right) and continued on to medical school with a scholarship at Columbia's Vagelos College of Physicians and Surgeons, where she fell in love with the opportunity to serve queer and under-resourced folks through a student-run primary care and sexual health clinic. And while she's older than most of the residents who supervise her specialty rotations, she recognizes that her first career as a teacher wasn't a mistake or a waste of time. Rather, it gave her an incredible ability to connect with patients, to break down complex information into digestible snippets, and to share what she knows with her classmates and colleagues. "I have learned that so much about teaching is, at its core, equipping people with the tools and practices to teach themselves and providing a lifelong journey of learning," she insists. Catherine will turn forty as she launches her second career as a physician but the seemingly unfathomable "zag" is actually what she needed to succeed.

Another huge benefit of the zigzag model? The ability to exit an organization or industry that is on the decline or being disrupted, transporting your skills to another sector with more viable prospects.

Dr. Robert Lang did just that when he stepped away from his lauded career as a physicist and engineer to become a full-time origami artist. As a research scientist and research and development manager, he worked at NASA's Jet Propulsion Laboratory, Spectra Diode Labs, and JDS Uniphase, where he was an expert in semiconductor lasers, optics, and integrated optoelectronics. Over two decades of work, he wrote more than eighty technical papers and was awarded nearly fifty patents for his innovations.

But in the wake of the dot-com bust of 2001, his work had transitioned from making things to laying people off, and he was ready to trade his focus on semiconductors for the art and mathematics of complex origami creations. "Over the course of my engineering career, I had written, by that time, six instructional books on how to fold different origami shapes that I had designed. And I could write those books while holding down a full-time job and raising a family just by working evenings and weekends and odd moments," he told me. (He had been a moonlighter!) But he had an idea for a book about how to design original origami, not just execute on his preset designs. And after ten years of thinking about this book but never really making much progress, he came to the conclusion that unless he was working on it full-time, it would never get done. "Weighing the joys and turmoil of the dot-com bust, I decided that whatever I might do as a laser physicist, there's plenty of other laser physicists in the world who could do it without me, but I really felt like I was the only person who could write that book."

Robert had first discovered origami at the age of six, and his interest in the art form grew during high school and undergrad as a way to escape the pressures of his academic work. Even during his doctoral work and early professional career, it remained an amateur, though still serious, endeavor. But after making waves in the origami world for his mathematical breakthroughs in design and folding techniques, he decided to go all-in on this new professional path. Over the last twenty years, in addition to making unique origami creations, he has written computer software to algorithmetize the design process for new origami shapes, developed lasers to help score paper for complex folds, and found real-world applications for his work in industrial design, optimizing the folding patterns of everything from car airbags to expandable space telescopes to medical devices.

Now, there are certainly tensions and trade-offs to the zigzag model. Depending on how much overlap there is between your zig and zag, you can feel like you're living a double-agent life, literally switching from one identity to another on your lunch breaks or off hours as you work to get up to speed in the new field before going all-in, like Robert writing origami books on the side of his full-time physics role. Time management is essential, and this model requires real focus and planning during transitions. Free time may become scarce for a while and you may have less time and energy for other things you love. Or money may be tight if you step away from the first role while preparing your transition to the second one, as Catherine did by going to medical school. But take heart that those transition periods are temporary, and once you make the switch, you will regain breathing room as you focus on a single role again.

Another key challenge of this model is that it requires you to craft a strong story for why and how you are making the switch since it may not seem obvious from the outside. You will have to explicitly connect the dots for potential employers or collaborators or investors, helping them see why your work in your previous world actually positions you to be even more effective in this new one.*

ZIGZAGGING MIGHT BE RIGHT FOR YOU IF . . .

- You are serious about wrapping up the current chapter of your life and making a bold jump into something new.
- You have the resources, time, and determination to get up to speed in a new field (or the ability to juggle both worlds simultaneously while making the transition).
- You can find the narrative thread to connect your different pursuits, helping outsiders understand why you made the leap and what unique perspective you bring to it.

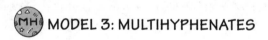 MODEL 3: MULTIHYPHENATES

While zigzaggers invest their energy in one principal area at a time, multihyphenates dig into multiple fields at the same time, either by pursuing several lines of work simultaneously or by merging two (or more) fields into a new line of work altogether. These are people who place more of an equal emphasis on their various professional interests, unlike moonlighters, whose side project(s) often need to take a back seat to their day job. The challenge for multihyphenates is how to fit their interests together, which often requires crafting a custom career path rather than following a road that's already paved.

Kat Mustatea is a playwright and a technologist. She studied philosophy at Columbia University and sculpture at Pratt Institute, worked

---

* This is why we're spending an entire chapter on telling your story in Part III.

as a software engineer and product manager, and founded a theater company in Berlin. For more than a decade, she lived both lives simultaneously, writing plays that were produced in New York, Chicago, Berlin, and Oslo, while developing code and building technology products for startups around the world. When I first met Kat in 2013, her challenge was whether to make both sides of her life visible to each other. In the world before the internet, she could cultivate industry-specific résumés and keep her work separate, but with just one LinkedIn account—and in the era of a simple Google search—it didn't seem realistic. Yet how would each community feel about her interdisciplinary career? Would it be a sign that she wasn't serious about either?

Kat decided to be transparent and tell one, integrated story, and in writing that integrated story she discovered an opportunity to build an integrated career. "The lightbulb moment for me was in realizing that my plays, which were already about uncanny and absurd things like people turning into lizards, had a natural expression using cutting-edge technologies, which are themselves uncanny and absurd," she told me. Kat realized that the two things she knew best, which previously had seemed diametrically opposed, actually overlapped, creating an opening to make something entirely new.

Just a few years after combining her worlds, she was invited to join the TED Residents community and build a body of work at the intersection of art and technology, examining the meaning of art made in an age of intelligent machines. "It turns out that overlap, while it was considered marginal and obscure even a few years ago, is now a rapidly growing area," she observed. "I just kind of found my way there before the mainstream did." Her experience as a multihyphenate positioned her to be one of the experts in an emergent field, which was not something she could have planned for just a few years earlier.

Tyler Thrasher is another example of a multihyphenate. He was three months away from finishing his degree in computer animation at Missouri State University when a guest speaker changed his life (and not in the way you'd expect).

The department had brought in a professional animator to help students learn about the career they were about to enter, and by the time the presentation was over, Tyler knew he needed to find a different path. "He didn't hold anything back. He told us that it's a very intense, almost grueling artistic field and can be a very unrewarding job. And there's a thing called the 'animator's widow'—it's like people cannot stay in healthy relationships with animators."

But Tyler didn't want to switch majors and stay in school longer. So, in the three months he had left, he took a close look at his skills and interests and decided to forge his own path as a scientist-artist. Inspired by the caves in the Ozarks and propelled by self-study of chemistry and molecular geometry, he started to grow crystals on organic artifacts like dead cicadas, barnacles, and skulls. By the time he graduated, he had sold a couple of his distinctive sculptures online, and within a few months he sold a few more. Now Tyler is making a living as a full-time scientist-artist in Tulsa, Oklahoma, where he lives with his wife and son.

Multihyphenates will tell you they find their work incredibly fulfilling, standing in two (or more) worlds simultaneously. But they'll also warn you to prepare for skepticism that you can be focused and dedicated to great work in one area while also pursuing another. I find this is most common when a component of your portfolio is a more traditional job while the other is more self-produced or creative (like Kat working as a software developer at a tech company while writing and producing plays). Small slipups or miscommunications that might otherwise be chalked up to being human, like dropping the ball on an important email, can suddenly become evidence that you're not "giving 110%" or whatever equally unrealistic and unsustainable bar the business world sets next.

If you choose to adopt a multihyphenate model, you will need to find colleagues who support your various workstreams, or at least are understanding enough that you can be transparent about how they may impact each other. I once had a role where I didn't have this conversation up front and when I suddenly got press for my podcast, well, they kinda freaked out. I hadn't done anything wrong or broken my employment contract or deceived them in any way...they just weren't expecting me to have a public life outside their company (and frankly, they didn't like it). Which is why I've always brought this up in interviews ever since and have walked away from potential roles where having an identity outside of the job wasn't welcome. I focus on overcommunicating both that I'm working across a portfolio of projects and that this is going to make me better at my primary job.

Here's the best argument for why this way of working can be a net positive for your colleagues and collaborators: Many people who balance multiple pursuits find the time away from one way of thinking and working fills them up and leaves them refreshed to go back and take another pass at it when they switch back.

For more than a decade, American ballerina and quantum physicist (yes, really!) Dr. Merritt Moore has balanced a professional life dancing with national ballet companies around the world while working as a research physicist studying quantum optics at places like Harvard and University of Oxford. She credits the extreme differences between her two worlds, and the opportunity to regularly toggle between them, as one of the reasons she has been so successful in both. "My brain gets tired after thinking about physics for hours. So when I go into a dance studio or step onstage, I'm so appreciative of being there. And when I come back to academia from dancing, I could not be happier to be sitting in a library all day long and not moving my very sore legs. Literally my toes all have blisters on them. Please, make me sit down in a chair and read for hours!" In the same way that some people get refreshed by a long workout or by volunteering in their community, multihyphenates use variety in their multiple professional worlds to unwind and recharge them.

The second tension to acknowledge in the multihyphenate model affects those who seek to merge their disparate interests into a new, interdisciplinary line of work. While this approach can set you up to be one of the foundational figures in that new field, it can also be lonely, challenging, and financially frustrating until the rest of the world catches up with you. Whether it's because funders and investors don't understand what you are doing, or because there's literally no box to check on an application form, or because people don't know to look for someone like you, this can be a longer road than a more straightforward path. Surround yourself with the support and resources you need to persist, from collaborators and cheerleaders to the cash to pay your rent or mortgage until this new path becomes more lucrative.

A MULTIHYPHENATE MODEL MIGHT BE RIGHT FOR YOU IF . . .

- You feel compelled to dedicate your time and energy equally(ish) to two or more worlds concurrently.
- You can see how a mash-up between multiple fields could create a new field altogether, and you're willing to be a pioneer in forging that path.
- You can overcommunicate to managers, colleagues, and professional partners how your work in other fields is a net positive rather than a distraction.

A LIFE THAT YOU ARE PROUD OF LIVING

Stacey Abrams may just be one of the most well-known examples of a Portfolio Life alive today. A former, and likely future, elected official, she also works tirelessly across several fields, advocating against voter suppression, crafting policy initiatives for the South, addressing pandemic recovery, and writing romance novels. She calls her schedule "work-life Jenga" but wouldn't want it any other way. "I can't put any of them away because they're part of who I am, and they reinforce each other."[6]

Growing up, she remembers her mother telling her she needed to focus or risk being a "jack of all trades and master of none." But instead of feeling chastised for her varied interests, what she heard was that to live this life, she'd have to be really good at everything she chose to work on. "I've always been very comfortable with the multiple strands of my identity, whether it's the creative piece or the activist piece or the policy part of me, the nerd part of me. I don't spend much time thinking about the conflicts. My responsibility is to figure out how to integrate them, not into a single thing, but into a life that I live and that I'm proud of living."

I couldn't have said it better myself.

These three models are not the only ways to construct a Portfolio Life, but they are a great starting point for how you might think about crafting a business model that works for you. Which skills and interests do you want to monetize, and which are better kept as hobbies or volunteer projects? How might the experiences in one part of your Venn diagram set you up to be successful in another part when you're ready to make a big leap? Do you have a unique perspective from standing in multiple worlds that might position you to be a pioneer in forging a new field altogether? Who are the "customers" for your work, and are there opportunities to broaden or diversify that base, giving you more control, stability, and earning power? Are you leaving space for rest in your business model?

As we head into the final chapter of Part II, where you will craft your portfolio, I want you to take a moment to look at how far you've come. You've sought out a second opinion as you worked to truly see yourself, searching not only for where you stand out against your peers but also when you have been happiest and what your hidden superpowers might be. You've broken out of your narrow job-title-box and constructed a Venn diagram that better captures your rich, three-dimensional identity. And you've examined the need for a sustainable business model for your life and analyzed three common approaches. Now we're ready for the last step: sketching out your portfolio.

CHAPTER 6

Craft Your Portfolio

I knew who I was this morning, but I've changed a few
times since then.

—Lewis Carroll, *Alice's Adventures in Wonderland*

There are many ways to craft a Portfolio Life. But at a high level, the
goal is to design a combination of work, community, hobbies, volunteering, and personal time (including rest!) that collectively meets
your needs by utilizing the skills, networks, and interests in your Venn
diagram. You can't do everything all at once—even Beyoncé only has
twenty-four hours in her day—but you should be able to make progress
on your most important priorities at any given time. And when your
priorities change or your needs transform, you can rebalance or rebuild
your portfolio altogether. Just like financial advisors recommend you
rebalance your financial portfolio over time (like trading out stocks for
bonds in your 401(k) as you get older so your retirement investments
become more stable the closer you get to needing them), you should
rebalance your Portfolio Life when, for example, you move to a new city
or you break up with a romantic partner or your kids graduate and leave
you with an empty nest. Think of it as a fresh approach to a new season
of life.

There are two big questions that will guide this final exercise: First,
what do you wish for your life? Rather than starting with what you studied, or what you're currently doing, or even what you imagined you'd be
when you grew up, I want you to start by wishing. This is about more

than a job or a career; this is about your life. As you imagine six or seven or more decades of your life, what do you hope to experience? What do you want to achieve? Who do you want to deeply know? What kind of person do you want to be? What mark do you want to leave behind? This is about taking the long view—you can't possibly do all of these things at once, right now, this year. But starting with wishing allows you to zoom out and dream big, ensuring you don't limit your life to what feels feasible today.

The second question is just as audacious: What support do you need to be your best self? The answer to this is obviously very personal. Some people may need freedom, adventure, and growth. Others may need security, dependability, and community. Your answer will also change over time. What you need at twenty may look very different from what you need at thirty-five or at fifty-five. That's to be expected: As our lives change, our needs change. It makes sense, then, that the mix of career, personal interests, family, and friends will change to match those shifting priorities. So the work we're about to do in crafting your portfolio is only a starting point. There are no right answers, only answers that are right for you, right now.

Once you have a sense of what you wish and what you need, we'll take a moment to reflect on how you are currently spending your time. It may surprise you how much of a disconnect there is between where you want to invest your energy and what you are actually doing from one day to the next. (Or maybe it won't surprise you. Maybe you are acutely aware of how your current path is not the one you want to be on.) Getting a clear look at which of your activities aligns with your wishes and needs, and which aren't serving you, is an integral step in evaluating what to keep and what to change.

To wrap it all up, you'll take pen to paper to map out a portfolio for your life: What combination of work, relationships, personal time, hobbies, volunteering, and community activities will you choose to meet your needs, make progress toward your wishes, and give you the stability and sustainability you desire?

The first time you do this may take half a day. (If you have the luxury of setting aside a full day for it, even better!) Later on, when your life changes and you revisit this exercise, you may only need an hour or two to make updates and tweak your portfolio. Remember, this isn't a one-and-done activity; it's a trusty tool you can turn to time and again to ensure you're living the life you want. Now grab those sticky notes and let's get started!

STEP 1: 100 WISHES

This first step I've borrowed from two talented UX (user experience) designers who have used it in very different contexts: Tautvydas Gylys and his girlfriend used it to "pair design" their relationship while Ximena Vengoechea kicked off her "Life Audit" with it, a process she dubs "spring cleaning for your soul."*

Here's what you do: Take a new sticky pad (or scraps of notebook paper if you're chaotic like that) and write out one hundred wishes for your life. Don't limit them to professional goals—include anything you hope to do, see, experience, create, or contribute to. Many people run out of steam after thirty or forty, but I encourage you to keep going. Mine your childhood and adolescent aspirations, those moments in your life where you dreamed without the constraints of practicality. Consider things that may feel too bold or impossible or far away. Just keep going until you hit a hundred.

Here are a few of my random wishes from one of the first times I did this exercise: travel to all seven continents, run for political office, build a happy and healthy family, make music on a regular basis, give a TED talk, learn to bake actually delicious gluten-free treats, run a half-marathon in under two hours, write a memoir, have dinner with my family most nights of the week, teach my children to love music, stay healthy and active well into my retirement years, get to know my neighbors, serve on a corporate board, learn all of the lyrics to "(Not)

---

* In the spirit of open source work, both were generous enough to publish their processes on the internet and I highly recommend reading their articles if you're interested!

Getting Married Today" from *Company*, and pay off my student loans. Your wishes can be bold, silly, ambitious, or practical. Don't judge them; if it matters to you, write it down.

Once you have your wishes on paper, give yourself a high five and, similar to what we did in the Venn diagram exercise from Chapter 4, start to group them by themes. A bulletin board or blank wall or big kitchen table is really useful here. Being able to visualize the groupings rather than just piling them in stacks will help with the next step. Here are some examples of categories you might end up with: professional goals, health, family, personal growth, financial goals, travel, community, BHAGs,* etc.

When they are arranged by group, do you notice any serious imbalances? For example, are the majority of your wishes professional goals while your personal development wishes are sparse? Did you exclude any BHAGs because they were just a bit too bold to put down on paper? Have you forgotten health or financial wishes entirely? Take a minute or two and add a few more wishes if you need to. This first scan is a good pulse check on what parts of our lives we might be ignoring.

Lastly, we want to add a layer of timing to our wishes: Are these things we can or want to do stat, soon(ish), or someday? Grab three markers or highlighters and leave a dot on each wish to denote timing. I like to use green (stat), yellow (soon-ish), and blue (someday?), but you can pick any three colors that work for you.†

STEP 2: A HANDFUL OF NEEDS

Put your wishes aside for a minute, and grab a fresh sheet of paper or another stack of Post-its. Think about the times in your life that you were the happiest, most fulfilled, or most at peace. What was it about

---

* That's Big Hairy Audacious Goals—the things you almost didn't dare to write down because they are that audacious, but you did anyway because you really do want to reach them. (Good job!)

† We'll use our wishes in this exercise, and we'll also return to them in the next chapter, so don't throw them out!

those circumstances that brought out the best in you? What did you have? What was missing? Jot down as many of these factors as you can. You may be able to put your finger on them right away, or this might require some digging around.

Here are a few of mine, in case they jog your thinking: dependable, high-quality childcare; visibility into my income (lumpiness is okay as long as I can reasonably forecast when the cash is coming in); at least six consecutive hours of sleep; and the resources to eat well and take care of my health. Those are the bare minimum, which is a great start. But in doing this exercise, I realized there are other things I had when I was at my best: control over my schedule; a community of peers or colleagues that I could regularly bounce ideas off of; a quiet work space with a door; and diversity of work throughout my day/week/year. Friends and colleagues have shared that some of their needs include a tight-knit community to support each other and learn from; a three-month sabbatical every five years or so; the flexibility to work from home when needed; a predictable work schedule to budget and manage family responsibilities around; and proximity to nature (fake plants don't count!).

When you have a robust pile of needs, look them over and start to refine them. Get specific! Instead of "enough money," put some numbers down: How much money do you need to feel secure rather than trying to survive? What is it about your "good work environment" that allows you to flourish and not just tolerate your day? Do you like to feel stretched, in a role that always feels a bit too big, or do you prefer a job where you know you can excel in every part of it? Do you actually like managing people, or do you tolerate it because it seems like that is a required part of rising through the ranks in your industry? When it comes to your schedule, do you value predictability or novelty more?

By the end of this step, you should have a handful of crystal-clear needs and, perhaps, another handful of "nice to haves" that help you feel like the best version of yourself. The more specific you can be, the more you'll be able to ensure your portfolio meets those needs.

While your wishes may stay consistent or perhaps grow over time, your needs are likely to change pretty dramatically as your life changes. The things you need as a young, single person are likely very different from the things you need when you are midcareer and caring for children or an aging parent, for example. Perhaps what you need most right out of college is opportunity for growth while what you need after having a child is flexibility (and excellent health care). As you go through transitions between chapters of your life, be sure to reconsider what you need to support the next phase ahead.

STEP 3: AUDIT YOUR TIME

Now we need to take a look at how we are currently spending our time. For many of us, our days are a mix of things we have to do, things we want to do, and things we just do, perhaps more out of habit than anything else. The goal of this step is not to find every waking moment and turn it into a productivity-driven hellscape. It's just to be aware of how we are currently spending our most precious resource, our time. To be honest, I am always a bit surprised by the gap between what I think I'm investing my time in and where I'm actually spending it. Whether it's frittering it away on distractions that don't add anything to my life (ahem: social media) or giving it over to other people's priorities (ahem: the tyranny of email) or just not allocating enough to accomplish what I say I want to accomplish, the difference between what I say and what I do is sometimes quite stark.

If you have a fairly regular schedule from one week to the next, you can choose one representative week to analyze. If your life is more variable, you may want to select a handful of days or even several weeks that best represent how you spend your time. Be sure to account for both your work life and your personal life, tracking time spent with friends and family, exercising, exploring new interests, and actual, restful downtime. Don't forget to include the things you may not typically calendar, like the hour you spend using a language-learning app or listening to your favorite science podcast while commuting to and from work each day.

Now count how many hours are spent on each activity over the course of the week. You can break it down to whatever level of granularity you find helpful. For example, you might group daily walks, workouts, and a weekly pottery class as "self-care" or you might separate the physical activity into "health" and the class into "personal growth." Once you've added up how much time is spent in each category, take a full-sized piece of paper and draw out a pie chart to help you visualize your time. Here's an example:

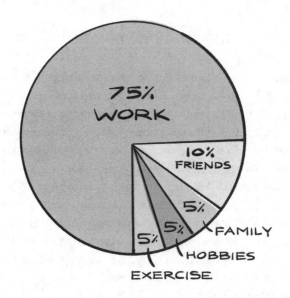

Once you've sketched it out, take a good look at how you are currently investing your time. This is your de facto portfolio—how you spend your life if you make no adjustments. Now that you can clearly see what's in your current portfolio, you can assess how well it is meeting your needs and granting your wishes. Only then can you make the necessary adjustments to align it with your priorities.

STEP 4: MATCH IT UP

Now it's time to match each activity in your time audit to the needs that it meets. I like to take my "needs" Post-its and stick them right on the different slices of the pie chart. Perhaps needs like "income," "predictable schedule," and "health insurance" map to your "work" activity but you don't feel like "opportunities to learn" or "part of a community" or "being creative" fit there. Maybe you spend time on a hobby like learning to code or being part of a writers' group, which meet your learning and creativity needs. Or perhaps your community need is met through the time you spend at your mosque or through volunteering at your kids' school. Your objective here is to see which needs are being met by your current portfolio and which are not.

Next, refer back to your wishes. Are most of the groupings of wishes represented in some way on your time pie chart? Does your overall time distribution roughly map to the distribution of your wishes? For example, if you spend 75% of your time on work, are 75% of your wishes professional goals? Or are more than half of your wishes focused on things outside of work, and yet you spend the majority of your time working?

This is meant to give us a starting point for the next few exercises, so rather than jumping to judgment, just make observations about what surprises you and where your self-perception differs from what you see on the page.

STEP 5: CRAFT YOUR DESIRED PORTFOLIO

Okay! You've done all of the hard work to draw out the themes and values that drive you (your wishes); to understand the factors that bring out the best of you (your needs); and to assess what's in your current, de facto portfolio (your time audit). You've also previously mapped out all of the different worlds you inhabit when you drafted your Venn diagram and considered different business models to power your portfolio. Now it's time to be intentional and put them all together. (Feel free to take a stretch and hydrate first; this is hard work!)

Start by taking a look at the needs that are not being met by your existing portfolio. What's missing? Are there ways to adapt your existing activities to include these needs, like negotiating a growth project at work, or taking a hobby you enjoy on an ad hoc basis and carving out a regular time for it in your week? Do you have a community that you don't get much time with and want to prioritize, or do you need to find or build one? Do you have existing skills or side projects you might consider monetizing or developing in a more formal way like through a class or community, or have you been so consumed by your day job that you need the space and time to cultivate outside interests? How many of your "stat" and "soon-ish" wishes are you set up to achieve and how many feel like a pipe dream?

Based on what you see, you'll likely fall into one of these three buckets:

1. Not too shabby!
2. Close, but no cigar
3. Nope, not even a little bit

Let's talk about what to do for each.

NOT TOO SHABBY!

If the majority of your needs are currently being met by your de facto portfolio—and you are feeling pretty fulfilled by the path you're on—then you're in a great place! Take a quick look at the one or two needs that don't have a home on your pie chart and consider whether there are opportunities to make small tweaks to accommodate them. Could you clear out some space in your day for a more disciplined approach to a hobby? Would taking a class or joining a club create accountability for developing a new skill? Perhaps taking on a leadership role in your community group would strengthen those relationships and offer connection through volunteering.

Refining your portfolio to meet your existing needs will give you the boost you currently need. But don't forget that needs change over time, and when yours shift, don't be afraid to make bigger adjustments to your portfolio.

Stella* had already made some big changes to her portfolio when she became a mom. A long-time small business owner, she had accepted an offer to sell her accounting practice to a larger firm in Chicago when she was pregnant with her first child. "I loved being my own boss and building my client list over the last decade. But the hours could be crushing at times, and the stress of my income being feast or famine didn't seem sustainable once I had a kid. I was ready and willing to trade freedom for stability. Also, I needed better health insurance!" she told me. She also swapped out much of her socializing, travel, and personal development time for childcare and family-focused commitments. "It's a big shift from what I needed in my twenties, but I'm ready for it. I see it as a season of paring back and focusing on my young family. It won't be this way forever."

For the most part, Stella was content with her new, streamlined portfolio: full-time employment at the larger accounting firm, volunteering with the food pantry at her synagogue, and a lot of unstructured time to give to her husband, daughter, and aging mother who lived with them. But she realized she had two unmet needs: regular physical activity and a community that wasn't centered around her role as a mother, wife, or caregiver. So she took a look at her Venn diagram to see what parts of her identity might line up with those needs and quickly saw an opportunity.

A former competitive field hockey player, she had carved out a name for herself through high school and college as a force to be reckoned with on the pitch. But she'd put it aside after university as she poured herself into building her accountancy. Now seemed like an ideal moment to reconnect with that part of herself, and she started researching recreational field hockey clubs in the Chicagoland area. "It's only a few hours a week, but it helps me remember who I am outside of being a mom. I really need that." While Stella admits she could have found more ad hoc ways to exercise or to make non-mom friends, she appreciates the commitment and camaraderie of joining a team for this season of her life.

---

* At her request, some identifying details have been changed.

CLOSE, BUT NO CIGAR

If a good chunk of your needs is being met by your existing portfolio but you know you can't match them all through small tweaks, you may have to make some bigger adjustments. Start by seeing if one or two could be taken care of through your current activities. Is there a way to stretch your current role to feel more fulfilling? Or could you keep the same line of work but shift to a different company or adjacent industry that better meets your needs? If you did less of X, would that free you up (either literally or emotionally) to take on Y? Being clear on the specific changes you are seeking will ensure the move is worth the effort.

After making those small tweaks, take a look at the needs that are still left out and take stock of the skills and networks in your Venn diagram that are currently being unused. How can you make space in your portfolio for new activities to meet those remaining needs? Is there a side business you want to start or a social group you want to join? Are there wishes you wanted to achieve "stat" that aren't represented anywhere in your portfolio? How might you match up that wish with a need and satisfy both through one of the elements in your Venn diagram?

Let's use Amelia* as an example. Her college degree was in photography and she had additional interests in songwriting and fashion design. But with sizable student loans and the need to pay her own rent, she wasn't comfortable with pursuing her artistic interests full-time. So, when she graduated, she accepted a job as a receptionist at an early-stage startup in Austin. The company had a great culture and lots of young people she enjoyed working with, and it gave her a predictable schedule with lots of free time, decent pay, incredible health insurance, and matching 401(k) contributions. On the flip side, she felt that her day-to-day work was pretty unfulfilling, and then felt even worse complaining about her "good enough" job when many of her college friends were piecing together contract work. Still, this wasn't what she thought

---

* Amelia was one of my coaching clients. At her request, some identifying details have been changed.

she'd be doing with her life, and two years in she was feeling a little stuck.

When I met Amelia, we identified which needs were currently being met by her portfolio (income, stability, insurance, and community) and which weren't (creativity and growth). We also identified which parts of her Venn diagram were currently unused or underused (photography, music, and fashion). We then strategized how she could add what was missing. She negotiated with her company to work freelance with the marketing team for their photography needs (read: get paid extra for wholly unrelated work, rather than just take on additional work for free). She also set up an Instagram account and an LLC for a small photography business, starting out by shooting her friends and coworkers at a discount and then gradually raising her rates for outside clients. And she decided she wanted to get connected to the community of musicians in Austin, so she started attending open mic nights, first as an audience member and eventually getting onstage to play some of her songs.

One night, after playing a set, a trio of musicians approached her and asked if she might want to join their newly formed band as the lead singer and a co-songwriter. While they all had day jobs, they were serious about the endeavor and wanted to make sure Amelia was willing to commit the time and effort to rehearse, record a few tracks, and perform regular gigs. The predictability of Amelia's day job and the autonomy she had over her photography business made that kind of commitment possible, and she readily agreed. This new portfolio of her day job, freelance work, side business, and serious hobby was the perfect combination of activities to meet all of her needs and leave her feeling fulfilled at the end of the week.

NOPE, NOT EVEN A LITTLE BIT

Now, if you realize your current work has almost nothing in common with the wishes you listed out in Step 1, you may have to make some bigger changes. In this case, I find it's easiest to start by sketching out how you would ideally spend your time. For example:

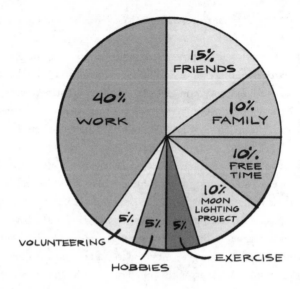

Then laying out your needs on one side of your pie chart, the big themes of your wishes on another, and your Venn diagram at the bottom, start brainstorming how you can craft a new portfolio that combines all three. Be prepared: Big changes may be required.

Diego* found himself in that position when he woke up one morning in his early thirties and said out loud (much to his surprise), "I don't want to do this anymore." A successful lawyer in New York, he had given nearly every waking moment of his life since completing his JD to his job. Because it was a client service role, and because he was on the partner track at his top-tier firm, he worked intense and unpredictable hours, often missing events with his friends and family like weddings and birthday parties. And as a single man, he found it hard to protect his time the way some of his married colleagues with children were able to. First dates weren't respected by the partners in the same way that a kid's ballet recital or parent-teacher conference was. So, his physical and mental health had slowly deteriorated while his bank account kept going

---

* At his request, some identifying details have been changed.

up. Meanwhile he struggled to find a single wish out of the 107 he wrote down that had anything to do with corporate litigation.

Creative writing had always been an important part of Diego's Venn diagram, and one of his wishes was to write and publish a novel. He also wanted a family someday, which required enough free time to meet and build a relationship with a partner. And many of his wishes were public service oriented, which was consistent with his strong track record of community service in high school and college, and his dual degree in public policy alongside his JD. Yet he found himself defending pharmaceutical companies against medical malpractice suits and doing risk assessments for incredibly profitable Fortune 500 firms for upward of one hundred hours a week. When a mutual friend introduced us, Diego's first words were "I don't know what I'm running to, only what I'm running from."

Because Diego had been able to pay off his student loans and build up his savings from his big-law job, his income needs were not nearly as high as they were right out of graduate school. His biggest needs were control over his schedule, a creative community, and time and space to explore his interests again. Rather than tweak his current job, he opted for a bigger change. He kept using his legal skills, but stepped off of the partner track and transitioned to become a part-time, contract resource for the firm for the next six months, the income from which bought him time to decide what to do next. He then enrolled in a low-residency MFA program in fiction, became a regular volunteer with the Food Bank for New York City, and started up conversations with his city council representative, who urged him to apply to serve on his community board.

As his six months came to a close, his firm asked if he would consider staying on indefinitely in an ad hoc way, contributing to cases here and there when they needed extra hands. Diego realized he could make enough money from that sporadic side job that if he downsized to a smaller apartment and traded his regular takeout for cooking, he could focus on writing his novel for the next two years.* The next week he met his future husband during his volunteer shift at the food bank.

---

* Reducing your expenses is a great financial strategy during a transition. More on this in Chapter 11!

For Diego, moonlighting (and a simplified lifestyle) covered his financial needs so he could satisfy his creative, family, and public service needs through unpaid work and community service, helping him get one step closer to seeing his wishes come true.

CHANGE MAY BE UNCOMFORTABLE, BUT IT'S NECESSARY

Don't be afraid of making changes—major or minor—to your portfolio when it is no longer serving you, even if you fear it will be uncomfortable. Don't worry: It definitely will be!

Prince Harry and Meghan Markle, the Duke and Duchess of Sussex, rebalanced their portfolios in early 2020 when they stepped away from active duty in the British royal family and relocated to Southern California. While they had proposed keeping some lines of royal work active while gaining some space and pursuing other personal projects, Queen Elizabeth II rejected their request. They had to be all in or leave "the Firm" entirely. So they took a hard look at what they needed, what they cared about, and the skills and networks they brought to the table, and crafted a new portfolio that worked for their values and priorities at this stage of their lives.

They created a foundation, signed development deals with Netflix and Spotify, joined an ethical investment firm as impact partners, continued their charitable work, and took on personal projects: Harry joined mental health startup BetterUp as chief impact officer while Megan started writing a collection of children's books. In his role at BetterUp, Harry had a front-row seat to the "Great Resignation" of 2021 as workers worldwide grappled with the same question of whether their current life was serving them. "With self-awareness comes the need for change," Harry said in an interview with *Fast Company*.[1] "Many people around the world have been stuck in jobs that didn't bring them joy, and now they're putting their mental health and happiness first. That is something to be celebrated." No matter your stance on the British monarchy, you have to agree he's got a point.

WHAT NOW? OPERATIONALIZING YOUR PORTFOLIO

By now you've got a Venn diagram, a draft of a business plan, a sketch of your target portfolio, and a floor full of sticky notes. You have a sense of how you want to apportion your time and talents and are ready to make the changes necessary to get there. But you might also be feeling overwhelmed by the chasm between strategy and execution. I get it! This is a normal reaction to both the incredible amount of work you've put in and the reality of how much you still have to do.

In order to build a truly sustainable Portfolio Life, you need more than a strategy—you need a plan to put it into practice. That's exactly where we're headed next in Part III: the operational tools and tactics to turn your strategy into reality. We'll dig into money, time management, storytelling, the team you'll need (both personally and professionally), and the systems and metrics you can put in place to be sure you are managing across your entire portfolio rather than just the project that's in front of you at the time. Grab a highlighter or take notes in the margins—this is meant to be as hands-on as possible!

PART III

HOW

CHAPTER 7

Define Your Personal Balanced Scorecard

> Strategy without execution is the slowest route to victory,
> and tactics without strategy is the noise before defeat.
> —Sun Tzu, *The Art of War*

Up to this point, we've been focused on the "work" part of your portfolio, because for many of us, our work is central to the life we lead. It often determines where we live, what kind of income we bring in, and how much control we have over our time, which in turn, can affect our relationships, health, and personal growth. Yet work is only a part of our story, and any conversation about happiness, fulfillment, or success must be broader than just our careers. Which is why I expanded Charles Handy's original definition of "portfolio life" to include, well, life: relationships, hobbies, health, finances, community, growth—anything that is important to you.

The most common framework for the relationship between work and life is the idea of "work-life balance." While the term was first used in the early 1980s in the UK as a movement advocating for maternity leave and flexible work schedules for women, it has evolved to incorporate questions of time management, flexibility, and satisfaction from work and life for people across the gender spectrum.[1] The ideal work-life balance is typically visualized as something like a seesaw, with work on one side and life on the other, equally weighted, the seesaw suspended in near-perfect parallel to the horizon.

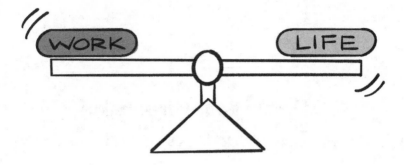

As you probably already know, this ideal is not realistic. More than thirty years of research have been dedicated to unlocking the promise of work-life balance and the general conclusion is that it's not possible.[2] Studies show that the vast majority of organizations indoctrinate workers with an "ideal worker" norm, which tends to mean prioritizing work above all other responsibilities.[3] Whether that is enforced through punishing hours, mandatory face time, or "anywhere/anytime" flexible work that translates into "everywhere/all-the-time" work,[4] the expectation is that the demands of life should be subjugated to the demands of your employer.

Thus, when work and life are seen as two opposing poles, every hour spent on one is an hour taken from the other. Not only does this lead to a constant state of work-life conflict, but most people recognize that a neat 50/50 split between work and life isn't actually what they want. What they tend to mean when they refer to "balance" is more about agency—that is, we want work that doesn't come at the expense of our lives. One subject in a 2019 study on the failures of flexibility in the workplace summed it up: "It's not about balance . . . [It's about] having the discipline to identify what's important in your life and establishing boundaries around those important items and then defending those fearlessly and limitlessly. I feel like if I can do that, no matter what those priorities are and how they shift over time, it gives me a sense of control."[5]

In a world that feels increasingly chaotic and unpredictable, it's no surprise that we're all craving more control. And what many of us want control of the most is where to invest our time and attention at any given point in the day. The aim of a Portfolio Life is to sidestep the rigid accounting of trade-offs between paid work on one hand and everything else you do on the other and instead see your life as one integrated entity. Anyone who has ever needed to renew their driver's license or schedule a medical appointment knows that life doesn't stop when you start work for the day—the same way that work doesn't necessarily stop when you're home eating dinner. The successful management of a Portfolio Life is about the dynamic sculpting and dissolution of boundaries as needed to manage inevitable work-life friction when it arises.

But how do you define those boundaries and determine when to defend them "fearlessly and limitlessly" and when to bend them to support the bigger picture? I think it comes down to two things: articulating what matters to you and tracking whether or not your efforts are getting you closer to or farther away from those priorities.

HOW WILL YOU MEASURE YOUR LIFE?

In the fall of my second year at Harvard Business School, I won the lottery. My prize wasn't cash, alas, but one of just eighty coveted seats in the section of "Building and Sustaining a Successful Enterprise" taught by the renowned professor Clayton Christensen. (If you've ever heard the word *disrupt* in the context of the tech industry, you can thank his doctoral thesis on the theory of disruption.)* It's hard to overstate the influence that the late Dr. Christensen had on the business world. He truly was a giant in the field.†

The course introduced his approach to management and innovation, teaching us how to diagnose a problem and apply a relevant theory to solve it. He didn't teach us the "right" way to do something; he taught us how to think about an issue. He was as beloved as he was idolized

---

* You also read about some of his work in Chapter 2 when we discussed the "innovator's DNA" and the power of associative thinking.

† At six foot nine, he also loomed large in real life.

and was truly one of the most wonderful human beings you could ever meet. His wife, five children, and flock of grandchildren adored him, as did nearly every student he had ever taught.

Toward the end of the semester in 2009, Professor Christensen told us that he had been diagnosed with cancer and this might be his last semester teaching. He asked if we'd mind if a few visitors joined us for the final class, a special lecture he did each year that took a turn toward the personal. A "few" guests turned into dozens, and with jam-packed aisles filled with family, friends, and alums who needed to be there one last time, he opened the class with a simple thought: That our future happiness would depend so much more on the choices we would make every day about where to invest our time, how to prioritize an infinite number of responsibilities, and the seemingly impossible trade-offs we would need to make, than on our ability to rise to the top job in our field. And that the business tools, frameworks, and theories he had been teaching us throughout the semester could be applied just as easily—and to greater impact—on our personal lives.

As he pointed out, none of his classmates sat in our seats and said, "I want to go to jail someday" or "I hope I'll get divorced three times" or "I need to make a lot of money because spoiling my kids is the only way they'll spend time with me," and yet, many of his MBA cohort ended up exactly there.

The classic axiom from management guru Peter Drucker is "what gets measured, gets managed" and Professor Christensen urged us to measure—and manage—our relationships, child-rearing, investment in our communities, personal finances, and mental health as actively as we were about to manage our careers. By the time he finished, there wasn't a dry eye in the classroom, and I knew I had just experienced the most important eighty minutes of my MBA education.*

---

* After that class I asked Professor Christensen if he would deliver the same lecture to the entire HBS 2010 graduating class, which he then adapted into an *HBR* article, and ultimately, expanded into the incredible book *How Will You Measure Your Life?* While his theory of disruption may be his best-known contribution to the business world, surely that legacy will be eclipsed by the exponential impact of his lecture on the happiness and fulfillment of the myriad people he never met.

His exhortation to not just let life happen to us but to proactively manage our happiness fundamentally changed how I approached my career, finances, and relationships. Rather than waking up one day asking, "How did I get here?" I knew I had an opportunity to set my path and intentionally put in the work. And while there are many things in life outside of my control, the things that I can affect are my responsibility.

WHY MEASURE AT ALL?

In short, metrics help you identify how you are doing and they tell you where to invest your time, resources, and energy. Defined and monitored appropriately, they can give you a clear sense of what's working and what's not. Then it's up to you to use your judgment about how to respond to what you've learned.

While the Peter Drucker quote has become a guiding mantra for many leaders in the business world, there is certainly a counterpoint that not everything that matters can be measured. (And its corollary: not everything that can be measured matters.) This is a valid criticism, though I don't think it means we should measure *nothing* but rather that we must choose the right metrics and then put that data into context when making decisions. And this part is key: You may well put more time and effort into deciding *which* metrics matter to you than you spend to track them once they are defined. There are myriad things to measure, but which actually matter? Well, it depends.

For example, if you were focused on improving your health, you could measure your steps, miles run/walked/biked/swam, calories burned, calories consumed, macros, resting heart rate, max heart rate, blood pressure, oxygenation levels, blood sugar levels, hours of sleep, quality of sleep, menstruation cycles, basal body temperature, mood...the list goes on and on. You could create a spreadsheet and track each of these data points every day if you really wanted to.

But the question of any data set always comes down to: So what? What does this mean and what actions (if any) should I take as a result?

Perhaps the only metrics that matter for your health goals are steps, sleep, and macros—that is, you care about whether you moved your body, got enough rest, and ate a balanced diet each day. Then tracking everything else is, at best, a distraction and, at worst, an opportunity to feel overwhelmed and drop the habit altogether. Plus, not every metric is an *actionable* metric. Some, like blood pressure or resting heart rate, are the *outcomes* of the actions you take elsewhere. Checking in on them periodically might offer useful signposts along your health journey, but you can't decide to spend an hour a day practicing your blood pressure, for example. (Still others are *vanity* metrics, which are things that you can track and may look impressive but don't matter at all. I suppose how fast my hair grows could be a vanity metric for my health journey. It grows super-fast, for the record, but so what?)

So the question Professor Christensen posed remains the central one to answer: "How will you measure your life?"

TYPES OF METRICS

Actionable metrics are things that tie specific actions to observed results. They highlight what is working and what isn't, giving you insights to inform your efforts going forward. These metrics are focused on *inputs*.

Vanity metrics are things that are measurable but aren't meaningful. They may look impressive, but they don't offer any insight into how things are going, and improving them doesn't move you closer to your goal.

Outcomes are measurable *outputs*. These metrics may tell you if you succeeded or failed at a goal, but they are unlikely to point out what you should do differently to change the result. They are worth keeping an eye on, but aren't as useful for refining your efforts as actionable metrics.

THE PERSONAL BALANCED SCORECARD

When I first sat down to consider how I would measure my life, I realized there were several factors at play for me. I cared deeply about my work and the impact I would have through my professional endeavors. But a laser-like focus on my career to the exclusion of all else would leave me unhappy in the end. I needed more. I needed meaningful relationships with friends and family, and wanted a life partner and children one day. I also wanted the financial stability and independence to make the decisions that were right for me, rather than the ones that paid the most. I didn't want to feel backed into a corner by money (or the lack of it).

My "extracurricular" projects were also pivotal to my happiness, whether long-standing interests like producing theater or new interests I was exploring like studying computer science more rigorously. They rounded out my portfolio and gave me community, creativity, personal development, and often, an on-ramp to my next professional venture.

At the root of the things I cared about was a need to invest in my physical health. I had been lucky up to that point in my life that my health was pretty solid with minimal concerns, but I didn't want to take that for granted. As I was getting older, I knew I needed to pay more attention to how I was moving and fueling my body, as well as keep on top of preventative care. In short, I had a number of big categories and many more granular indicators that would feed into how I wanted to measure my life. To be honest, it was all starting to feel a bit overwhelming.

While digging around for a way to organize all of these concerns, I remembered Professor Christensen's advice to apply business tools to our personal lives and I decided to adapt a management framework called the *balanced scorecard*. The balanced scorecard is used to connect the dots between a company's mission (purpose), strategic priorities (big themes they care about right now), and activities (how they are executing that strategy), and help management see how the company is performing across those areas via a single dashboard. I liked this format because it started with the big picture, then forced me to articulate the priorities that would help me get closer to that vision, and then set specific, quantifiable targets that I could work toward. At the end of the year, I would be able to give a clear yes or no to whether I had met those targets and see whether my efforts overall were constructive or ineffective. It would be my "*personal* balanced scorecard" (PBS).

I designed my PBS to track progress in the four principal categories of my wishes: financial health, physical health, professional achievement, and personal relationships and, crucially, I decided to set a roughly equal balance between each category since, at that point in time I wanted to spread my focus across all the verticals of my life rather than narrowly focusing on professional goals as I had in the past. (Of course, the balance you choose will be personal, based on your needs and how you're investing in your wishes, and may vary dramatically from one year to the next. More on that in a minute.)

Within each vertical, I then identified four or five priorities for the year. These priorities could be multiyear efforts, or they could be something I wanted to work on just for the next twelve months. In either case, I knew I needed to pinpoint what exactly I could actually achieve within the timeframe of one year.

For example, one of my financial health priorities was to get out of debt. I was working very hard to pay off my student loans, which was a multiyear endeavor. So for this priority I did the math on when I wanted to have them paid off in full and how much I was going to commit to paying off in this specific year, breaking it down then by monthly payments as well as the larger lump sum payment I planned to make when my year-end bonus came through. In another instance, a priority for my physical health was "don't be stupid," which I defined as not incurring any injuries that required a cast, stitches, or surgery. (I'm both a bit of a klutz and an adventure seeker and the combination of those traits often leads to the emergency room. As I neared thirty, I knew that those injuries could turn into chronic issues if I wasn't careful and it was best to avoid them whenever possible.) For every priority, the key was to define a set of targets that I could evaluate at the end of the year with a clear yes or no for whether I met them.

Here is an excerpt from one of my first personal balanced scorecards (with some details redacted):

CATEGORY	STRATEGIC PRIORITIES	TARGETS	CURRENT	ACTIVITIES & COMMENTS
FINANCIAL	Be debt-free	Pay off student loans	$xx	On track to pay off by 2017!
FINANCIAL	Plan for the future	Retirement at 1x salary by age 33	$xx	X% salary to 401(k) + 1099 income to SEP IRA
HEALTH	Be active!	Run 365 miles this year	off track	You won't make your goal. Was it the wrong target?
HEALTH	Don't be stupid	No new significant injuries (requiring surgery or stitches)	on track	Have fun and keep making good choices!
PROFESSIONAL	Podcast	Incorporate as LLC, open bank account, register trademarks	done!	Whew! This was a heavier lift than expected!
PROFESSIONAL	Writing	Make personal creative projects a priority	??	This was a terrible goal. How to measure?
PERSONAL	Travel	Take at least 1 trip not attached to a speaking gig or work trip (aka a "vacation")	done!	You even put your phone away! Good job!
PERSONAL	Music	Practice cello 3 times per week	nope	This wasn't the right goal. Reframe for next year.
		Total goals	8	
		Achieved	5	
		Score	62.50%	
		Are you happy?	Yes	

WHAT ARE YOUR PRIORITIES?

Here's your opportunity to look back at your stickies from Chapter 6 and reexamine your wishes and needs. In that exercise, we focused on dreaming big to articulate one hundred wishes (or more!) and then identified the things you need to be happy and to do your best work. Then we mapped those wishes and needs to our desired portfolio of projects, prioritizing which things we wanted to focus on stat and which things might be saved for soon or someday.

Use your "stat" wishes plus your needs—that is, the stickies that made the cut for your newly crafted portfolio—to create the priorities on your personal balanced scorecard. Gut check: Does the list of priorities look manageable or is it longer than *The Lord of the Rings*? You may quickly realize you don't have the bandwidth for everything you want to do now while still meeting your needs, and some things may have to take a back seat for a while. That's why we call them priorities: What matters most to us when our time, energy, and resources are limited? If we bite off more than we can chew, our portfolio won't be sustainable or bring us joy.

Once you have a clear set of priorities, you can start to allocate your time, money, and energy across your full portfolio rather than doing the thing that seems the most urgent or demanding at the time. You'll feel the shift from being reactive and frantic to intentional and strategic. You'll also have clarity around when and how fiercely to defend your boundaries.

EVALUATING AND MEASURING PROGRESS

Once you set a metric, you have to decide how and when you'll evaluate it. I decided to check in on my progress on a semiannual basis. Every month felt too frequent and waiting until the end of the year to see if I was on track or not seemed too far off. But checking in at the six-month mark and using that as an opportunity to redirect my energy for the back half of the year felt like the right cadence for me.

When the year wrapped up, I assessed my progress, marking my scorecard green if I hit the target, red if I missed it, and yellow if I wasn't sure. I also left myself notes for each target, a combination of high fives, observations on where it was hard or why I might have missed the mark, suggestions for the next year if that priority was going to carry over, and some tough love if I dropped the ball. Sugarcoating my failures wasn't going to help me do better the following year.

WHAT TO DO WITH FAILURE?

The first couple of years using my PBS had a steep learning curve, and there were a number of ways I failed along the way. For example, at the beginning, I wasn't particularly good at defining measurable targets. A target I set one year was "make personal creative projects a priority." Unsurprisingly, when I tried to evaluate my success at the end of the year, I was stumped. I could think of some instances where I spent more time and energy on my personal projects than binge-watching *The Office*, sure, but then there were other times when my projects took a back seat to the demands of my job or my mental health. So did I succeed or fail at that target?

And in other cases, I realized there was a gap between what I said my priorities were and the actions I took on a day-to-day basis. For example, I once set a priority to recommit to playing my cello, targeting at least three practice sessions a week. But at the end of the year, I had to admit I was so far off the map on that target that perhaps it wasn't really a priority for me. (I think I opened my cello case twice that entire year.) You could say I failed at achieving my goal, but I would be more inclined to say that I set the wrong goal. What I *really* cared about was keeping music in my life in an active way (jamming, performing) rather than just a passive one (attending concerts, buying records). It didn't need to be playing my cello, nor did playing my cello need to mean practicing scales and études like it did in high school. In fact, I had spent a good part of that year singing in an a cappella group of tech nerds where we rewrote lyrics to pop songs to be relevant to the startup world and performed at tech meetups and for VC events.* So while I failed at my original target, I felt I had succeeded at the priority, which begged the question: Does that count or not?

Here's the thing: This isn't a test and no one is evaluating you except you. The point of the personal balanced scorecard isn't to hand out grades like in school, but rather to give you a framework for considering, setting, and revising strategic priorities; measuring your efforts and commitment toward achieving them; and noticing when and where there is a gap between what you say you want and what you actually do. It's a way to remind yourself of what you care most about and whether you're devoting enough time, attention, and resources to those priorities.

ARE YOU HAPPY?

For a business, the bottom line is profit; for our lives, the bottom line is our happiness. So the last item on my PBS was one simple question: "Are you happy?" It might seem reductive after the in-depth analysis of priorities and targets you just went through, but ultimately, it's the only metric that matters. I knew it was very possible to set—and even achieve—the wrong goals, and this entire endeavor would be pointless if I aced my scorecard but was miserable. So I added this final metric to force myself to slow down and ensure that all of this activity was actually delivering on what matters the most. If I wasn't, it was a flashing neon sign to reassess my priorities and portfolio for the following year.

---

* We called ourselves NYC# (pronounced NYC-Sharp, a play on the C sharp programming language as well as the musical note). I told you we were nerds.

Your Personal Balanced Scorecard

CATEGORY	STRATEGIC PRIORITIES	TARGETS	CURRENT	ACTIVITIES
	Total goals			
	Achieved			
	Score			
	Are you happy?			

Download a template at www.portfoliolife.com/scorecard to use for your own Personal Balanced Scorecard.

SO, WHAT'S NEXT?

The personal balanced scorecard is meant to give you something of a blue-print for your year, distilling your portfolio down into specific priorities and targets you can work toward. From here, we'll focus on the resources you need to execute on that blueprint: your team, your story, your time, and your money. To do that we'll look at your portfolio through the eyes of a chief executive officer, a chief marketing officer, a chief operating officer, and a chief financial officer. Then we'll wrap up this section with a focus on the future and some real talk about how the massive disruptions of the last couple of decades aren't going to slow down anytime soon. So with a giant grain of salt, we'll take a look at strategies for fore-casting the future like a chief strategy officer and being prepared for the unknowns that are guaranteed to come our way.

CHAPTER 8

Build Your Team

If you care about someone, and you got a little love in your heart, there ain't nothing you can't get through together.
                                                        —Ted Lasso

The first thing any investor wants to know about a business is its team: Who are the founders, the employees, the advisors, the strategic partners? More than how much money the business will make or how it will grow over the next five years, before they put money in a company, investors want to know if the firm has the right people leading, supporting, and surrounding it. Why? Because ideas are a dime a dozen; what differentiates a good company from a great one is execution. And successful execution depends on diverse individuals working together in pursuit of a clearly articulated goal. Which means a CEO's job is first and foremost about recruiting, developing, and managing their team.

To pull off a Portfolio Life, you'll need to build your team like a CEO. While the healthiest, most successful and fulfilling lives—portfolio or linear—come from relationships, portfolio living necessitates a specialized team. Straddling multiple industries and interests will require you to cultivate a more diversified network. This will demand more time and energy to develop and maintain, but the investment will ensure you have the right people to lean on as you weave together the strands of your portfolio. Crafting a custom path will also demand a custom-built community of advisors. Rather than being able to rely on professional development through formal mentors and a transparent career trajectory over many decades of focused work, you'll need to recruit and regularly refresh a personal board of directors to guide your growth. And finally, if you choose to build your Portfolio Life with a partner, you will have to communicate and coordinate more proactively in this model, working together like co-founders in a company, aligning your values, vision, and velocity to ensure you're headed in the same direction and pursuing the same goal.

While this approach to team-building decidedly takes more effort, it also leads to a more fulfilling and intentional community of collaborators, coaches, and confidantes to provide the support you need to thrive. So let's start with the broadest part of your team—your networks—and then we'll zoom in on directors and partners.

INVEST IN ORTHOGONAL NETWORKS

We need to start by discussing your "networks," plural, because every world you are a part of—every circle in your Venn diagram—will have a different community of folks you'll want to meet and build relationships with. The hard part of straddling these different worlds is the amount of time it will take to meet and stay connected with these various communities. But one huge advantage this gives you is the opportunity to be a "super node"—a connector—to link otherwise disparate networks, which is a unique position you can put to use at any stage of your life.

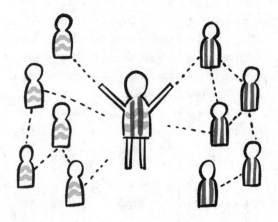

Venture capital investor Alex Taussig wrote an article for *Fortune* magazine in 2012 targeted at junior folks who wanted to enter his industry.[1] His number one piece of advice? Build and share access to your "orthogonal" networks. *Orthogonal* is a mathematical term that basically means "nonredundant" or perpendicular to the set of things currently being considered. Applied to social networks, it means having relationships with people who aren't part of the same circles. When you are the unique connection between different worlds, you can create value no matter how young or inexperienced you are.

Here's an example from my undergraduate days: I once served as the assistant director for a production of a new play about Isaac Newton and the "miracle year" in which he developed integral calculus, refined his theory of gravity, and experimentally verified the composite nature of light. Over the course of the play's development process, I was able to connect the creative team with professors in the math department who could offer expert advice on the more technical aspects of the script. Then a few months later, I brought fellow actors over to the math building to coach awkward graduate students who were terrified of presenting their research in front of an audience. My unique perspective and relationships in both departments allowed me to see that there was an opportunity to link these vastly different worlds, fostering an unlikely, yet productive, collaboration.

CULTIVATING ORTHOGONAL NETWORKS

Not sure how to build an orthogonal network? It's easier than you think. Picture your core group of friends. What do they have in common? Did you all go to college together or work in the same industry? Maybe you are all obsessed with the same hobby, like USWNT superfans or Dungeons & Dragons nerds. Whatever your shared culture, there is a clear connection between you. Now think of that random friend outside the group, someone who would feel out of place and miss all of the inside jokes if they tagged along to a party with your tight-knit circle. That outsider is the beginning of a new, orthogonal network for you. They represent an entirely different community you can get to know. Instead of dragging them along to your friend hangout, ask them to drag you along to theirs. Be the outsider to their circle and start to build new relationships there.

Orthogonal networks put you in a position to create value through connection. They also form the foundation for your team, giving you a rich community to draw from as you build your personal board of directors. Never heard of a personal board of directors? Well, read on!

FORGET MENTORS, SEEK DIRECTORS

You likely are familiar with the term *mentor*. You may also be someone who has repeatedly wondered, "How exactly do I get a mentor?" This may have been followed by "What does a mentor do? Why would someone want to be my mentor? What is my job in this mentor relationship? Honestly, who actually has a mentor, and can they please explain this whole charade?"

I'm with you on this. My generation has been told repeatedly* that we are to seek out mentors (or, perhaps, "sponsors") who will explain the unwritten rules of our industry, open doors for us, and champion our work in the rooms we haven't yet been invited into. In big companies, there are formal mentor programs† with mentor budgets to fund mentor lunches and mentor happy hours. In smaller companies, nonprofits, startups, and noncorporate sectors like entertainment and hospitality,

---

* As of this writing, there were 287 million results for "What is a mentor?" on Google, followed by 214 million results for "How to find a mentor," 134 million results for "Why is it so hard to find a mentor?" and 188 million results for "Do I really need a mentor?" In short, a lot of people have opinions on this and yet I don't know anyone under the age of forty who has someone in their life that they would call their mentor.

† Many of my peers who have participated in those programs say it's mostly just awkward professional small talk.

supposedly you just one day find a mentor and you all live happily ever after? Maybe this worked for our parents, who worked their entire lives at one company, or at least in one industry, but for today's young professionals, the mirage of a mentor is both stressful and haunting. Which is why I'm telling you to drop the idea of one perfect person who has experience and clout and social capital, who opens doors and shares secrets and cares as much about your advancement as you do. Instead, like any CEO, you need a board of directors.

The role of a board of directors for a company or nonprofit is to oversee the big picture for the organization: They set the mission, advise the chief executive, evaluate and set compensation for the CEO, and represent the interests of the shareholders or stakeholders. Directors are often recruited for the board because of a specific skill or experience they bring, quite literally, to the table, and they serve on smaller committees along with chiming in on big, strategic conversations once a quarter. A diverse board of directors is imperative, ensuring that for any question or concern there is someone who can offer counsel. As a CEO, you don't ever want to feel like you're flying in the dark.

A personal board of directors is much the same: It's a collection of folks you go to for advice, introductions, a fresh perspective, or some hard truth. They bring their experience, judgment, and network to the table, providing counsel, access, and feedback. Rather than looking for one mentor who can be all things for an indefinite period of time, you can seek out directors who may do a rotation on your board for a few years, maybe more, maybe less. To be clear, you don't need to specifically ask them, "Would you like to do a rotation on my personal board of directors?"* These are just folks you make a point of connecting with on a regular basis because you appreciate their experience and trust their advice.

You may go to each one for a specific thing, like asking one for help negotiating a job offer and consulting another for a second opinion on

---

* You certainly *can* tell them if you think the formality or accountability will help you follow through, but there's no need to make custom T-shirts or throw an annual director retreat. (Unless you really want to, I guess.)

an important email before you hit send. Or you may look to a cross section of them on a fairly regular basis to weigh in on big decisions before you make your move. Fun fact: You may also play a role on *their* personal board of directors. This isn't about a one-directional relationship where one gives and the other takes. Even with an age or experience differential, there is nearly always something you can offer.

These relationships needn't be solely focused on careers. Your personal board of directors can help you navigate a health care crisis, a breakup, a cross-country move, or even weigh in on the decision to get bangs or adopt a pet. If it's part of your life, it's in play.

Case Study: "A Nice One, a Mean One, and a Neutral One, like Switzerland"

Jeanette Cajide is no stranger to pulling together a team to support her work. An entrepreneur and software executive by day, she moonlights as a competitive amateur ice-skater. The forty-five-year-old skated for just over a year as a teenager before focusing her energy and time on ballet. When her professional dancing career was cut short, she shifted her attention to academics and earned degrees in business and public policy, then kicked off a career in startups. She loved the work and the community she found there, but when her mental and physical health started to suffer from the long hours she spent at her desk, she realized she needed to reengage the athletic part of her portfolio. So she returned to skating. "I thought, if I'm going to do this, I want to do it well. I'm going to be serious about it," she recalled.

She built her team, just like she did as a startup CEO, lining up coaches ("a nice one, a mean one, and a neutral one, like Switzerland"), a physical therapist, an acupuncturist, a nutritionist, and a specialist in muscle activation. "I'm like a professional athlete without the funding of a professional athlete!" she laughed. "But I need each of them to challenge me or work with me in a different way, mentally, physically, emotionally. One does my choreography, another helps me with the mental game of competing, another understands how to use data and biohacking to help me get in peak physical shape."

It's not that far of a leap to see how a personal board of directors serves a similar function in advising Jeanette in her career and broader portfolio. "I have classmates, colleagues, people I used to report to who know me and understand my style. They know how to challenge me and help me grow," she told me. "And as much as I want to excel in my career, right now I'm also seeking balance, with skating, traveling, and trying new things. They get my priorities." Jeanette understands the importance of having the right team to support her, both on the ice and off.

 ## Building Your Board of Directors

So who should be on your personal board of directors? First, think about the industries, networks, geographies, and functional experience you may want to stay connected to, and assemble a diverse board of directors that can support the complex and robust Portfolio Life you are building. (Reams of research back me up on this: A diverse board matters—including across generational lines, gender identities, ethnicities, geographies, and experience.) In addition to considering their functional and industry expertise, you'll want to "hire" directors with an eye toward what specific role you want them to play on your board.

There are five roles that belong on most personal boards: coach, negotiator, connector, cheerleader, and truth teller. (Feel free to add to this list any others that fit your situation.) Let's look at each in more detail.

1. COACH

A huge challenge of a Portfolio Life is that your combined interests, activities, and priorities leave you very few, if any, road maps to follow. Your unique path is as far from a prescribed career ladder as they come, and you will bear more responsibility for navigating your way through life. But that doesn't mean you have to journey alone as you make hard decisions and balance trade-offs. You don't need someone whose footsteps you can follow; what you need is a coach.

The ideal coach isn't necessarily a subject matter expert, but rather someone who is focused on helping you unlock your potential. This is different from a teacher, who knows the thing and is imparting that knowledge to you. Instead, a coach is someone who believes that you innately know what to do and merely need some help to make sense of the situation and get out of your own way. The key skill of great coaching is asking the right questions.

So where should you look for your coach? This could be a former colleague or classmate you've stayed close with. It could be a parent, if you have a great relationship with them. You could hire a professional career or life coach for a particularly challenging or opaque chapter of your life. It could even be a therapist. The central attribute to look for is someone who has a track record of asking great questions and withholding their own judgment about what you should do. They should care deeply about helping you uncover the right decisions for you, and be able to suspend their own ideas or desires to give advice.

2. NEGOTIATOR

One of the jobs of a board of directors is to set CEO compensation, and your personal board is no different. You have likely seen the research on the various pay gaps for women, people of color, and junior folks who lack negotiating leverage. Often this comes down to two things: one, these populations have less data on what "market rates" are for a given role, industry, and geography, so they often peg their target compensation to what they are currently making, feeding a vicious cycle of underpayment; and two, they may lack the skills and vocabulary of negotiating because it's something most people only do every few years.*

So how do you overcome this information and experience gap? You seek out the advice of a professional. This role on your board of directors should be played by someone in your industry who has hired folks at or above your level. While you can benefit from the input of an experienced negotiator outside your industry, they won't be as helpful in vetting specific salary and bonus numbers, or have a sense of what else could or should be on the table, like equity, professional development stipends, vacation days, flexible work support, or other perks. You need someone with current market intel.

You may consider having two directors who play the "negotiator" role, particularly if you are from an underrepresented group in your industry. Here's why: I'd want to seek market data from someone in the dominant group (e.g., childless white men under forty in the tech world) since they are the most likely to be paid fairly. But I'd like to seek advice on how to approach the negotiation—the opening ask, the cadence of communication, the tactics for holding firm or walking away—from someone who has experienced the particular power differential I might be facing. They will likely have a more applicable toolkit to deal with the microaggressions or complex power dynamics I'm up against.

You may also need more than one negotiator on your board of directors if you are paid across several different industries or contexts. You'd need different inputs for setting the rates you charge for your small photography business in Vermont than you would for negotiating your promotion in your marketing job at Nike, for example. Likewise, you'll want expert advice for negotiating a book deal, setting ad rates for your podcast, charging for piano lessons, baking custom cakes, taking on freelance clients, and more. And

---

* Unless your job is literally a negotiations job, like a lawyer or business development professional.

don't forget about the personal components of your portfolio that could be ripe for negotiation: This director could be a key partner in navigating a tricky health insurance situation or helping you advocate for yourself when buying a home.

How do you find these directors? There are a couple of strong places to start: a former boss who you maintained a good relationship with; a friend's parent who is in your industry; a former classmate; or even a peer who you know has been successful in negotiating excellent deals for themselves and is willing to share their secret sauce. If you run a small business or charge for your side projects, you could also build a roundtable of other folks in your space to bounce rates and terms off of. (We'll talk more about money in Chapter 11, and in particular, about the importance of sharing pay rates, contract terms, and other key compensation details among friends and colleagues in order to level the playing field just a bit more.) Companies won't pay you a dime more than they have to, and they are relying on social norms and shame to keep compensation as opaque as possible.

3. CONNECTOR

You know that friend who somehow knows everyone? The person who delights in setting up blind dates, always has the scoop on job openings, has friends in that random place you are traveling to next month, and seems to know at least one person in basically every industry? That, my friends, is your connector, and they are a must-have on your board.

In any social network* there are often a few folks who serve as the main points of connection for all of the other members of the community. They are called "super nodes" and they are what makes a network efficient. Most people stick to their own smaller subgroup of friends or colleagues or classmates, but these super nodes

---

* By which I simply mean a network of people, not any specific technology platform.

have friends throughout the community so information flows fastest through them. They are the ones who actively cultivate orthogonal networks. And they delight in their role as connectors. For example, making pitch-perfect introductions is something these folks take great pride in. They don't just throw out a generic email; they thoughtfully advocate for both sides and highlight the mutual benefit of the potential relationship.

The keys to a great relationship with the connector on your board of directors are to ask for their help strategically, provide them with the most important details to make a great introduction, and to follow through on that connection like it's your job. You don't want to overuse your connector's relationships for asks that aren't particularly important because each introduction requires them to spend both time and social capital on your behalf. You also want to do as much of the work for them as possible: making specific asks ("Could you connect me with X about this opportunity they just posted on LinkedIn?" rather than "Do you know anyone who is hiring right now?") and offering any background context they might need to provide the connection (even better if you draft the email for them to tweak). And you want to honor the work they did on your behalf and follow up on that connection in a timely and respectful manner.

Finally, remember that your relationship with your connector goes both ways, and they may reach out to you to be a connection or advocate for someone else. Be sure to invest in the relationship as much as you benefit from it.

4. CHEERLEADER

Everyone needs a hype person from time to time. There's nothing embarrassing about admitting that you need positive reinforcement, particularly when imposter syndrome sets in. But impersonal praise from someone whose opinion you don't value isn't worth much. Which is why your cheerleader needs to be someone you know and trust.

This person is likely the one on your board of directors that you've known the longest and can drop into a text thread or make an unplanned phone call without much context for a quick five-minute pick-me-up. You don't need to set aside an hour for a full catch-up when what you might need is simply a reminder that "You got this!" They see the best in you and have enough shared history that they (and you!) believe the hype they are sending in your direction.

I have a couple of cheerleaders on my board of directors, and while we've all taken different paths in life, we share the ups and downs of our careers, families, fertility, health, dreams, frustrations, and more. Through that extreme vulnerability we are able to authentically lift each other up in a way that fuels bravery and belief in ourselves.

5. TRUTH TELLER

Lastly, to balance out your cheerleader(s), you need a truth teller. This is the person you trust to call you out in a way that you can hear it, and to do so with your best interests at heart. They aren't there to make you feel bad, but rather to push you to do better because they know you can. If you're wondering if the person you have in mind could play this role for you, they cannot. There should be no doubt. This person is the living, breathing embodiment of Luvvie Ajayi Jones's book *I'm Judging You: The Do-Better Manual*. (Go read the introduction on Google Books and you'll see what I mean.) They give it to you straight.

You need a truth teller on your personal board of directors for several reasons. The first is that you need someone who sees all of you—your full Venn diagram of talents and interests and the big picture of the Portfolio Life you're building—and can reflect back to you whether what you are saying and what you are doing are actually lining up. In every other part of your life, your colleagues and connections have an incomplete picture of your talents, commitments, and priorities, and when things aren't going well, it will be easy to discount their feedback because of that limitation. You can sidestep blame and write off criticism if that is your nature. (You can also take everything they say too personally and stew in it unnecessarily if that's more your style.) But having a director who sees the big picture, cares deeply about your success, and can tell you with love and devotion that you are screwing up is vital for your development.

Second, you need an accountability partner, particularly over the long haul. When you are zigging and zagging, changing roles or companies or industries every few years, it can be easy to develop and sustain bad habits that won't serve you in the end. Having a director who can challenge you to meet your goals, grow personally and professionally, and help you see an accurate representation of yourself along the way will make the difference between being good and becoming great. Their high expectations for you will help you thrive beyond your wildest dreams.

What do you do if you don't feel like you have the people to serve in these director roles? Maybe you're just starting out, or perhaps you're going through a radical life change and looking for a fresh start. It's okay to not have all of these seats filled on day one; building relationships takes time. Comb through your community and see what roles you do have covered, then make it a point to start "recruiting" for the unfilled roles. Maybe someone can do double duty for a while, serving in multiple capacities while you look for other leads. Or perhaps you can ask your existing "board members" for suggestions or introductions to folks who might be a natural fit for the missing directors. Bottom line: You don't need to stress, but you do need a strategy to fill the seats.*

Now that you've invested in your orthogonal networks and built your personal board of directors, it's time to talk about partnerships. While

---

* Remember, these "board seats" are metaphorical. They aren't formal roles; rather, this is a framework for you to think about who you have around you for support and advice.

the typical narrative around life partners is rooted in romance, for the next few pages I'd like you to think of this role as a co-founder. Why? Because as much as a life partnership is about love, it's also very much a business relationship. (After all, marriage is a contract: You accept rights and benefits but also take on legal and financial obligations.) And research shows that choosing the right life partner is the most important decision you will make when it comes to both your career and long-term happiness.[2] So if you choose to have a partner, there is no one who will have a greater impact on your Portfolio Life.

PARTNERS AND PARTNERSHIPS

In the startup world, we often say a co-founder relationship is like a marriage. Co-founders are the folks who start a new venture, taking on the financial and emotional risk of the unknown and building something together, from the ground up. So it's not that far of a stretch to make the reverse analogy: marriage—or any kind of life partnership—is like a co-founder relationship. But just like in business, there are many models for a life partnership, so before you can find the right partner, you need to determine what kind of partnership is right for you.

Some folks find the serial monogamy approach works best for them: one person at a time, whether for the long haul or just a chapter of life. Perhaps you intend to grow together over time or maybe you'll agree to part ways when your paths diverge; either way, this model is anchored in an exclusive partnership between two people. Others take a portfolio approach to partnership and prefer a polyamorous path: Not expecting any one person to meet all of their needs in work or at home, they cultivate concurrent relationships that each provide a particular aspect of what they need. This approach recognizes that the diversification or rebalancing of priorities might naturally lead to a diversification or rebalancing of partnerships. And then there are those who are happy without a life partner, finding companionship, intimacy, and joy through other relationships. So which model is right for you?

WHAT ARE YOU LOOKING FOR?

When my entrepreneurship students come to me for advice on finding a co-founder, I always start by asking, "Why do you want one?" Often, they don't have a good answer, instead defaulting to an assumption that they *should* have one because so many of the entrepreneurs they admire did. But if you don't know why you want a partner, how will you know when you've found the right one? Without a clear understanding of what you are looking for, you may latch on to the first warm body that seems like a "good enough" fit.

So I prod my students to do some self-reflection and report back. Are they looking for someone to fill a specific gap in their skill set or just another set of hands to help share the workload? Do they want an equal to help them wrestle with big decisions and push their thinking, or do they want a deputy who is happy to let them call the shots alone? Are they waiting to start their company until they find their co-founder, or are they content to get started on their own and maybe bring someone on down the line if they find the right person? There are no right answers to any of these questions, but they need to know what they want out of the partnership before they can possibly attract and select the right person.

If the analogy to life partners seems a bit too on the nose, let me take a minute to point out it took me more than a decade of dating all the wrong people before I came to this realization. All throughout my twenties I had zero clue about what I was looking for in a partner. I picked dates like I was reviewing résumés and kept breaking up with (mostly) lovely, interesting, accomplished guys who were all wrong for me. As I approached thirty, I was infuriated by how well my professional life was progressing compared to my stunted personal life. So, ever the entrepreneur, I decided to take myself on a "relationship offsite," solo camping in Acadia National Park to figure out what I really wanted.

I had never been to Maine and my last pseudo-boyfriend had an extreme aversion to anything below four-star hotels, so it felt like an appropriate exercise of my newfound freedom to wear flannel and cook dinner over a fire pit and sleep on the ground for a week. I packed my gear, loaded up on instant coffee, s'mores supplies, and honey whiskey, and set off for the great lobster state.

My goal was to spot bad habits or problematic patterns and devise a strategy for improving on my partner-selection process. So as I basked in the warmth of my bonfire, I jotted down a decade's worth of boyfriends, bad decisions, and everything in between, asking questions like what initially drew me to them, what ultimately caused things to end, how far I was into the relationship before I knew deep down that it was doomed, and how long I stuck around after that realization.

What I came to were two lists: "The Nonnegotiables List" (the traits, habits, values that I knew I needed in a life partner) and the "Couldn't Care Less List" of criteria that didn't make one whit of difference in whether we would make a good team. Has a passion for their work and the drive and discipline to make an impact? Yes, absolutely a nonnegotiable. Specific career? Nope, doesn't matter. Makes time for me and for our relationship, despite the complications of life? Super important. Lives off a convenient subway line? Nah. (Also, height or alma mater? Not relevant!)

Looking at the two lists side by side with my relationship history, the issue was clear as day: I had developed a set of proxies for the things I thought would make a successful partnership and was treating them as signals that *this* might be my person without actually testing whether the potential partner and I had shared values, vision, or velocity.

VALUES, VISION, AND VELOCITY

When I meet a startup founding team, there are just three variables I look at to predict success: common values, compatible vision, and comparable velocity.*

---

* This doesn't mean their *startup* will be successful—there are more elements at play like market size, business model, competition, speed of learning, and more— but these variables are usually a good test of whether the team will stay together or implode at the first real pressure point.

There are so many unknowns when starting a company, from the product to the business model to the competitive and economic forces that might impact what you build, that it's impossible for co-founders to discuss and agree on everything in advance. But if they share a common set of values, it's more likely they will see eye to eye when it comes time to make difficult decisions. Do they prioritize profit or people? Do they care more about speed or scale? How do they rank collaboration versus cooperation? Which is more important: learning or winning? There are no right answers to these questions, but co-founders who don't agree on values are unlikely to make it very far.

Along with common values, successful founding teams have compatible visions for the future. Whether it's a sustainable, cash-flow business still humming along twenty years later or a venture-backed startup seeking hypergrowth and an IPO, the founding team must agree on what "success" means for their company. Otherwise, they'll clash on the tough questions as they attempt to build very different futures.

Lastly, the founding teams that have what it takes are those that are running with comparable velocities—that is, they are going in roughly the same direction at roughly the same speed. They don't have to be in lockstep with each other; they may have marginally different priorities, need slightly different resources, or make decisions in different ways. But when you zoom out, it's clear they are running the same race and they're on the same team.

Building a Portfolio Life is a lot like building a startup: Most of the time there are more unknowns than knowns, and what it looks like at the beginning will bear little resemblance to what it looks like one, two, five decades in. Which means it's impossible to discuss all of the possible variables up front with a potential life partner. But if you look for common values, a compatible vision for the future, and comparable velocity, you are much more likely to set your partnership up for success.

Not too long after my week of flannel and honey whiskey in Maine, I got an email on OkCupid from a Brooklyn lawyer, actor, and writer named Chas. At first glance he wasn't my "type." I had long ago sworn off attorneys (they like to argue too much), he was two years younger than me (a red flag for being ready to settle down), and we were the same height (which, in online dating terms, meant he was probably shorter, let's be honest). But I remembered how little those details actually mattered and decided to meet up with him anyway. I'd give him one hour and one drink to suss out whether we were even in the same ballpark for values, vision, and velocity.

One hour turned into five, then a second date, and a third before we stopped counting them altogether. As it turned out, our values were completely aligned, even though we arrived at them through very different life experiences. Chas and I also shared a similar life vision of mashing up creative projects, political engagement, impact-driven career choices, and a desire to build a community of similarly inspired and driven friends. And our velocity was evenly matched: We were running in the same direction at roughly the same speed, a key point since we were discussing marriage and children. Within a year, we shared a washer, dryer, and two houseplants, and shortly thereafter tied the knot, bought an apartment, and had two kids. (See how important shared velocity is?) He even gets a seat on my board of directors, serving both as my negotiator and pro bono general counsel.* And it turns out he wasn't lying about his height; we really are both six feet tall.

As the CEO of your Portfolio Life, you are in charge of ensuring you have the right people on your team to support, advise, and partner with as you build a life that is fulfilling and sustainable. Serving as the connector between orthogonal networks will foster community and fuel collaboration and creativity. Cultivating a personal board of directors will ensure you are surrounded by a diverse set of folks to nurture growth, open doors, and cheer on your success. And seeing your life partner, should you choose to have one, as a co-founder will position you to build a foundation of shared values, vision, and velocity to power your partnership. This team will help you steer the ship. Now it's time to tell them where you're headed.

---

* There are a few upsides to marrying a lawyer.

CHAPTER 9

Tell Your Story

About all you can do in life is be who you are. Some
people will love you for you. Most will love you for what
you can do for them, and some won't like you at all.

—Rita Mae Brown

The scariest thing you can say to someone with a Portfolio Life is, "So
tell me about yourself."* This is a hard question to answer, and most
Americans default to our jobs for an easy out.† But someone who combines several strands of work and personal endeavors—and crucially,
defines their identity in that intersection—will face a quandary: Do I
share everything I do (and risk coming off as a braggart or dilettante), or
do I shrink who I am to fit into a neat box that is easy to describe?

Most of the time, neither of those is the right approach, yet opting
out of talking about yourself altogether is a terrible one. When you're
crafting a Portfolio Life, you have to actively seek the opportunities you

---

* Okay, this might be the second scariest sentence. The scariest is probably "I'm
from the IRS and you did your taxes wrong." But don't stress about this just yet.
We'll discuss the financial realities of a Portfolio Life in Chapter 11.

† This is truly an American response, since we view work as identity. Interestingly
enough, talking about your job or asking someone what they do is considered rude
in many parts of the world. In much of Europe, for example, asking about someone's
profession can come across as inquiring about where they stand in the hierarchical
class structure. In the United States, where there is no history of an aristocracy, we
see it more as a quick way to learn about someone or to look for what we might have
in common.

want; they are highly unlikely to just be waiting for you on a job board somewhere or just find their way into your inbox. And while you know you aren't defined by your job, or by just the things you *do*, you do need some way to describe how you allocate your time and talents. So you need to be clear about who you are, what you're offering, and what, specifically, you are looking for so that your tribe can show up for you.

HOW VISIBLE ARE YOU?

When I founded Quincy, I joined an online network called TheLi.st—a community of women and nonbinary folks who work in tech, media, politics, and entertainment. It can be hard to explain what we are exactly; it's a cross between an email LISTSERV, real-life friendships, and the good-old-boys-club of professional networking. The founders, Rachel Sklar and Glynnis MacNicol, describe it as a platform that gives members visibility, which turns into access, which leads to opportunity. One of the things this network does on an almost daily basis is provide a forum to practice bragging, which we define as "sharing our wins and our wants" with the group. Because the community is full of investors, journalists, potential business partners, and potential hires, it is a community ripe with opportunities. But only if they know what's going on with you.

Author, public speaker, podcaster, and member of TheLi.st, Luvvie Ajayi Jones is a strong supporter of being open about what you are doing and what you need to move forward. "Don't hoard your dreams to yourself. Speak them out loud so your helpers can find you," she insists. "There are people who have the key to doors you want to enter, but if they have no clue about where you want to sit, they can't offer you the key to that room. Speak up. Say what you want. Dream audaciously."

I know that for some, "bragging" feels like a dirty word. And, yes, it can be obnoxious if done to the extreme. But there is a difference between tone-deaf monologuing about your perceived awesomeness and being honest about your achievements. To make a Portfolio Life possible, you have to be willing to be your own chief marketing officer. That means telling the story of who you are, what you're doing, what you need, what you're proud of. That's not being obnoxious; that's just being visible. Sharing your story not only allows others to help you, but it also makes it clear how you can help them, strengthening your relationships in both directions.

For example, when Dana Hork made a recent transition from being an in-house corporate marketing leader to launching an independent consulting and media business, she needed to do a fair bit of bragging. She was making a big jump into the nascent world of web3 and wanted to connect with others who were similarly building companies based on decentralized and token-based technologies. But her résumé was just one part of her story. She also had relocated to the suburbs with her husband and two children during the pandemic, and had navigated a difficult health diagnosis, which she also shared with her friends and network. The point of her "bragging" was to share the news of her new professional endeavors and ask for help, yes. But it was also to offer help: She had a wealth of experience from her previous work, ranging from e-commerce and fashion to partnering with the White House to address the diaper gap. And anyone thinking of making a similar move to the suburbs or dealing with the same health diagnosis was more than welcome to reach out for advice on those personal fronts. She wasn't puffing up her professional success to put herself on a pedestal. Sharing her story was a way to both give and receive support.

You may think crafting a story is just something you need to do for networking events or updates you post on LinkedIn, but the way you market yourself can have more of an impact on your life than you realize. Sometimes opportunities are waiting for you in the grocery line or at the dog park or even in the bathroom at the ballet.

Maria* was washing her hands during an intermission of the American Ballet Theatre's *The Sleeping Beauty* when the woman next to her complimented her lipstick. Maria thanked her, paused, then added that it was a shade she was testing out for the next season's collection of the beauty brand she'd founded. As she and the woman struck up a conversation about Maria's experiences as a dancer-turned-entrepreneur, a woman in line for the toilets spoke up. "This may be a bit odd, but I heard

---

* At her request, some identifying details have been changed.

you mention you started a beauty company and I used to be an executive at Estée Lauder. Now I'm retired and invest in and advise a handful of companies. If you have any interest, I'd love to get your card and meet up for lunch this week to learn more about your brand."

Maria was thrilled. As she dug into her bag to find a business card for the executive, the woman next to her at the sinks chimed in. "I'd love your card too. I'm throwing a luncheon for the female leaders in our company next month and would like to talk to you about speaking at the event. Your story is so inspirational. Perhaps we can include that lipstick in the gift bag!" Maria was stunned. Her company had been struggling and she had begun to wonder whether she should shut it down. Now she had two incredible leads that could provide much-needed momentum, and all because she bragged about her brand instead of batting away the compliment with an embarrassed "thank you."

DO I HAVE TO?

I know that some of you are still not convinced. "Why do I have to talk about myself in the first place? Why can't I just do great work and wait for the recognition that I deserve?" I understand the reticence. Many of us see folks who are all talk and very little substance, who are constantly bragging about their work but don't seem to have much to back it up, and want to avoid coming off as obnoxious as they do. *Brag Better* author Meredith Fineman calls them the "lackluster loud." And she agrees, they are obnoxious. But that doesn't give you permission to skip out on talking about your work altogether. Effective bragging "doesn't require false bravado, talking over people, or pretending to be more qualified than you are," she insists. Instead, it's about "turning up the volume" for the group she calls the "Qualified Quiet," the people who have done the work and just don't talk about it.

Bottom line: You need visibility to get opportunities. It's often not the people you already know, but the people *they* know who will fuel your success.[1] Stay top of mind for your network.

THE STRENGTH OF WEAK TIES

In 1973, American sociologist Dr. Mark Granovetter published his seminal paper[2] on social networks titled "The Strength of Weak Ties."* In it, he introduced a new idea called "weak tie theory" to explain why the speed and novelty of information spread between loosely connected people far surpassed that of networks more closely connected. While strong ties between people are vital for real community, they can also be self-limiting, favoring the resharing of news, ideas, and information that is likely already known within the largely homogenous group. Weak ties, on the other hand, were far more likely to exist between heterogeneous groups, and as such, introduced new ideas, promoted creativity, and increased the speed of information dissemination.

When it comes to networking—the seeking and sharing of professional and personal opportunities—those weak ties are going to be where you find the most traction. However, by definition, these are also the people who are likely to know you *the least*. So your responsibility is to provide a clear, concise, repeatable narrative that outlines who you are, what you offer, and what you need. Arm them with a memorable story and they can get to work on your behalf.

When I was ready to move on from Startup Institute and go build something of my own again, I emailed TheLi.st. I outlined what I had done: opening the New York office, winning a $250,000 grant, launching nearly 150 young professionals into new careers, advising on the opening of three more offices, winning big stories in prestigious media outlets, and more. And then I told them what I wanted to do next: focus on getting more women in tech, which meant getting more girls in the Science, Technology, Engineering, and Math (STEM) pipeline.

One of the Listers was friendly with a philanthropic foundation that wanted to fund programs for girls in STEM. She introduced me to a trustee, and we began talking about a venture that could teach girls

---

* At the time, social networks were largely physical, though further research has since proved his findings translate seamlessly to the digital world as well.

and other communities underrepresented in tech how to code through the context of science—using scientific data sets and inquiry-based learning to get students excited about computer science. The trustee wanted to fund an initiative like that based at the American Museum of Natural History, and I agreed to build it. In the end, the Helen Gurley Brown Foundation awarded us a five-year grant of $7.5 million to fund BridgeUp: STEM. One email that summed up my wins and my wants led to a distant friend making an introduction, which funded my next venture in full. But that weak tie only knew how to promote me because I had promoted myself first.*

SO HOW DO YOU CRAFT YOUR STORY?

Okay, you believe me that you need to be your own CMO. But what story is it that you want to promote? Before I answer that, let me introduce a marketing framework known as "what are they buying/what are you selling?"

Imagine you just moved into a new home and are trying to hang a heavy mirror on the wall. You realize you need to drill a large hole and install an anchor so the screw won't pull out of the drywall. There's only one problem: You don't own a drill. So, you go down to the hardware store. Most likely, the sales associate you beg for help will start rattling off the product features. They'll tell you the technical specs or the details behind the fabrication or the complex science behind why this tool is 10% better than its nearest competitor, trying to close a sale.

The thing is, you're not there to buy a specific drill with a certain power rating or the ability to recharge the battery in under an hour. To be honest, you aren't necessarily even there to *buy* a drill at all. You'd be happy enough to rent one for the afternoon. Or, better yet, hire someone

---

* TheLi.st has been equally powerful in my social and personal life, whether referring me to lawyers to negotiate my prenup, introducing me to new friends when I relocated to Boston, surfacing political and nonprofit volunteer opportunities, or sharing childcare leads, another example of how professional and personal often overlap.

to come and do the work for you. Because what you're really there to buy is a way to safely and securely hang your mirror.

See the problem? They're trying to sell you a product when you're really there to buy a *solution.*

Now let's translate this framework to the context of work: Imagine you're interviewing to be the executive assistant to a solo entrepreneur. Rather than focusing on you, reciting facts and figures from your résumé, you home in on what problems you can solve for them: You can make sense of that pile of receipts, triage their inbox, and streamline their upcoming travel, turning a nightmare into something just shy of pleasurable. You can offer them leverage and free them from logistics so they can zero in on the big things that make the most impact on their business. You can transform them from frazzled into focused, catapulting them to the top of their game. Get the idea?

When it comes to telling your story, you must focus on the solutions you offer, not the "product specs" listed on your résumé. This becomes exponentially true for folks with Portfolio Lives whose backgrounds are a veritable cornucopia of skills and experiences. So when someone asks you about yourself, rather than reciting a three-minute monologue of your résumé in reverse chronological order (sans breath), your goal is to share what kind of solutions you bring to the table.

Not sure what that means exactly? Here's an example. Before Mike Slagh was the founder and CEO of Shift.org, he was a naval officer specializing in bomb disposal. When he left the military, he wanted to get a job in the tech world, but he couldn't get his foot in the door. No hiring manager could make heads or tails of his previous experience except for a glimmer of recognition that his education at the US Naval Academy and the Harvard Kennedy School of Public Policy was "kinda impressive." And there was a real question about whether his work in a highly regimented world like the US military would set him up to fail in the fast-moving and often nebulous world of Silicon Valley.

Mike's credentials and service record got him initial interviews at tech companies, but he kept losing out on offers because he wasn't telling a compelling story. "Instead of spending the entire conversation trying to explain the system of military occupational specialties, I should have just led with 'veterans exhibit good judgment in chaotic situations because it's as natural as breathing.'"

Holy wow is that an introduction that would stop me cold! In just one sentence I have learned a ton about Mike—that he is comfortable in unknown and unpredictable situations (which, incidentally, is the very definition of early-stage startups); that he has deep experience in making tough calls with limited information ("it's as natural as breathing"); and that he knows enough about this new world that he's seeking to join to show me how it connects to his old one. You may point out that his statement is about all veterans, not Mike specifically, which is true. But the fact that he could synthesize his value and answer the question that way *does* tell me about him—it reveals his understanding of the context and his communications skills.

"Now that I've got your attention, we can talk about how my experience in bomb disposal makes me one of the world's best problem solvers," he points out. "Or how most outsiders' perception of the military misses out on how gritty and entrepreneurial we had to be in foreign countries, operating in the gray with painful resource constraints and no playbook." I don't have to understand a word of Mike's hyper-technical résumé to be able to see what he could offer my organization. He's helped me understand how his previous experience has prepared him to solve my current and future problems.

This isn't easy for most people, and it's even harder for anyone who has worked in a jargon-heavy world like the military or medicine. But connecting the dots in straightforward language is the key to working across multiple fields or making unexpected career jumps.

SHIFTING FROM JARGON TO ENGLISH

So how do you break free of industry lingo and write your story in plain English? First, find a translator. And second, refine your delivery like a stand-up comic. Let me explain.

When I wanted to make my first big zigzag from opera to the business world, I struggled to convert my work into experiences and skills that would be relevant elsewhere. (Somehow, scheduling a rehearsal for a horse, a dog, and a goat for a production of Prokofiev's *War and Peace* didn't reflect the corporate cultures I was targeting?) Then one day a business school classmate, Jen, asked me about my work at the Met. Jen came from an operations background, managing manufacturing plants for a large health care company. I wasn't sure where to start; she had never even been to an opera.

So she reframed the question: "Tell me about a time you had to do something crazy hard at your job." As I shared one particularly hairy story involving feuding divas, missing charter buses, restrictive union rules, the politics of the New York City Department of Parks and Recreation, and about four dozen child choristers, she interjected with follow-up questions: "What, specifically, made that so difficult? What support did you have? Why does the opera world do things that way?" When I finished, she reflected back to me what she heard, translating my unique experiences into a more general context that those outside my niche industry would understand. While my title had been "rehearsal associate," my work was classic operations management, and my expertise in navigating the big personalities of opera singers easily transferred to the context of client services. Just as important, I was adept at coordinating between the business side and the creative side of an organization, juggling competing priorities and cultures and coaching folks to work together on the same team.

Armed with new vocabulary and the confidence that my work was relevant beyond the red velvet-covered walls of the opera hall, I sought out opportunities to practice telling my story. Like a stand-up comic on tour, refining a set in comedy cellars across the country, I told my story over and over again until the narrative clicked. I used conversations in line at Starbucks, while introducing myself to classmates, even on a few first dates to get comfortable with the new language and learn from my audience: Where were they skeptical? What was unclear? Did they understand not just what I used to do, but why I was making a change? The interplay between storyteller and listener is key; by telling your story to an audience, rather than just reciting it in private, you are giving them the opportunity to revise and refine it with you, co-creating a narrative that can really sing (pun intended).

Case Study: From the ER to the C-Suite

Charlotte Lawson had to completely rewrite her story when she left her first career as an emergency room physician to earn an MBA and found a software startup. A self-described overachiever, Charlotte was a twelve-season varsity athlete and graduated summa cum laude from the University of Pennsylvania with a degree in neuroscience before continuing on at Penn for medical school. She moved to North Carolina to complete her residency in emergency medicine with no intention of ever going back to school to study business (or anything else).

But as she progressed in her career, she became frustrated with the process of introducing new technologies to the clinical environment. She saw technology impacting all other parts of her life, from transportation to groceries to travel planning, but in the ER she was stymied; the American health care ecosystem wasn't set up for entrepreneurial tinkering in how doctors delivered care. Just as frustrating: She had big ideas but lacked the skills and network to implement them. Charlotte cared enough about the opportunities for radical change in health care that she was willing to trade in her stethoscope and doctor's coat for contracts and complex financial models.

Charlotte had also made a pivot in her personal life. During her residency, she came out and got divorced, finding the courage to bring her whole, authentic self to every part of her life. "In coming out, I gave myself permission to speak aloud who I was, what I wanted, and what I needed." By the time she started her MBA, she had remarried and her wife was expecting their first child. That's when everything sort of clicked for Charlotte.

During her first-year entrepreneurship course (which, in full disclosure, I taught her), she realized that her training in the emergency room was incredibly relevant to the job of an early-stage startup founder. "I got comfortable making high-stakes—literally life or death—decisions with limited information and even more limited time. I often had to do my best with what I knew in the moment and learn from my mistakes to do better next time, rather than beat myself up for not being perfect. And I couldn't do it alone. In the ER, it is always a team sport."

By the end of her first year, she had the kernel of an idea for a software solution to enable at-home diagnostic testing and health care delivery at scale, and quickly found two co-founders to jump on board. Over the next year, she found herself telling her story over and over as they raised capital, built out a team, and landed their first paying clients, a major regional health care system and two national in-home service providers.

She refined her story's delivery with each repetition, eschewing the (albeit impressive) details of her time in the ER and instead highlighting that while the day-to-day work as a software CEO was a far cry from her clinical work as a doctor, the muscle memory for effective, high-stakes decision-making she built in medicine would fuel her success as an entrepreneur. Plus, she reminded them, her experience as a health care industry veteran gave her the credibility to attract talent, resources, and customers for her health-tech startup. Rather than being questioned about whether she was qualified to build her company, Charlotte was able to frame her previous career as an "unfair advantage."

Notice that the story you tell *must* be context-specific. When Charlotte answered a page on an airplane that was asking, "Are there any doctors on board?"* she was wise to mention she was an emergency room physician, which was far more relevant to the man having a heart attack in first class than the vascular surgeon or internist who were sitting closer to the passenger.

But when talking with interested investors or potential customers, those details are irrelevant because what they are "buying" is an ambitious and visionary CEO, not a medical provider.

---

* While en route to a sales meeting for her new startup, naturally.

Her background as a doctor is only relevant for "selling" her track record of excellence, ability to work with a team in a high-stakes environment, and understanding the industry she is building a company in.

BUT WHAT IF I *HATE* TALKING ABOUT MYSELF?

Now, I fully understand that many people struggle to talk about themselves. That no matter how clear they are on why they should, it still feels uncomfortable at best and self-aggrandizing at worst. So let's talk about some ways to get more comfortable with this indispensable skill.

First, try writing your story in the third person. Why? Almost everyone—even the people who cannot stand to talk about their own successes—gets excited to brag about their friends' accomplishments. We're generally pretty great at pumping up the people we love and making sure everyone around us knows how awesome they are too. So while you get used to talking about yourself, do it in the third person and pretend you're describing your amazing friend who just happens to share your name.

Second, think back to your coffee chats from Chapter 4. How did your friends and colleagues talk about you? If you can't remember the specifics, follow up with three or four of them and ask them how they would describe you to a stranger. Or just tag along with them to a party and take mental notes on how they introduce you. You may be surprised by how easy it is for them to extoll your greatest achievements and attributes.

Lastly, don't think about this as talking yourself up. Think about it as solving a problem for your biggest cheerleaders. Imagine your best friend randomly gets into an elevator with the person you most want to meet in the world. They've got one minute, maybe two to shoot their shot and tell this person why you are the best thing since sliced bread. If you've given your friend a clear story that they can easily recall and share, they can make your dreams come true. But if they only have the vaguest sense of what you are currently working on or why this stranger should meet you, they will fumble the pitch or, worse, just stay silent. The people who love you want to help you, but they need the tools to do so. It's up to you to provide them.

 ## One Page, One Paragraph, One Sentence

Okay, it's time to get to work! Take out a notebook or your laptop and let's craft your story. We're going to borrow a technique from the marketing world called "one page, one paragraph, one sentence." We'll start by writing the full-page version of your story. Think of this as the bio on your personal website or the introduction someone reads before giving you an award. Then we'll whittle that page down to just one paragraph: five to seven carefully crafted sentences that get right to the heart of who you are and what you can offer. Think of the paragraph as the email intro a friend might send on your behalf or the quick summary on an elevator ride. Lastly, with the deftness of a poet or a surgeon, we'll finesse that paragraph down to a single sentence. It won't capture all of you—how could it!—but it can provide enough of a taste to make the listener say, "Tell me more."

ONE PAGE

As French philosopher and mathematician Blaise Pascal once noted, "I would have written a shorter letter, but I did not have the time." Brevity is hard. *Really hard.* So we're going to start on the opposite end and write a full page about ourselves.

You can craft your narrative in any way that speaks to you, but I find it generally includes four principal components, roughly one paragraph per topic:

1. **Who are you?/What are you doing now?**
2. **What did you do before this?**

3. **What else do you care deeply about? (Think: board seats, volunteering, hobbies and personal projects.)**
4. **Biographical data that helps humanize you, like pets, family, and fun facts.***

Before you set pen to paper, glance back at your Venn diagram. Rather than telling a chronological story with specific job titles, pull up one level and look at the bigger picture. What are some of the circles in your Venn diagram, and how do you want to prioritize them in your story? For example, are you a jazz musician who codes, a software engineer who plays saxophone, or an engineer and musician who sees similarities between programming and improv? Weave in personal details that give color to who you are beyond your professional titles.

When you've finished a draft of your page, send it to your board of directors and ask if it captures the essence of who you are and what makes you stand out. Does your personality shine through? Are you bragging enough? Is it clear, concise, and memorable? Keep tweaking until the people who know you best agree that it sounds like you.

Here's a classic one-pager:

Stephanie Alderman is a business manager who works with established recording artists, major touring acts, and up-and-coming songwriters alike. Stephanie has spent two decades in the music industry, including more than fifteen years in business management. She believes that every artist deserves a financial partner to help them navigate and achieve their business and personal goals.

---

* These are "fun" in the same way that after-work social events are "fun"— they are not, but they are opportunities for colleagues to see each other as three-dimensional humans, which is useful even if it is still work.

A trained classical pianist, Stephanie's journey to business management was anything but linear. Between hours of études and sonatas in the practice studios of Interlochen Arts Academy and Michigan State University, she developed a keen interest in the business aspect of the music industry. After completing a degree in music performance from MSU, she moved to Nashville where she earned a second degree in music business from Belmont University.

After Belmont she kicked off her career in the industry by gaining a wide range of experience spanning artist management, publicity, and tour production. When she had the opportunity to join a business management firm, she knew she had found the perfect role that leveraged her robust financial management skills and her ability to understand and authentically connect with musicians and artists.

Originally from Lansing, Michigan, Stephanie is a member of Phi Kappa Phi, Beta Gamma Sigma, the Academy of Country Music, and the Country Music Association. She lives in Franklin with her husband, Shaun, and their three creative and energetic boys.

ONE PARAGRAPH

After all that hard work to get a perfect one-pager, your mission, should you choose to accept it, is to whittle that page down to 100 to 150 words. I'll help you make the first cut: So long, fun facts! We get seven sentences max* and no one *needs* to know about your houseplant obsession (unless you moonlight in horticulture). Instead we're going to structure our paragraph like this: an introductory sentence that paints the broad strokes of who you are. One sentence about what you currently do. Two sentences to sum up your previous experiences and skills, grouped by theme or impact, not chronology. Then one or two sentences that sketch an outline of your broader portfolio to round out a three-dimensional portrait. If you

---

* Now is not the time to go all James Joyce and push the bounds of commas and sentence structure. Keep it simple.

have an accolade that would be somewhat recognizable outside your narrow professional world, finish with that.

Here's how we could slim down Stephanie's page to one really strong paragraph:

> *Stephanie Alderman is a business manager with more than two decades of experience working with established recording artists, major touring acts, and up-and-coming songwriters alike. A trained classical pianist, Stephanie holds dual degrees in performance and music business. After kicking off her career by gaining a wide range of experience from tour production to publicity, she found her sweet spot in business management, leveraging her robust financial management skills and her ability to authentically connect with musicians and artists. A native Michigander, Stephanie now lives in Franklin, Tennessee, with her husband and three boys.*

Boom! Ninety-four words that pack a punch and leave you wanting to know a lot more about Stephanie.

ONE SENTENCE

Are you ready? This one is the hardest of the three. Again, the goal here isn't to sum up the whole of your humanity in two dozen words, but rather to sketch an outline of who you are, what world(s) you inhabit, and what role you take on in those worlds. Done right, it is clear and memorable enough to provide a scaffolding for getting to know you better. The best possible response to your sentence? "Tell me more."

Here are some of my favorite one-liners:

- Dustin Growick is a science communicator helping share the stories behind the absolute coolest places on Earth.
- Cindy Gallop is the Michael Bay of business: She likes to blow sh!t up.

- Elan Morgan believes in good design, quality writing, and genuine community, and much of their work revolves around furthering the internet to this end.
- Baratunde Thurston is a futurist comedian, writer, and cultural critic who helped relaunch *The Daily Show with Trevor Noah*, co-founded Cultivated Wit and the *About Race* podcast, and wrote the *New York Times* bestseller *How to Be Black*.

How might we parse Stephanie's experience into just one sentence? There could be several different approaches, depending on her audience. Here's my favorite version:

> *Stephanie Alderman is a financial fairy godmother for Nashville musicians and believes that all artists—from up-and-coming songwriters to major touring acts alike—deserve a business manager who can help them reach their goals.*

DIGITAL REAL ESTATE

Now that you have your page, paragraph, and sentence ready to go, where should they live? If the goal is to be visible, first and foremost, they need to live on the internet. Being findable on the web is the equivalent of being listed in the phone book fifty years ago. And unless your name is "Jane Smith" or you live off the grid, you likely already have bread crumbs about your work and extracurriculars online, but they may not add up to the story that you want out in the world. So, at a bare minimum, create a personal website to be visible on your own terms.

A website is a key opportunity for ensuring your work is discoverable without you having to constantly share it. Think of this as your chance to publish the details about your portfolio that will help people find you. Use the "one page" version of your story as the "About me" section. Invest in some high-quality photos that are consistent with how you want to be seen (e.g., no awkward corporate headshots if you are claiming to be an avant-garde performance artist). Include keywords that people might use to search for someone like you, both in the website copy and in the metadata (this is super easy to set up on a template from providers like Squarespace or Wix). And make sure you have a way for folks to reach out to you, whether through a contact page on the site itself or by sharing an email address you don't mind making public.

Other places you may want to consider publishing your page, paragraph, or sentence include LinkedIn, your social media bios, and any alumni directory listings you may be a part of. The less obvious your portfolio is to the outside world, the more you'll want to ensure you are telling a story that is clear, consistent, and easily findable.

We've covered the work you'll do as the CEO and CMO of your Portfolio Life, pulling together a team to support you and crafting a cohesive narrative to ensure opportunities can find you. Next up? Figuring out how to make all of these pieces fit into a twenty-four-hour day. That's the job of the COO—the chief operating officer.

CHAPTER 10

Manage Your Time

> How we spend our days is, of course, how we spend our
> lives. What we do with this hour, and that one, is what
> we are doing.
>
> —Annie Dillard, *The Writing Life*

First, I owe you an apology, and so does every time management book that has ever been written. Beyoncé does *not* have twenty-four hours in her day. She has an army of assistants, nannies, housekeepers, stylists, personal shoppers, travel managers, and financial advisors to help her shoulder the work of being the world's greatest living performer. There is no instance in which you should be comparing your portfolio or your productivity to Beyoncé's. And she's not the only one you shouldn't be comparing yourself to.

The reality is that twenty-four hours looks different for someone who is nineteen and doesn't have kids, someone who can afford to hire a housekeeper, someone who has a partner to share the load, someone who spends two hours commuting, and someone who is a caretaker for elderly relatives. The amount of time we have available to us is highly personal, and it's imperative to note we're not all starting out with the same resources. So as you read this chapter, try not to compare yourself with anyone (including former versions of yourself) and instead give yourself the grace to figure out how to make your portfolio work in your life as it is today.

Second, as I have mentioned before, I do not subscribe to "hustle

culture." The Portfolio Life is *not* about working nonstop. The fetishization of working long hours seemed to emerge out of the explosive growth
of tech culture in the wake of the 2008 financial crisis. Best personified
by WeWork founder Adam Neumann and the company's (in)famous tag-
lines "Hustle Harder" and "Thank God It's Monday," this ethos ignored
the structural problems in the economy and the modern workplace and
instead shifted the burden of success to individuals, insisting that their
ability to make millions of dollars (or, at least, enough money to pay
both rent and student loans) was entirely up to them if they just worked
hard enough. Finally, after a decade of this pernicious workist evange-
lism, Reddit co-founder and venture investor Alexis Ohanian publicly
denounced the cult of 24/7 effort at a prestigious tech conference: "Hustle porn is one of the most toxic, dangerous things in tech right now."[1]
Working hard for what you want makes sense, and there may be periods where multiple strands of your portfolio have simultaneous crunch
times, but our goal is to make that the exception, not the rule. "Rise and
grind" should only be a mantra for baristas.

And yet, it's hard to push back against that mindset when it sur-
rounds us every day. I know this quite well. Squeezing every productive
minute out of a day is how I took twenty-three credits a semester in college while working three part-time jobs, serving in leadership roles in
multiple student clubs, and graduating with high honors. It's also how I
landed in the hospital just a few months after graduation with pneumo-
nia and mononucleosis *at the same time*. And even then, I was so unable
to relinquish the idea that my value was irrevocably tied to my work that
I actually checked myself out against medical advice in order to play
piano in the pit orchestra for a performance of *Sweet Charity* that night,
then checked myself back in after the curtain fell. This is not a brag. This
is a confession of a misguided twenty-one-year-old with no sense of self-
worth beyond her achievements.

The American ethos is that we're only as worthy as our output and
we are replaceable in the blink of an eye. These dual convictions have led
to an explosion of work-related stress causing significantly higher rates
of depression, coronary heart disease, and chronic ill health in Americans who work long hours. And these aren't outcomes that can be offset

by a meditation app or a hot bath with organically sourced lavender oil. No amount of #selfcare will solve what some epidemiologists estimate is now the fifth leading cause of death in American adults.[2] This is "the result of how public policy favors businesses over workers, how US companies organize and manage work, and how we've embraced a cultural norm that devoting oneself to work not only gives us identity and value, but is almost a sacred duty," in the words of Brigid Schulte, founder of the *Better Life Lab* podcast.[3] No wonder our natural inclination is to put work above all else.

So we have to start this conversation around time management with a bit of reprogramming: Your worth is separate from your work. You deserve to be healthy and happy. Your relationships, personal growth, rest, and joy are not optional.

Just to make sure you heard that, let's say it again:

Your worth is separate from your work.

You deserve to be healthy and happy.

Your relationships, personal growth, rest, and joy are not optional.

I hope you already know these things. Even if you do, you may need help—or perhaps, permission—to manage your time differently in a world that is stacked against you. Because overwork doesn't just apply to the work you feel you have to do. It also applies to the work you *want* to do.

What happens when the pieces of your Portfolio Life that bring you growth and joy and community hit against the reality of limited time? The more you love the things you do, the easier it is to say "yes!" to each individual opportunity. However, for this model to thrive over the long-term, it is imperative that you build systems and set boundaries around your time, or you will put your entire portfolio at risk from stress and overwhelm and burnout. Take it from someone who has done that (more times than I care to admit!), burnout is not a good look. Instead, think of yourself as the chief operating officer of your life, responsible for allocating your most precious resource (time) and, just as importantly, saying no to the things that just don't pass muster.

In the business world, the field of operations management is one of my favorite places to look for inspiration and frameworks to manage scarce resources. There are three concepts from that sector that I have found particularly helpful when it comes to my schedule:

1. Capacity utilization
2. The critical path
3. Planned downtime

Together these three tools can help you create, manage, and trouble-shoot a schedule to (sustainably!) support your portfolio. If you're feeling stretched thin, evaluate your capacity utilization. Trying to juggle converging parts of your life? Analyze and adjust your critical path. Feeling burned out? Evaluate your planned downtime. Let's take a look at each in more detail.

CAPACITY UTILIZATION

Capacity utilization is a formula used to determine pretty much what it says on the tin: How much capacity is being utilized. We get that by dividing the amount of a resource being used by the total availability of that resource. Knowing how close we're running to full capacity will help us understand whether we have the space to say yes to something new or whether we're at risk for burnout. It can also give us a sense for how our capacity might change across seasons and help us proactively adjust commitments *before* they create unnecessary stress.

$$\frac{\text{RESOURCE IN USE}}{\text{RESOURCE AVAILABILITY}} = \text{UTILIZATION RATE}$$

For example, if a factory can make up to 100 widgets a day but is currently making only 50, then it has a 50% capacity utilization rate. Half of the day the factory is sitting idle, which means it has the ability to take on more work—up to another 50 widgets per day—without straining. Or they could choose to rent out the factory to another company during their downtime, making a little extra money from the spare capacity. They could also use the space and time for employee dance parties or impromptu chess tournaments or any number of things, depending on their priorities. This seems pretty straightforward, right?

Applied to our lives, "capacity" is a way to think about the total amount that we can take on in any given time period, and our "utilization" is effectively how busy we are.

$$\frac{\text{HOURS COMMITTED}}{\text{HOURS AVAILABLE}} = \text{PERSONAL UTILIZATION}$$

In a linear career, this is pretty easy to assess: Tally up the time you spend working your job (which, depending on your industry and role, could mean anywhere from seven to twenty hours a day, four to seven days a week) and divide by how many nonsleeping hours you have in the week. That's your utilization, and it is probably pretty consistent week over week. It's a little more complicated than that description allows, of course: There are periods of crunch times like tax season for accountants or the holiday rush for retail jobs, where you may put in up to double the hours of a normal workweek. But generally, your work takes up what it takes up and you have a roughly consistent amount of available time for the other components of your life.

A Portfolio Life is more complicated to manage, not just because multiple work streams and projects demand more time, but also because each likely has its own rhythm of commitment and crunch time. Each activity in our portfolio has two dimensions when it comes to time: *how much* time it takes up and the *cadence** of that time commitment. For example, coaching a community soccer team might require two hours of prep time, two hours of practice, and three hours for a game and

---

* In this context, I define *cadence* as the frequency and the flexibility of the work.

postgame debrief each week during the regular season, with additional commitments for practice and games if your team makes it into the league playoffs. The practice and game time is on a fixed schedule while the prep time is flexible, for a total of seven hours committed each week.

When it comes to managing our capacity, the default is often to add up the amount of time each activity requires on *average* and be sure that the sum of our commitments doesn't surpass our available time.* Maxing out the available time is called a *100% utilization rate*, but the problem with 100% utilization is that it doesn't give you any wiggle room for the crunch periods—the moments where the commitment surges beyond the average (like those extra practices and games during the playoffs). Nor does it allow for mishaps, sick days, unforeseen complications, or any of the curveballs that life throws at you. One hundred percent utilization is not sustainable.†

Operations management experts will tell you that world-class utilization of a manufacturing line is generally considered to be about 85%.[4] This means that there is a buffer of 15% of the total available production time on a line that is intentionally not being scheduled. This extra capacity allows for maintenance to keep the machines in top-notch condition; it gives flexibility in the event of human or equipment error to redo the work and still meet deadlines; and it provides some room for unexpected surges or rush orders that management wants to accommodate.

I'm going to repeat that for those in the back: The *upper limit* to the time you commit *across your entire portfolio* should be 85%. Not 100%. Not 110%. Eighty-five percent.‡ You have to leave capacity for the surges, breakdowns, do-overs, and maintenance.

---

* Though many of us tend to steal hours from sleep to squeeze in even more work, which means we're actually operating beyond 100 percent capacity. Those hours should be "unavailable," and yet . . .

† One of the many reasons I hate the phrase "give 110 percent."

‡ I know, I know. There are, of course, exceptions to this rule, and you may have seasons where you have to run at (or above) 100 percent capacity. But those seasons should be intentional and as brief as possible. It's not safe to operate a factory at 100 percent indefinitely, and it's not safe to live your life at that pace either.

What's Your Current Utilization?

Let's pause for a second and check in on your current personal utilization rate. It will offer some clarity on how much (or how little) space you have in your current de facto portfolio.

STEP 1: DETERMINE YOUR DENOMINATOR

The first decision you have to make is to determine what number belongs in the denominator for your calculation—that is, how many hours are you going to allocate as "available" each week? Some people will choose to deduct only time for sleep, marking all other hours as available. Others may want to block off time for personal care like showering, eating, meditating, or other nonnegotiable activities over the course of the week. My rule of thumb is to block off the time that must be 100% protected to get through your day. For example, for this season of my life, I mark sleep, time for basic personal care like showering and eating breakfast, the time my family needs to get up and out of the house in the morning, and dinner through bedtime for the kiddos as "unavailable." (If I'm stealing from that time, I am very much over 100% capacity.) That leaves roughly twelve hours available for my portfolio each day or eighty-four hours in an average week.* Choose however many hours you deem "available" and set that as the denominator in your utilization equation.

STEP 2: ACCOUNT FOR YOUR TIME

Once you determine what 100% looks like, go back and look at the time audit you completed in Chapter 6. How many hours are you currently using? Be sure to include *all* of the components of your portfolio, including time with family, participating in a religious community, exercise, volunteering, you name it.

---

* Yes, I'm including weekends here because my portfolio isn't just about work, but about ALL of the elements of my life, including friends, family, hobbies, personal development, and rest.

STEP 3: RUN THE NUMBERS

Grab a calculator and divide your committed time by your available time. That is your current utilization. Does it surprise you? Is it higher than 85%? (Is it higher than 100%?!?) If it's higher than you'd like, don't stress. It just means you may need to clear out some "clutter" in your calendar to make room for rest. We're going there next.

CREATE SPACE FOR JOY

At the root of this work is a belief that I want to make explicit: The Portfolio Life should bring you joy. Yes, it also offers diversification and downside protection, providing security amid an ever-changing and unpredictable world. But it also should give you the platform to develop and express your magical, multifaceted identity, foster connections and community that offer a sense of belonging, and provide a scaffold for growth and rest in whatever proportion you desire. To do all of that, you need space. Space for reflection, for redirection, for serendipity, for luck.*

Dorie Clark ✓
Leave time in your schedule for "good fortune." Nothing serendipitous can occur if you are scheduled wall to wall. By making sure you have time allotted every day for anything to happen, you not only have room for error, you have time for chance encounters.

---

* The saying "Luck is what happens when preparation meets opportunity" is famously attributed to Seneca, though there seems to be little evidence to back that up. Still, I like to believe that I can attract luck by being prepared for it.

A cluttered, overscheduled, always-working life leaves you with no space. If you struggle with this (as I do), I'd like to suggest the life-changing magic of Marie Kondo's approach to tidying up.

Japanese cleaning-consultant-turned-tidying-guru Kondo burst onto the American scene in the mid-2010s after her first book was translated to English. She introduced both a methodology for decluttering and a surprisingly high bar for the things that should remain in our homes: They must spark joy. *Joy!* Applied to socks and gardening tools and Tupperware and scratchy sweaters, *joy* seemed like a bit of a stretch. But one by one, folks gave her system a shot and most became evangelists. Perhaps it wasn't too much to expect joy from the things we shared our lives with.

As a longtime urban dweller in microscopic apartments and virtually no storage space, I am not plagued by clutter. I have had no choice but to be ruthless in the paring down of my belongings so as not to feel like I have given over my living space to *stuff*. So when Kondo first became a household name in the United States, I didn't think she had anything to offer me.

Then one day I published an article for Forbes for their "Day in the Life" series that highlighted a day in the life of a human Venn diagram. My day started at 6:00 a.m. with a workout and a mentoring coffee before heading to my full-time job and continued nonstop until I ate cereal for dinner while standing in my kitchen at 11:00 p.m. after a computer science class, time spent reviewing fundraising plans for a nonprofit I sat on the board of, and rehearsing a Portuguese folk song for an upcoming choir concert. Then the texts and emails started trickling in from friends and loved ones. Was I okay? Was this my usual pace? Was I going to end up rehospitalized for exhaustion?

It was a harsh wake-up call. I was *way* over 100% capacity* and had been going at that pace for months. And yes, I was exhausted. While each piece of my day was something I willingly chose—and in theory, reveled in—the reality was that many of my endeavors were leaving me

---

* In fact, terrifyingly, I was running at nearly 120% after repeatedly cutting into my sleep.

short-tempered or frustrated or annoyed, which was more of an indication of my overall state of mind than any specific activity or interaction. I would have struggled to identify any moment of actual joy at that point in my life. I decided something needed to change. And if joy was my goal, then Marie Kondo would be my guru: I would apply her method to tidying up my time.

HOW TO KONDO YOUR CALENDAR

The first step of the KonMari method, as it has become known by, is to gather all things that are alike so you can assess the set of them together. For many, this first step is shocking because it shines a naked spotlight on just how much of any given thing you actually have. Whether it's serving dishes or scissors or shoes, you must first confront the gulf between what you believe about your belongings and what is actually true. The corollary for your calendar is to consolidate your activities over the course of a week or two and stare down the distribution of how you spend your time. Lucky you: You already did this in Chapter 6! Pull out that time audit and look at it again with fresh eyes.

Once you've gathered all like items, Kondo instructs you to examine each one and ask whether it brings you joy. But as you take a deeper look at your calendar, don't ask whether each *category* of activity brings you joy. If you have kept it in your portfolio post-audit, it likely does! (If it doesn't, please pause immediately and reflect on why you've kept it in your portfolio. Does it really deserve a spot in your life? Or is there a way to gently set it aside?) Instead, take a look at each meeting, each interaction, each class, each event and ask whether that *specific instance* brings you joy. For example, I love to spend time advising young career changers, but I discovered that I found joy in investing in longer-term relationships rather than giving one-off advice to random folks that friends sent my way with little context.

For those who are tidying their homes with the KonMari method for the first time, there's a moment when you realize you find joy in just a small proportion of your possessions and everything else is either some-thing left over from a previous stage of your life, a gift you were guilted into keeping, a good deal you couldn't pass up that you never actually use, or something you thought you wanted only to discover you don't. My calendar was much the same way. I had commitments I clung to out of habit rather than choice, activities I felt I should participate in (even when I really didn't want to), and invitations to gatherings that I had FOMO* over missing but never enjoyed.

To clean things up, I embarked on a "Summer of Joy." (Somehow giv-ing it a name made me feel I had permission to enforce it.) Here are some reasons to say no that I compiled that summer:

- I don't want to.†
- I choose to rest.
- I already have a commitment.
- I don't believe this will be a good use of my time.

They all seemed so simple when I wrote them down, and yet *actually saying no* in the moment still felt like moving a mountain.‡ So I decided that I didn't owe anyone an explanation and practiced two phrases over and over: "Unfortunately, that doesn't work for me" and "I won't be able to participate in that." Armed with these responses, I went through my calendar and declined commitments I knew I didn't want to attend, rejected incoming offers that didn't bring me joy, and decided it was time to make a bigger professional change since 90% of the things I wanted to say no to—but couldn't—were part of my day job.

Remember, the entire point of a Portfolio Life is that it serves you, not the other way around. If the life you're living is burning you out, or doesn't reflect your passions, values, and needs, head right back to Part

---

* FOMO = fear of missing out

† This is really the only reason you need.

‡ Even though research shows people overestimate the negative consequences of saying "no."[5]

II and reassess your portfolio. If you don't have room for joy, then it's time to make some changes.

THE CRITICAL PATH

The second time management issue we have to face is the crush of bottlenecks. If you've ever been stuck in bumper-to-bumper traffic while three lanes winnow down to one, you are familiar with the idea of a bottleneck and its frustrations. It's the moment when too many things (cars, deadlines) are demanding the same resources at once (roadway, time on your calendar), creating congestion in the system. This is where the cadence of your commitments becomes really important. You might be great at keeping your capacity under control, but you still keep hitting serious stress points because everything is due at the same time.

To make bottlenecks visible before they become a problem, there's a concept in process management called the "critical path" that will help us identify how our commitments intertwine and how narrow or forgiving the way through is. Together with a tool called a Gantt chart,* we can visualize the critical path and then adjust our commitments or set different expectations *before* those bottlenecks occur. Let's use an example to make this more tangible.

Risa Puno is an interactive installation and sculpture artist who also orchestrates one of the most impressive Thanksgiving dinner spreads I have ever seen. The New York–based artist returns to her extended Filipino American family in Kentucky every November to produce an operation worthy of a Tony Award. Dependencies are mapped out, like the timing of kneading and rising of homemade bread. Conflicts are noted, like which recipes require different oven temperatures or when a particular pan needs to pull double duty. And the buffet is optimized for both traffic flow and the geometry of serving dishes. It's a four-day affair

---

* Named after their creator, Henry Gantt, these are bar charts that illustrate a project schedule and highlight dependencies within the plan.

spanning cooking, baking, decorations, playlists, and seating plans. There's even a dress rehearsal. "I started making a plan because I was so tired of eating Thanksgiving dinner at 10:30 p.m. when the turkey would finally be done but all the sides were cold," she told me.

Risa maps everything out (like on the sample Gantt chart below) so she can visualize the steps for each dish, seeing which have to occur at the same time, and identifying how many family members she'll need to rope in to help on any given day. Bottom line: She can see the shortest possible path from start to finish once everything is laid out, and how rigid or flexible that path is. A rigid critical path, like one that is so tightly mapped out that a five-minute delay on one dish causes a chain reaction that ends up bumping the turkey from ever getting into the oven, is divorced from reality and creates a ton of additional stress. Then, in addition to all of the work of making the food, Risa would also have the mental load of constantly checking her plan to ensure she didn't get more than five minutes off schedule. She can't possibly do her best work in this context.

On the other hand, if there is flexibility in the critical path—extra family members available to help, unscheduled oven time, extra ingredients in case they need to remake a dish—that gives her the confidence that she can recover from a setback and lowers the stress for everyone involved. Visualizing the bottlenecks gives Risa the opportunity to move things around, adding in buffers or simplifying processes to ensure her plan is not only feasible but also realistic. "To be clear, we're not a well-oiled machine. But more than once this strategy has ensured the critical path was safe and we ate dinner on time (even if the kitchen smelled like burnt biscuits)."

Often the stress of juggling the various streams of our Portfolio Life comes from the expectation of a perfectly optimized system that can run at nearly 100% utilization with no errors that put our critical path at risk. But that isn't real life. It leaves no room for being human. Give yourself the grace of a flexible critical path.

Dishes	Thursday			Friday					
	noon	2pm	4pm	8am	10am	noon	2pm	4pm	6pm
Pancit Palabok									
Make shrimp stock	◀								
Make palabok sauce		●							
Marinate pork belly			◀						
Warm up pancit sauce								◀	
Take shrimp out of fridge								▶	
Cook noodles								●	
Assemble pancit									
Peel hardboiled eggs							♥		
Slice hardboiled eggs						♥			
Tita Cielo's Lumpiang Ubod Sariwa									
Make lumpia filling		◀		●					
Make wrappers									
Assemble lumpia									
Warm up lumpia sauce								♥	
Chop peanuts / cilantro							✕	✕	
Put lumpia on bandehado								✕	
Crispy Pata									
Confit pork shank in pork fat (275 F)				●	●				
Deep fry pork shanks							■		
Reheat crispy pata (airfry @ 400 F)								▮	
Chocolate Flan									
Make flan batter				●					
Bake chocoflan (350 F)				●					
Flip chocoflan onto platter							●		
Dinner Time!									▮

KFY   ● Risa   ♥ Mom   ■ Ronnie   ◀ Dad/Tito Mike   ✕ Tita Ces   ▬ Ross

Map Your Critical Path

Now that you've seen how Risa uses a Gantt chart for Thanksgiving, let's put it into practice for a project in your portfolio. I'll use the example of throwing a benefit for your local library, but you should choose something that you're working on and fill in the specifics that apply for you.

STEP 1: WHAT TIMESPACE SHOULD I BE USING?

We want to visualize the entire project in our Gantt chart, so first we need to assess how long our project will take from kickoff to completion. For our example, imagine we have three months to organize and produce our benefit. Choosing months as our increment of time gives us only three "blocks" to visualize, while choosing days gives us ninety. One feels too few and the other too many. So instead, I'm going to split the difference and set my blocks of time to be weeks. I'll create thirteen columns (one for my task list and twelve for the weeks to complete them) and label each column.

Tasks	Week 1	Week 2	Week 3	Week 4	Week 5	Week 6	Week 7	Week 8	Week 9	Week 10	Week 11	Week 12

STEP 2: BREAK DOWN ALL OF THE TASKS AND MAP OUT THE TIMING AND DEADLINES

Write down all of the elements of this project in whatever level of granularity works for you. For example, I might first start by listing the big categories for my benefit: catering, rentals, entertainment, decorations, marketing, ticket sales, setup/cleanup, and volunteers. Then I might go back through each category and list out the specific tasks for each, like choose a caterer, lock in a menu, pay the deposit, and pay the balance of the contract. Then for each task I map out the block of time that I'll need to work on it and organize the tasks in the order they need to be completed.

Tasks	Week 1	Week 2	Week 3	Week 4	Week 5	Week 6	Week 7	Week 8	Week 9	Week 10	Week 11	Week 12
Catering												
Choose a caterer	■	■										
Lock in a menu			■									
Pay deposit				■								
Pay balance												■
Rentals												
Entertainment												
Decorations												
Marketing												
Ticket sales												
Setup/cleanup												

STEP 3: LOOK FOR DEPENDENCIES AND BOTTLENECKS

First, we want to check for dependencies to ensure we have the resources we need to complete each task. For example, in order to pay the deposit to our caterer, we need to have already sold some tickets, which also means we need to have kicked off our marketing efforts as well. But perhaps we've learned from previous years that we shouldn't start marketing until eight weeks before the benefit. So if our marketing task starts in week 5, we can expect to have the "early bird" tickets sold by week 7, which means we need to negotiate with our caterer to pay the deposit in week 8, rather than week 4.

Tasks	Week 1	Week 2	Week 3	Week 4	Week 5	Week 6	Week 7	Week 8	Week 9	Week 10	Week 11	Week 12
Catering												
Choose a caterer	■	■										
Lock in a menu			■									
Pay deposit				→				■				
Pay balance												■
Rentals												
Entertainment												
Decorations												
Marketing					░	░	░	░				
Ticket sales												
Early bird tickets						░	░					
Full-priced tickets								░	░	░		
Setup/cleanup											░	░
Volunteers												

Next, we need to check for bottlenecks. To do this, we need to assess whether there are any resources that are overtaxed at any given time. For our example, let's imagine we're doing all of the work of producing this benefit alone. So our time is the resource we want to check on. Then we could look at any given week and see if we have more things assigned to that week than we have time available for this project.

Tasks	Week 1	Week 2	Week 3	Week 4	Week 5	Week 6	Week 7	Week 8	Week 9	Week 10	Week 11	Week 12
Catering												
Choose a caterer	■	■										
Lock in a menu			■									
Pay deposit								■				
Pay balance												■
Rentals												
Order tables and chairs						■						
Order linens							■					
Delivery												■
Entertainment												
Select DJ				■	■							
Decorations												
Choose a theme	■											
Buy supplies								■				
Make decorations									■	■	■	
Install decorations												■
Marketing					■	■	■	■	■	■	■	■
Ticket sales												
Early bird tickets						■	■	■				
Full-priced tickets									■	■	■	■
Setup/cleanup											■	■
Volunteers												
Recruit									■	■		
Manage												■

In our example, we see that things start off pretty light, with only one or two tasks to manage for the first five weeks. But by week 7, we have four different things to keep track of, and it doesn't let up until the benefit is over. To avoid bottlenecks, could we shift any of these workstreams to reduce the strain on resources (our time) during weeks 7 through 12? (Perhaps we could buy supplies and make decorations in weeks 2 through 6.) Or can we bring on someone to help us by week 7 to split up the work and add resources, easing the bottleneck? (If we start recruiting volunteers in week 3 instead of week 9, we might find a deputy to share the load starting in week 7.)

STEP 4: CHECK AGAINST THE BIGGER PICTURE

So far, we've been using a Gantt chart to map out the critical path for a specific project. But what if we want to visualize our entire portfolio to see how different projects might overlap? Great question! To do that, we revisit our timescale and the level of detail we want to visualize.

Let's imagine we want to see how our various activities line up throughout the year so we can be sure the crunch periods don't conflict. Then we might build a Gantt chart on a monthly timescale and map out each of our projects, using darker shading to note deadlines or increased time commitments. We could also name those crunch times explicitly like in the sample below.

Projects	Jan	Feb	Mar	Apr	May	Jun	Jul	Aug	Sep	Oct	Nov	Dec
Sales job			Q1			Q2			Q3			Q4
Church choir				Easter								Christ-mas
Club soccer						Play-offs						
Dad surgery / PT				Sur-gery	PT							
Vacation								Beach house!				
Scuba class										Assess-ment		
Library benefit											Gala	

That helps us check in on where we might be overstretched (like in April or October in this example) and make any necessary adjustments. Perhaps we might recognize that the timing of the scuba class would add more anxiety than we'd like and instead we might look to take it in January and February instead of September and October. We also could see that kicking off work on the library benefit while trying to close out the third quarter at our sales job might be tricky. So instead, we might choose to recruit a partner from the start to help share the load. With that additional support, we would have the option of condensing the work from twelve weeks down to eight and waiting until October to dive in on the fundraiser.

Remember, the goal of this tool is to visualize the bottlenecks *before* they occur, so you can shift things around or procure additional resources to prevent them altogether. A rigid critical path is a recipe for unnecessary stress.

PLANNED DOWNTIME

Finally, we need to stare down one of the hardest challenges you'll face when it comes to your Portfolio Life: taking time off. Even while managing just one job, Americans are already terrible at taking planned time off.* Add in a portfolio of projects with different timelines and crunch periods, and you have the perfect conditions to literally *never* unplug. Somehow it seems like there is always (at least) one deadline looming. Unfortunately, this is a direct consequence of one of the biggest *benefits* of a Portfolio Life: Well-executed diversification across your projects means different activities hit their intense periods at different times. This helps balance your capacity! You have fewer bottlenecks! It's a good thing!

Except...when it means there's never a good time to turn everything off and take a breath. (And if you choose a life partner who is also

---

* A large part of this is because we worry that if we truly unplug for more than a few days, our boss will realize they don't actually need us, and our jobs won't be there when we come back. So, it's not fair to place the blame solely on the individual here; it's how Americans have been conditioned by their employers.

managing a portfolio, the likelihood their lulls naturally coincide with yours is pretty much close to zero.) Which is why you must develop the discipline to schedule downtime anyway. An assembly line that is never taken offline for routine maintenance ends up with unscheduled breakdowns that can be more costly than scheduled downtime would have been.[6] (Imagine trying to train for a marathon without ever scheduling recovery time. You'd be more likely to end up on crutches for a stress fracture than taking a selfie at the finish line.) Rest is a requirement, not a reward.

So what does that look like in practice? The same way financial advisors suggest paying yourself first by contributing to your savings before distributing the rest of your money to bills and discretionary spending, you must carve out regular downtime in your calendar *before* you schedule everything else. This could mean putting a vacation on the books that is nonnegotiable. Scheduling workouts and sleep the same way you schedule your commitments at work and to other people. Or investing in a sabbatical to refresh and recharge.

Sabbaticals may feel like a rich person's solution to the modern problem of burnout and overwork, but they are actually a very old idea. Likely connected to both the concept of the Sabbath, a day set aside for rest each week, and the Old Testament notion of a "sabbatical year" where farmland is to be left fallow one year out of every seven, these are periods away from work that can "unlock a deeper level of rest than shorter periods allow,"[7] according to Joe Pinsker, writing for the *Atlantic*.

DJ DiDonna is an entrepreneur and the founder of the Sabbatical Project, an advocacy organization. Staring down burnout after years of building his venture-backed company, he took a four-month sabbatical that included a 900-mile Buddhist pilgrimage through rural Japan. He had such an "identity-shifting, ego-shattering" experience that when he returned to his "real" life, he set out to study sabbaticals. Partnering with workplace well-being expert Matt Bloom at the University of Notre Dame, they conducted research on the effects of these extended pauses in our careers. "Our main finding is striking: Much more than an extended vacation, sabbaticals provide a psychological safe space to change one's personal identity and to figure out what it means to live a more authentic life."[8] And perhaps surprisingly, they found that while many sabbatical-takers did make drastic changes afterward (like quitting a job or deciding to have kids), the majority "simply returned to a version of their previous lives with a newfound, hard-won perspective." Sometimes we just need the space to take a breath and see things clearly.

Dr. Sabriya Stukes chose to take a "radical sabbatical" after her parents staged an intervention. She had recently completed her doctorate in microbiology and immunology and, feeling a bit unmoored after a painful breakup, threw herself headlong into work, accepting two full-time jobs (one was remote) along with a slate of freelance projects for a science startup. For four months she woke up before dawn and worked nonstop, often forgoing sleep, food, and everything else in her life. Unsurprisingly, this pace took a serious toll on her health and happiness. (And, she admits, she wasn't doing very good work.) So when her parents sounded the alarm for the then-thirty-three-year-old, she decided to take a much-needed break for three months to sleep, eat, go to group therapy, and get back on track. "I know that's an incredibly privileged thing to do," she told me, "and even then, it was hard. Allowing people to take care of me was a huge shift for me during this time in my life." But the extended rest gave her the space to reset, and she emerged from her sabbatical with a clearer sense of self, the energy to jump back into science, and the guardrails to protect her time, health, and relationships.

DJ DiDonna, the Sabbatical Project founder, is quick to acknowledge that formal sabbaticals are currently available only to a select few Americans. While McDonald's created the first corporate sabbatical policy in 1977, nearly fifty years later just 5% of US organizations offer paid sabbaticals,* according to the Society for Human Resource Management's 2019 benefits report.[9] This means most folks who want to experience the benefit of an extended break must do so on their own, either taking an unpaid leave of absence (which another 11% of US companies

---

* And the frequency with which younger workers change jobs makes this rare benefit even harder to access. Typically, companies require seven-plus years of tenure to qualify for a paid sabbatical while the average time in a job is two years, nine months for a millennial and two years, three months for Gen Z, according to research by CareerBuilder in 2021.

have formal programs for) or opting for a self-funded hiatus between jobs.

At this point I'm guessing I don't really need to offer you more evidence for the benefits of such a break. The sticking point is how to do it without blowing up your life (or going broke). DJ has some advice on this front: "First, plan ahead. Maybe you can't just get up and leave tomorrow, but could you look a year or two or five ahead and work toward it, just like if you were going to graduate school or making a big move? That way you can save for it, wrap up work, make arrangements for who is going to water your plants or sublet your place, etc."

Second, get creative about how to accommodate the responsibilities you *can't* take time off from. Sabbaticals shouldn't be just for childless, privileged twentysomethings and wealthy, retired folks. It may be more challenging to make them happen in the in-between years, but that can make it all the more valuable. "If you design your sabbatical to include your family, to include your kids, that creates memories that will last a lifetime," DJ advises. "It could actually transform your relationships."

 Design Your Sabbatical

Take a few minutes to perform a little thought experiment with me. What might a sabbatical look like for you? No matter how certain you are that this could never work, just humor me for a bit.

Let's imagine you want to take a three-month break, beginning one year from now.

First, think about what you might hope to get out of your sabbatical. Jot down a few reflections. Would you want an opportunity to travel to new places? Experiment with a different way of living? Are you thinking about this time as a chance to learn something new about yourself, about the world, or about your work? Do you need rest or inspiration (or both)? Defining what a sabbatical would mean for you is the first step toward making it a reality.

Second, consider the complications. According to DJ, there are three factors that often prevent folks from taking a sabbatical: cost, optics, and responsibilities. Start to think through how to mitigate these three factors for yourself.

Cost:

- Assuming you work for the 95% of American organizations that don't offer paid sabbaticals, how much money would you need to support yourself during that period? Are there ways to offset that number by reducing fixed expenses (like subletting your home if you want to travel somewhere else for your sabbatical)?

- Conversely, are there ways to earn some income during your sabbatical that won't interfere with your goals? For example, if you wanted to spend three months surfing in Costa Rica and recharging from your demanding health care job, might you consider working a few hours a week in a surfboard shop to help offset your costs? Working in other countries can add complications around visas and work permits, but planning ahead can give you the time to see what is possible.

Optics:

- A common fear is how it would look to take an extended break from work. Yet a survey the Sabbatical Project conducted among Harvard Business School alumni showed that they were seven times as likely to worry about how others would perceive their time off as they were to judge their own friends, colleagues, or employees for doing the same. So before you start to fret about how this might look, read the stories from other folks who have done it. Then start to imagine the story you might share with your network and future employers about how you used the time away.

Responsibilities:

- Besides work, what other responsibilities would you want or need to put on hold during your break? Are there periods during the year where that is easier to do?
- If you want to include others in your sabbatical, what does their calendar look like? Do they have natural lulls you could take advantage of (like summer break when kids are off school)?

Yes, it is challenging for nearly anyone to take a sabbatical on a whim, but with some forethought and planning, it can be within reach. Rather than rule it out from the get-go, try to imagine what it could look like and how you might prepare for extended downtime.

A CAVEAT: DO AS I SAY, NOT AS I DO

Anyone who knows me is undoubtedly rolling their eyes at this point. Limiting your utilization to 85% to leave space for rest and the realities of life? Building flexibility into the critical path to lower stress and reduce bottlenecks? Scheduling a sabbatical to refresh and recharge? Ha! That's not how Christina works.

And they are right. While I have gotten a little better since my post-college cycles of overwork followed by extreme burnout, I am still that person who thinks I can teach a full course load, complete research for an ambitious slate of case studies, and write a book while my husband works two jobs and completes a second graduate degree and we parent a toddler in a pandemic with the birth of our second child on the horizon. What can I say? I have to learn these lessons over and over and over too. It doesn't mean the research and the tools are flawed; it just means that I am human and still trying to redefine my relationship between work and self-worth.

So if you are struggling in this area, don't stress. It's a journey for all of us. My best advice is to avoid romanticizing the intensity of your workload and instead ask the "truth teller" on your board of directors to help keep you accountable. Keep working on these skills and remember that even slow progress is progress. Maybe you didn't get a fully unplugged vacation. Okay, not quite what you wanted, but did you take a vacation for the first time in years? Good job! You're growing. The more we practice, the more natural these tools and boundaries will feel. And then we get to learn them all over again when life throws us a new curveball.

Your time is your scarcest resource, and a Portfolio Life demands more active stewardship of it than a linear life does. It's not easy and it's not particularly intuitive when you've been raised in a society that demands productivity above all else. But it is worth developing the systems and structures to protect and invest your time in the pursuit of joy.

Finally, we have one last resource to discuss, and it's a topic that can make folks feel nervous and uncomfortable: Yup, we need to talk about money. It's time to change hats again, and this time we need to step into the role of a chief financial officer.

CHAPTER 11

Crunch the Numbers

Carpe per diem—seize the check.

—Robin Williams

I'm going to give it to you straight: There are both financial pros and cons of building a Portfolio Life. The big pro is that you can cultivate multiple income streams, if not simultaneously, then via the optionality to change course in the face of disruption. You're not putting all of your eggs in one paycheck basket, so to speak. Another pro? If your portfolio includes self-employment of any kind, you have some control over your income, from how much to charge to how many hours you want to work. You can decline projects that aren't profitable. You can decide to charge what you are worth. You can ramp up or ramp down hours based on what works best for your portfolio. Yay!

But, here's the bad news: The entire American financial system was constructed with the assumption that you have exactly one job that compensates you roughly the same amount every pay period. No more, no less. Paying taxes, getting a mortgage, saving for retirement, all of these things are trickier when you have multiple income streams and/or lumpy cash flow.

So in addition to managing your team, your story, and your time, there's one last operational dimension of a Portfolio Life you will have to master: Managing your money. I know that people have varying degrees of comfort and interest in personal finance, but staying on top of your money is the best way to future-proof your life. Think of this as becoming your own CFO.

There are several important dimensions to managing your finances, and depending on your previous experience, you may want to jump around to the parts that are new (or newly relevant) to you. Go ahead! This is one chapter in particular that you'll really want to get into the weeds on.

We're going to delve into four key topics:

1. Finance 101: Budgets, cash flow, and contracts

Start here if your approach to managing money is using your unpaid bills as coasters or if you've never heard the term *net 30*. We'll cover the basics of why you need a budget, how cash flow is different from income, and how you can influence not just what, but *when* you get paid through smart contract and invoicing strategies.

2. Taxes

If you've never done your own taxes or remain mystified by the IRS, don't worry, you're not alone. That said, when you stop having just a single W-2 land in your mailbox every year, things get extra complicated. Here's what you don't want: a giant, unexpected bill on April 15. We'll discuss how you can set yourself up for success: Track those write-offs, consider setting up an LLC, and enlist the help of a professional to get ahead of those estimated quarterly taxes.

3. Getting paid (more) for yo`ur work

How do you know if a project is worth your time? We'll chat about setting rates, managing billable hours, and firing unprofitable clients. Plus you'll learn why you should be telling both your friends and your competition how much you get paid.

4. Establishing a f*#!-off fund

Emergency funds aren't just for a rainy day. If you want to make a big life change, you need a cushion to do so. Whether you're thinking of zigging and zagging with your career, rebalancing the proportion of paid and unpaid work in your portfolio, or going on a sabbatical, you'll need a chunk of change ready and waiting. We'll talk about why and how to sock away savings while still paying for all of your other priorities.

#1. FINANCE 101: BUDGETS, CASH FLOW, AND CONTRACTS

Let's start at the beginning: You need a budget. If you don't have one, do not pass Go and do not collect $200. If the mere thought of creating a budget has you breaking out in hives, take a deep breath and stick with me here.

Many folks think of budgets as report cards, judging you at the end of every month for all the ways you failed. Or they fear budgets are the quickest way to kill the party, having to sort through a pile of receipts (does anyone even keep receipts anymore?) and painstakingly add up every coffee, cab ride, and cocktail only to realize they don't quite have enough to cover rent. But while budgeting won't magically turn one dollar into ten, it will give you necessary visibility into your needs and how to maximize what you've got.

Think of a budget as your GPS on a road trip. Before you hop in the car, you want to plot out the route to your destination so you can make appropriate plans. You'll need a preview of the trip so you can stock up on snacks, water, and gas. You'll want a sense for when and where you might stop and stretch your legs. If there are several routes that could get you from point A to point B, you'll have to choose which path to take, perhaps making trade-offs between picturesque scenery, construction delays, toll roads, and frequency of Waffle Houses. All in all, having a rough sketch of where you're going and what your travels will look like is vital for a successful drive.

But it doesn't mean your trip is set in stone. You can be opportunistic if you pass a killer estate sale or get back on track after taking a wrong turn. Your GPS just updates the route and revises your arrival time, giving you an early glimpse into what has changed and how it might affect other parts of your trip. It also gives you the flexibility to adjust your plan: If you opt to stop for antiques now, you might forgo the pit stop you'd planned for later. It's a judgment-free tool to help you get where you want to go.

The same is true of a budget. You'll want a plan for how you'll put your money to work each month, knowing where things could get tight and where you might have to make trade-offs. Especially for folks building a Portfolio Life, you need to be clear on what matters most and fund that first. But your budget is more than a map to the road ahead. It can also help you think through bigger changes down the line, arming you with data as you debate how and when to rebalance your portfolio.

My favorite tool for first-time budgeters is YNAB (You Need A Budget), but there are dozens of apps, templates, and tools you can choose from (many of them free). The goal is to have a bird's-eye view of your revenue and expenses each month so you can make informed decisions like a CFO would.

Once you have a grasp on how much money is coming in and going out, the next step is getting clear on *when* those inflows and outflows occur. We call this *cash flow*, and anyone who has ever had to wait until after payday to restock groceries or deal with that utility bill understands the principle, even if you didn't know the term.

As an employee, you can rely on a regular paycheck, usually biweekly or monthly. But as a freelancer or small business owner, you have to negotiate payment terms, submit invoices, and get set up in a client's supplier system in order to get paid. Some companies have standard terms for working with small businesses; others are open to negotiation. Either way, it's on you to be up-to-date with your accounting. Otherwise it could be months between when you do the work and when you finally get paid, a recipe for a cash-flow disaster.

Here is the most important term to know: *net days*. When you agree to do a piece of work, you need to specify how many days you'll give the company to pay you after you submit your invoice. *Net 30* means they'll pay you a month after you bill them (which usually happens after you complete the work). Very few companies pay upon receipt of the invoice. A few might pay net 15. Many more will try to push for net 45, 60, or even 90. And be aware that even if they agree to pay a certain number of days after invoicing, they may choose to delay payment beyond that. Many businesses intentionally delay payments to suppliers as a tactic for managing their own cash flow. So before you take on work, be clear on when you'll be paid and what options you have should they not hold up their end of the bargain.

For example, when you negotiate the initial contract with them, can you include terms like a 2% late fee for every thirty days payment is late? Or can you ask for an initial deposit on signing the contract and bill the balance upon completion of the work? If they are a larger company, speak with their procurement team about any special terms they might offer to small businesses and/or women- and minority-owned businesses. Or ask around to see if there are local laws that protect freelancers, such as New York City's Freelance Isn't Free Act.

Bottom line: Cash (flow) is king. You need to manage both *how much* and *when* you have money coming in.

#2. TAXES

I know, I know. But we have to. The last thing you want is the IRS knocking down your door, and if we're not on top of our stuff, Portfolio Lifers can be highly susceptible to audits. Whether full-time or part-time, salaried or hourly, the process for having taxes withheld by your employer and then any overpayment refunded to you when you file your return in April was established under the assumption that you have only one job. Anyone who has held down multiple jobs simultaneously can probably tell you about the unpleasant surprise bill come tax time when you discover your combined income puts you in a higher tax bracket than the withholding formula assumed. And let me tell you how much fun it is when you file jointly with a partner who *also* earns from multiple sources. (Bonus points if one or both of you earn money from a different state than you live in!)

So we're going to get into the weeds on this, but I promise I'll leave out the IRS-speak and keep it accessible.* We'll delve into a trio of topics you'll want to understand: relevant business deductions, limited liability companies, and how to find an accountant or tax professional who understands your Portfolio Life.

Relevant Business Deductions

So the downside of having self-employed income is that you have extra self-employed tax liabilities. (Ugh.) The upside is that you can reduce your tax bill by deducting relevant business expenses from your revenue. But before you go all David Rose from *Schitt's Creek* and try to declare everything you buy as a write-off, the key word here is *relevant*. So what counts as a valid business expense? More than you might realize.

There's the obvious stuff: equipment you might buy (like a fancy DSLR camera or a new computer for work purposes), office expenses (printing costs or software licenses), marketing costs (brand photos, collateral you distribute like posters or business cards, or hiring an SEO consultant), web services (domain registration and hosting services, cloud storage, social media tools), and travel expenses (including mileage incurred on a personal vehicle). But there are other non-obvious things as well. Do you pay professional membership dues? Pay for a P.O. box or rent a desk at a coworking space? Have a dedicated home office? Pay for subscriptions to publications that you use for research purposes (like newspapers or platforms with proprietary data)? Invest in professional development or continuing education courses that maintain or improve your skills in this line of work? All of this is probably deductible.† But

---

* As a math nerd who took exactly one tax law class at Harvard, I have done my own taxes every year. It's gotten more complicated over the years as I've added an LLC, a husband, a mortgage, a couple of kids, and a whole bunch of freelance work requiring estimated quarterly tax payments in multiple states, but I keep doing them because I'm stubborn. But I need to include the disclaimer that this is not financial advice. Go talk with a licensed professional now that you understand the basics!

† But really, consult a tax professional. There are nuances to all of these that can trip anyone up.

you'll have to keep great records to ensure you can take advantage of these write-offs.

Limited Liability Companies

When you are self-employed, you have two choices when you agree to do work for someone: You, the individual, can enter into the contract with the client. Or a corporation that you own can enter into that contract and then that corporation can pay you to do the work. Are you doing the exact same work in both cases? Yes. Does this seem like extra red tape for literally the same outcome? For sure. Is it a waste of time to go through the extra effort of option two? Nope. It's very likely worth the initial headache.

Here's why: If you, the individual, do the work and something goes wrong, then your client can sue you, the individual. And any assets you, the individual, have from other parts of your life could be taken if you lose that lawsuit. But if you set up a limited liability company (LLC) that you own 100% of, and that LLC pays you to do the work it has agreed to do for a client, and something goes wrong, then the client can only sue the LLC. Which means only the assets inside the LLC (e.g., the money you made from doing work for other clients) are at risk. Your personal savings accounts, your spouse's retirement fund, your house, your family heirlooms—none of that can be touched.

The other big benefit of an LLC is that it greatly simplifies your taxes at the end of the year by keeping your self-employed earnings and expenses separate from your personal finances. This is as easy as opening a second checking account and keeping a dedicated credit card to consolidate your LLC's spending. Come tax time, you can download your data, sort it, and easily tally up deductible expenses. (Also remember to keep receipts for any expense above $75. Your easiest option: take a photo and save it to a folder in the cloud labeled with the tax year. You can also save any emailed receipts or invoices to the same folder.) As a bonus, if you ever get audited by the IRS, you will suffer one-tenth as much as you would if you commingle your personal and self-employment finances.

The downside to setting up an LLC is that extra red tape: There are some initial expenses to getting the entity set up (both in legal fees and in state and federal filing fees) and the LLC has to file a separate tax return each year (versus just including your income and expenses on your personal tax return's Schedule C). Annoyingly, small business tax software is even less user-friendly than the software designed for individual tax returns. So if you go this route, you will want to enlist the help of a tax professional.

Find an Accountant

Did those last two topics get your heart racing? I see you. The IRS really doesn't make anything easy, but it's *especially* challenging for Portfolio Lifers. So unless you are stubborn like me and insist on doing it all yourself, your best bet is to find a great certified public accountant (CPA) to be your financial partner. At a minimum, they can file your taxes for you and help you estimate quarterly taxes for the year ahead. If you want a more meaningful partnership, they can also help you think strategically about ways to structure your various income streams and expenses, and advise on how to establish that LLC.

So how do you find the right CPA for you? Here's my favorite hack: Ask an artist or performer who lives in your state. Accountants who are accustomed to working with creatives are well-versed in multiple 1099 (independent contractor) income streams, lumpy cash flow, unexpected business expenses, and the complications of earning money from several states. This is likely going to be a better fit for your Portfolio Life than a CPA who works mostly with high-income families or folks juggling assets and complex transactions across international lines.

Get recommendations and then ask for a free consultation to get a sense of their style. You should walk away from that conversation feeling like you have a financial partner who takes you seriously and wants what's best for you. If you leave the consultation feeling stupid, condescended to, or like they don't have time for your questions, go find someone else.

Also, pro tip: Look for this person over the summer or in early fall.

From October through April, they are going to be slammed with end-of-year matters and then the crunch of tax season.

#3 GETTING PAID (MORE) FOR YOUR WORK

Given all of the economic factors we discussed in Part I, it is *highly unlikely* you are being overpaid. Perhaps you are being paid fairly. Most likely there's some room to negotiate a better deal. But how can you know for certain what your work is worth? It's simple: You've got to start talking about money. With your friends. With your colleagues. Even with your competition. No matter how uncomfortable it may be, or how gauche it may feel, the onus is on you to uncover what market rates are for the kind of work you do.

Now I know how awkward it is to talk about money. Sex? Fine. Religion and politics? Okay! Money? Um, hahahaha, no thank you. If it comes out that you are making significantly more or significantly less than folks in similar positions, things can get weird. Does this mean you should be picking up the check at lunch? Or perhaps that you aren't as valuable an employee? It can be even harder when you're talking with friends in other industries. Suddenly you start to see the stark contrast between industries that society rewards and those it deems less important, even if the workload and the caliber of talent are similar. But a lack of pay transparency only benefits employers. You will only be paid what you are worth if you actually know what you are worth (and then fight for it).

Author and journalist Jessica Bennett wrote about her "salary whisper network" where she shares what she is getting paid with her friends.[1] "For younger workers, one of the ways of moving up is often to take on additional duties, only to then realize, as one friend recently did, that you won't necessarily be paid for the work." So Jessica made it a habit, just a few years into her career, to talk with her friends about salaries, day rates, and consulting fees. Author, podcaster, and digital marketer Aminatou Sow is also a big advocate for talking openly about money. "I'm in a cohort that shares salary information all the time and refers each other to jobs. I always tell women to ask the men in their lives about their salaries."[2] This last point is key: If you suspect you might be underpaid, you can't only talk with folks who may also be underpaid. You need as broad of a data set as you can get.

Getting paid fairly is one way to keep your earnings growing faster than your expenses, which is vital for balancing your budget. Another way is to bring in an additional revenue stream, whether a sporadic moonlighting gig or a regular freelance practice, to provide the buffer you need to live well below your means. But if you've never set a price for your work before, it can feel especially daunting to try to monetize your talents. Getting this wrong means you could lose money on a project or feel resentment when you realize you are delivering more value than you are earning. But charging too much might feel equally risky.

So how do you set your rates? There are a few inputs to consider. The first is what market rates are for the work. See if there's a local freelancers community or check out the websites of folks doing similar work to get a sense of what others are charging. Depending on your industry, there may be other resources like the Freelancing Females rate sheet or pay ranges for tech jobs on AngelList.

You may argue that your rates shouldn't be set to market—maybe you are just starting out as a photographer or computer programmer or SEO specialist and are happy to charge much less to gain experience and build your portfolio. Or perhaps you are an expert Spanish teacher or can build a financial model in Excel for a small business in just a few hours (exclusively using keyboard shortcuts, natch) and want to be compensated for your expertise. Both scenarios are totally understandable! You'll still want to know what range of rates your field is charging in your area.

The next input to consider is whether you expect this to replace (now or perhaps in the future) regular full-time work for you. If not, you may have more flexibility (though you do want to be aware of not underpricing so far that clients don't take you seriously or you inadvertently pull down market rates for those who *are* making a living doing this work). If you expect it to be your primary income stream, you need to figure out the equivalent of the full-time salary you'd want to earn and calculate from there.

There are two ways to set rates: time-based and project-based. In both cases you'll need to account for all of the costs of providing free-lance labor that an employee doesn't face. What does that mean? You need to gross up from what you want to "take home" to cover the costs of taxes (including the employment tax your employer would pay if you worked for a company), overhead costs (like marketing, equipment, soft-ware licenses, cloud storage fees, etc.), nonbillable hours (time spent building your client base, crafting proposals, sending invoices, etc., that you can't charge for), and paid time off (you know, like sick days and vacation, because you *will* be planning for some downtime).

The rule of thumb for setting hourly rates is to start with the annual "salary" you would want to earn for this work, then divide it by 46 to 48 weeks (to allow for 4 to 6 weeks of paid time off between vacation, holidays, and sick leave). Now divide that number by 30 to 35 hours (to account for nonbillable work, which may be more substantial in certain lines of work). Now take that number and multiply it by 1.4 ("grossing up" by 40% to cover taxes and overhead). That's your hourly rate.

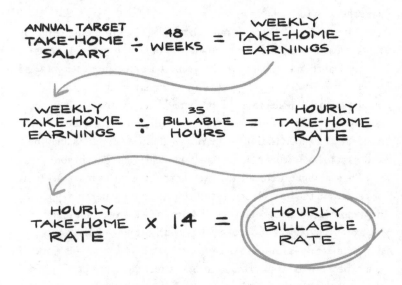

(Or you can skip all of the math and just use a shortcut by taking that annual "salary" number and moving the decimal point three spots to the left, so a $100,000 take-home salary would translate into roughly a $100/hour rate.)

But what if you want to price by the project instead of by the hour? This is a tad trickier and is a strategy I would recommend only for those who have been doing this kind of work for some time. Why? Because you need to have a really clear sense of how much time and effort you put into various types of projects, you have to scope the project clearly so you don't end up getting roped into doing extra work for free, and you need to set clear expectations with the client for revisions, timing, and deliverables. It's certainly an easier strategy for work that you can "productize" (i.e., have set packages or outcomes like a newborn photo shoot or a three-tier cake that serves fifty people) versus more customized work (like ghostwriting articles for a CEO you've never worked with before).

Finally, you need to consider how much you want to do this work, at this time, for this particular client. If you have a lot of time and really want to build your body of work, you might consider being flexible on your rates to win more projects. (In that case you should always quote your "usual" rate and then frame the lower rates as a one-time discount so you aren't anchoring too low if you end up doing more work for them in the future.) Or if you have worked with a client before and want to give them a volume discount for larger projects that you know you'll enjoy and learn a lot from, great! Offer to work within their budget. On the other hand, if you are tight on time and someone is demanding you squeeze their project in, or it's work you don't really want to do, or you know from experience that there will be far more hand-holding and headaches than usual to work with a particular client, feel free to increase your rates. You are entitled to price in the cost of friction and emotional labor a project will incur.

So now you have these three data points: the market rate, your ideal hourly or project rate, and the discount or multiplier you would apply to the given situation. Now do you quote a price for your work? Nope. To the best of your ability, try to avoid going first in a negotiation. Why? Because the first number in a negotiation "anchors" all further discussion to a narrow band in that neighborhood. And you have a lot less information than the client does, which means if you put a number on the table first, you are likely to undershoot the range that they would have been willing to pay.

Instead, say something along the lines of "My rates vary based on the timeline and scope of work. Can you give me a sense of what you're looking for and your rough budget for the project?" (Getting their "rough budget" forces them to anchor the negotiation.) *Then* you can start putting together a quote that will suit the work at hand: "I think I have the information I need. I'll get back to you with a proposal in twenty-four hours."

If it's the first time you're working with a client, you should be prepared to negotiate. They'll likely want to talk you down from your initial quote (and if they don't, you probably priced it too low... Good to know for next time!). Negotiating is totally normal. But know at what price you're willing to walk away from the work and hold that boundary. Otherwise, you'll lose money on the project, resent the client, let word get out that your rates are decreasing, or all of the above.

Lastly, once you agree on a rate and *before* you start the work, sign a contract with the client. It can be as simple as one page or as complex as you want it to be, but you must put in writing what you have both agreed to: scope, pricing, deliverables, deadlines, payment terms, and the circumstances that allow either party to break the contract. There are templates online that you can adapt to your purposes or your CPA can recommend a lawyer if you need something more customized. This is a necessary step to ensure you know exactly what you are signing up for.

Remember: You are the CFO of your life, and a CFO never apologizes for trying to make more money. It's literally their job. Get paid what you are worth.

#4 ESTABLISH A F*#!-OFF FUND

You've likely heard the exhortation to have three months of living expenses in an emergency savings account, but perhaps it never seems to hit your top three financial priorities. It might feel like an arbitrary amount for an arbitrary reason: "in case you need it." What does that even mean? In case you get laid off? In case your apartment becomes uninhabitable and you need to move quickly? In case of a worldwide pandemic? (Is three months even close to enough in that case? Seems not.)

In my twenties I had a lot of competing demands on my money and a three-month emergency fund never quite felt pressing enough to build up. It wasn't until I came across a brilliant story on The Billfold by author and writing coach Paulette Perhach called "A Story of a Fuck Off Fund"[3] that I realized what "in case" meant. It means "in case you need the freedom to make a radical life change."*

Perhach narrates the tale of a young college grad who starts to build a life: from the precarious leap from an internship to finally landing an entry-level job that doesn't quite make ends meet (complete with a boss who inches—then runs—toward inappropriate behavior), to falling in love and moving in with a partner, to the micro-financial decisions along the way that make you feel like a proper grown-up like eating out, upgrading your car, splurging on real furniture and a nicer wardrobe, and making liberal use of your credit cards to close the gap between your income and your lifestyle. By the end of her parable, the young professional realizes they are cornered, unable to leave the boss or the partner because either or both would require more money than they have saved up. They feel frozen and helpless. So they stay.

I'd love to tell you that you won't ever find yourself in that scenario. Unfortunately, the lack of a financial safety net can feel more precarious and destabilizing than you might realize. Suddenly the choice is between a rock and a hard place, which isn't much of a choice at all, and so you start to overlook or rationalize the little things that eventually turn into really big, seemingly intractable things.

But here's where the story takes a turn: It doesn't have to end up this way. Perhach rewinds the clock to graduation day and has our protagonist choose a different adventure: one that opts for a touch more

---

* In case it's not clear: a F*#!-off Fund is the same as an emergency fund, but with better branding to help you understand the urgency here. It would be ill-advised to build a Portfolio Life without one.

frugality than they would otherwise prefer in order to build up a buffer of cash. Rather than feeling cornered by bad situations—a toxic relationship, a nightmare roommate, an abusive boss—our young professional can say "f*#!-off" and extricate themselves before it gets even worse.

But guess what? A "F*#!-off Fund" doesn't only save you from nightmare scenarios. It can also provide the cushion to absorb the impact of big shifts in your portfolio. Want to zig and zag into an entirely new field like Catherine Jennings, the science-teacher-turned-doctor? Or need to rebalance the proportion of paid and unpaid work in your portfolio, like Joseph Solosky when he left the FBI and followed his wife's career to Germany? Or maybe you're burned out like microbiologist Sabriya Stukes and need to invest in a multimonth sabbatical. Whatever the reason, having the funds set aside gives you the freedom to make your portfolio serve your life, not the other way around.

The only way to be able to save for a "F*#!-off Fund" is to live below your means. One way to do that is by keeping costs low and surrounding yourself with friends who understand and support this financial priority. Another way is to increase your income. Yes, this is where an additional revenue stream could come in. But it's also where getting paid more for the things you are already doing becomes an equally valuable lever.*

IMAGINE THE POSSIBILITIES

Now that we've covered the basic financial tools you'll need, let's look at an example of how they can all work together to power your Portfolio Life.

Alex lives in Detroit and works as a graphic designer making $50,000 annually at one full-time job. They are single, live alone, and this is their current monthly budget:

---

* Remember, this is not about monitoring every nickel you spend or promoting hustle culture. It's about ensuring you have the visibility to make the most of your resources.

	BASE CASE $
FT JOB	4,167
FT TAXES	(1,067)
RENT	(900)
UTILITIES	(150)
FOOD	(400)
CAR PAYMENT	(250)
INSURANCE	(150)
GAS	(100)
STUDENT LOANS	(500)
HEALTH	(150)
SAVINGS	(200)
MISC	(300)
NET	0

Let's say Alex is considering leaving their job to go all-in on freelancing and is wondering whether or not that would be feasible. The most straightforward calculation is what would they need to earn as a freelancer to take home as much as they are currently taking home in their full-time job?

Right now, they balance their budget on a monthly take-home income of $3,100. Given the additional self-employment taxes they'd face as a freelancer, they'd need to earn around $4,626 monthly to have the same net income. So, first question: Can they earn that out of the gate? Alex believes they can charge $30 to $40 an hour given their current experience level, which means they'd need to bill 29 to 39 hours a week to meet that revenue target. That feels unlikely in their first month of freelancing, so we start to ask other questions and gather information.

First, we dig into their expenses: Are there ways to reduce their burn rate? They're proud of their modest expenses, but they are open to reducing them if it means they can make the transition smoother.

In this case, Alex currently lives alone in a cozy two-bedroom apartment and is considering either getting a roommate or moving to a smaller apartment when their lease is up in three months. There is a one-bedroom in the same building that will be available then for $725, and since it's in the same building, there would be no application or broker fee. They would have to cover the cost of moving, though. A roommate would reduce their rent to $500 since the second bedroom is a bit smaller and would likely rent for $400.

Student loans could be deferred for up to twelve months, if necessary, but accrued interest would be capitalized with the outstanding principal and Alex would like to avoid that if possible. They could lower their food expenses to $300 per month by cooking slightly larger recipes and freezing meals. Their savings contribution could always be lowered, though they'd really prefer to *increase* it given the potential volatility of their future earnings once they're full-time freelance. The only other big option would be to give up their car and switch to public transportation and occasional ride-sharing. Alex estimates that that would lower their expenses from $500 per month for transportation to $225 if they are disciplined about using the bus. Still, they see this as a last resort.

So altogether, Alex could lower their expenses by somewhere between $275 (smaller apartment and lower food budget) and $1,475 (roommate, defer loans, lower food budget, stop savings contributions, and give up car), depending on how austere they want to be. They would like to start by considering the $275 scenario and seeing if that would be feasible before making more extreme cuts to their costs.

The second set of questions is about timing: What do they believe the ramp-up might look like for their freelance work? Let's say they have a small list of clients they've worked with before that are eager to work with them again, and they think they can balance up to 20 hours a week on the side of their full-time job before they worry about burnout. While they previously charged $30 to $40 an hour, they think they can start at the $40 mark and maybe even increase their rates in a few months when they have a broader portfolio of work to point to.

Overall, they estimate they can start at 5 hours per week for the first month, 10 hours for months 2 and 3, 15 hours for months 4 and 5, and 20 hours for month 6.

So with this information in mind, we can model out how this revenue curve and revised costs play out for their budget.

	BASE CASE $	MONTH 1	MONTH 2	MONTH 3	MONTH 4	MONTH 5	MONTH 6
FT JOB	4,167	4,167	4,167	4,167	4,167	4,167	4,167
FREELANCING	0	800	1,600	1,600	2,400	2,400	3,200
FT TAXES	(1,067)	(1,067)	(1,067)	(1,067)	(1,067)	(1,067)	(1,067)
FREELANCE TAXES	0	(264)	(528)	(528)	(792)	(792)	(1,056)
RENT	(900)	(900)	(900)	(900)	(725)	(725)	(725)
MOVING EXPENSES	0	0	0	(500)	0	0	0
UTILITIES	(150)	(150)	(150)	(150)	(150)	(150)	(150)
FOOD	(400)	(300)	(300)	(300)	(300)	(300)	(300)
CAR PAYMENT	(250)	(250)	(250)	(250)	(250)	(250)	(250)
INSURANCE	(150)	(150)	(150)	(150)	(150)	(150)	(150)
GAS	(100)	(100)	(100)	(100)	(100)	(100)	(100)
STUDENT LOANS	(500)	(500)	(500)	(500)	(500)	(500)	(500)
HEALTH	(150)	(150)	(150)	(150)	(150)	(150)	(150)
SAVINGS	(200)	(200)	(200)	(200)	(200)	(200)	(200)
MISC	(300)	(300)	(300)	(300)	(300)	(300)	(300)
NET	0	636	1,172	672	1,883	1,883	2,419
ACCUMULATED ADDITIONAL SAVINGS		636	1,808	2,480	4,363	6,246	8,665

Alex notices a few things: The costs of moving expenses net out against the savings of moving to the smaller apartment in the short-term, though going forward they would reap the benefits of the lower rent. And the additional income over six months allows them to save over $8,000 to provide a nice buffer for when they do quit their job and pursue freelancing full-time. They also see that the more extreme measures to lower their costs seem unnecessary, and perhaps even moving to the smaller apartment may not be required if they can indeed ramp up their client work fast enough. After all, if they used the second bedroom as a dedicated office space, they could deduct that on their taxes as a business expense.

Overall, they are feeling pretty good about this transition, but have two questions on their mind: First, what if they can't charge $40 right away and need to start at $30? And second, how should they think about the unpredictable (and somewhat lumpy) nature of freelance cash flow?

Sensitivity Analysis

The partner tool to financial modeling is sensitivity analysis, a technique that tests how much our model is affected by changes in assumptions. If our model looks feasible on the surface but falls apart if our key assumptions turn out to be a little off, then the scenario is high risk. Similar to the critical path analysis we did with our Gantt charts, we want to use sensitivity analysis to vet how fragile or robust our financial forecasts are.

Like a CFO, you want to keep an eye on the bigger financial picture and how it could impact your Portfolio Life: If the economy suddenly hits a recession, will that affect the demand for your work or the pricing power you have over your rates? Are there expenses that could see a sizable change, like the cost of living significantly increasing in a fast-growing city? What about one-off costs that you don't regularly budget for like a hefty health or car expense? Do you have a plan to mitigate them? Are there other potential potholes you haven't considered? In short, what assumptions are built into your model and what is the likelihood that they might be wrong?

In the case of our freelancer, Alex wants to run their model at the lower rate to see how it impacts their buffer. Changing only their rate from $40 to $30, we see their accumulated savings decrease from $8,000 to $6,000 by the end of month 6. But that's not the real test of whether they are ready to jump into full-time freelancing. They want to extend their model out to the end of month 12 with their freelance hours steadily increasing every 2 months and losing their salaried income after month 6. Keeping their conservative rate of $30 an hour, we see how their savings buffer is put to use over that transition period.

	Base Case $	Month 1	Month 2	Month 3	Month 4	Month 5	Month 6	Month 7	Month 8	Month 9	Month 10	Month 11	Month 12
FT JOB	4,167	4,167	4,167	4,167	4,167	4,167	4,167	0	0	0	0	0	0
FREELANCING	0	600	1,200	1,200	1,800	1,800	2,400	2,400	3,000	3,000	3,600	3,600	4,200
FT TAXES	(1,067)	(1,067)	(1,067)	(1,067)	(1,067)	(1,067)	(1,067)	0	0	0	0	0	0
FREELANCE TAXES	0	(198)	(396)	(396)	(594)	(594)	(792)	(792)	(990)	(990)	(1,188)	(1,188)	(1,386)
RENT	(900)	(900)	(900)	(900)	(725)	(725)	(725)	(725)	(725)	(725)	(725)	(725)	(725)
MOVING EXPENSES	0	0	0	(500)	0	0	0	0	0	0	0	0	0
UTILITIES	(150)	(150)	(150)	(150)	(150)	(150)	(150)	(150)	(150)	(150)	(150)	(150)	(150)
FOOD	(400)	(300)	(300)	(300)	(300)	(300)	(300)	(300)	(300)	(300)	(300)	(300)	(300)
CAR PAYMENT	(250)	(250)	(250)	(250)	(250)	(250)	(250)	(250)	(250)	(250)	(250)	(250)	(250)
INSURANCE	(150)	(150)	(150)	(150)	(150)	(150)	(150)	(150)	(150)	(150)	(150)	(150)	(150)
GAS	(100)	(100)	(100)	(100)	(100)	(100)	(100)	(100)	(100)	(100)	(100)	(100)	(100)
STUDENT LOANS	(500)	(500)	(500)	(500)	(500)	(500)	(500)	(500)	(500)	(500)	(500)	(500)	(500)
HEALTH	(150)	(150)	(150)	(150)	(150)	(150)	(150)	(150)	(150)	(150)	(150)	(150)	(150)
SAVINGS	(200)	(200)	(200)	(200)	(200)	(200)	(200)	(200)	(200)	(200)	(200)	(200)	(200)
MISC	(300)	(300)	(300)	(300)	(300)	(300)	(300)	(300)	(300)	(300)	(300)	(300)	(300)
NET	0	502	904	404	1,481	1,481	1,883	(1,217)	(815)	(815)	(413)	(413)	(11)
ACCUMULATED ADDITIONAL SAVINGS		502	1,406	1,810	3,291	4,772	6,655	5,438	4,623	3,808	3,395	2,982	2,971

Alex is feeling reassured that their model still works at the lower rate. Now we want to turn our analysis to their second question: What if their assumptions around growth in freelance hours are too aggressive and their cash flow is lumpier than in this model?

Here we start our analysis with the question, What is the minimum number of hours they must work each month to break even on their expenses once their only income is from their freelance work?

MONTHLY EXPENSES WITH REDUCED RENT	$ (2,825)	$ (2,825)	$ (2,825)
REQUIRED TAKE-HOME PAY	$ 2,825	$ 2,825	$ 2,825
ESTIMATED FREELANCE TAX RATE	33%	33%	33%
REQUIRED FREELANCE GROSS INCOME	$ 4,216	$ 4,216	$ 4,216
FREELANCE RATE	$ 30	$ 35	$ 40
IMPLIED WEEKLY HOURS TO BREAK EVEN	35	30	26

This analysis makes Alex a bit nervous. The thought of maintaining 35 billable hours a week just to break even on their expenses seems a bit ambitious when they are still in their first year of business. Also, that weekly hours projection doesn't allow for time off or nonbillable work like invoicing and business development. The 26 billable hours per month at the higher rate of $40 feels more doable, but Alex isn't confident they can reach that rate right away. Before they jump in, they want to know how much of a savings buffer they need to survive their first 6 months of full-time freelance work at a conservative projection of 25 billable hours with a $30 rate.

MONTHLY EXPENSES WITH REDUCED RENT	$ (2,825)
FREELANCE RATE	$ 30
CONSERVATIVE BILLABLE HOUR ESTIMATE	25
GROSS FREELANCE INCOME	$ 3,000
ESTIMATED FREELANCE TAX RATE	33%
TAKE-HOME FREELANCE INCOME	$ 2,010
MONTHLY SHORTFALL	$ (815)
ESTIMATED CUMULATIVE 6-MONTH SHORTFALL	$ (4,890)

Given our freelancer estimated that they will have a savings buffer of more than $6,000 from the 6 months they are working at their salaried job while building their freelance practice at the $30 rate, they feel comfortable with this estimated shortfall with such conservative projections. It feels feasible to make this leap and Alex is ready to move forward!

BE YOUR OWN BATNA

This entire chapter boils down to one thing: Thinking like a CFO gives you the financial flexibility to build the life you truly want. Because when it comes to achieving your definition of success, knowing what you want is only half the battle. The other half is having the freedom to walk away if what's on the table doesn't work for you. Which is why the best leverage you have in any situation is a backup plan.

The official term for this is a BATNA: best alternative to a negotiated agreement. When you've set up your Portfolio Life to give you financial stability and flexibility, you become your own BATNA, which basically makes you a modern-day superhero.

We have just one chapter left and it is all about forecasting the future like a chief strategy officer. With all of the unknowns and moving pieces, it might feel like a waste of time to worry about the future. But there are ways to combine art, science, and some educated guesswork to think through what the future *could* look like and consider how you want to be prepared to respond in those scenarios. Rather than being surprised by disruption, forecasting puts you squarely in the driver's seat, building a life that is sustainable amid the thousand natural shocks that may come our way. Let's take a look!

CHAPTER 12

Forecast the Future

It is not in the stars to hold our destiny but in ourselves.
—William Shakespeare, *Julius Caesar*

As much as I would love to exhort you to "live in the moment!" it would be malpractice not to suggest you keep one eye on the future. We got here in large part because of the political, economic, and ecological disruptions of the last few decades. So while any given disruption may be unlikely, we've seen over and over again that it is *highly likely* there will be frequent and significant disruptions ahead—ones that may impact our lives for both good and bad.

That's right: Disruptions aren't necessarily negative events. They can be dramatic new changes of behavior (like the acceleration of work-from-home spurred by the pandemic), the widespread adoption of new technologies (like the massive shift iPhones brought into the world), or exceptional outside forces (like the growing acceptance of legalized marijuana) that suddenly create life-altering opportunities if you're prepared to take advantage of them. And because you're building a Portfolio Life, you've got the optionality and the flexibility to be opportunistic when it counts.

With all of that in mind, the last hat we're going to put on is that of a chief strategy officer. A key part of the CSO's job is to observe and respond to market changes, identifying new strategic opportunities and mitigating potential downturns when they arise. Applied to your life, thinking like a CSO will help you prepare for the unpredictable so that when (yes, *when*, not if) disruptions occur, you aren't caught entirely flat-footed. And so that no matter what happens, the answer to "Where do you see yourself in five years?" includes some version of "Happy, resilient, and making progress on my wishes."

LIVING AMID DEEP UNCERTAINTY

What does it mean to keep one eye on the future? When nearly everything can change in the blink of an eye, are we fooling ourselves if we plan more than five minutes ahead? How can we be strategic in the face of such deep uncertainty?

Amy Webb is a quantitative futurist,* the founder and CEO of the Future Today Institute, and an assistant professor of strategic foresight at New York University. Her entire career has been focused on the future, from trend forecasting to scenario planning to helping people and organizations think more flexibly. "It's difficult to imagine yourself in the future, and there are neurological reasons for that. Our brains are designed to deal with immediate problems, not future ones. That, plus the pace of technology improvement is becoming so fast that we're increasingly focused on the now. Collectively, we are learning to be 'nowists,' not futurists," she told Klaus Schwab and Thierry Malleret in an interview for their book *The Great Narrative*.[1]

But here's the problem with a "nowist" mentality according to Webb: When faced with deep uncertainty, most people become inflexible. We revert to preset plans and refuse to consider a new mental model. And it's this mental rigidity that makes disruptions, both large and small, feel so overwhelming. Instead, to effectively respond to unexpected events, we need to increase our flexibility.

Webb will be the first to tell you that it's impossible to predict the future. But that's not the point of her work, and neither is it the point of

---

* A futurist is a person who uses research, modeling, imagination, and intuition to make educated projections about the future. The point of their work is not to predict but to provide the opportunity to create states of readiness, make long-term plans, and aid in decision-making.

a Portfolio Life. In both cases, "the goal is to be prepared for alternative outcomes." By keeping one eye on the future, we can be proactive about adjusting our portfolios to ride the waves of disruption.

FLARE AND FOCUS

A key tool for managing uncertainty is the ability to toggle back and forth between two modes of thinking: flaring and focusing. A model first developed by Stanford's d.school for "design thinking" work and later adapted by Webb for use in her work as a futurist, this is a process for dealing with ambiguity that requires shifting between *divergent* thinking—brainstorming, looking for fresh inputs, considering a range of alternatives—and *convergent* thinking—winnowing down a set of possibilities to settle on specific solutions.[2]

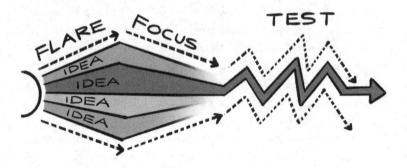

According to Webb, flaring is about gathering information and seeking inspiration from radically different points of view to spot new behaviors, hacks for problem-solving, trends at the fringe, and early signals of outside forces.[3] This stage isn't about what is likely to happen in the future but simply keeping an open mind to spot clues of what could happen, how folks might deal with it, and who might be impacted by those events.

Focusing, on the other hand, is about applying a critical lens to the clues and bread crumbs to build scenarios about what is probable, what is plausible, and what is possible. Webb points out that this allows us to look for data, consider timelines, and think through how we might respond in those scenarios well ahead of time.[4]

Combined, this is the art and the science of forecasting: recognizing patterns in the present, thinking about how those changes will impact the future, and charting a feasible path to be actively engaged in building what happens next, rather than waiting to let the future surprise you. Let's take a look at flaring and focusing in more detail to see how we can put these tools to work.

FLARE: INVESTIGATE THE HACKS, THE EXTREME USERS, AND THE OUTSIDE FORCES

Flaring allows us to imagine realities beyond our current one and consider the circumstances under which those realities might become true for us. Rather than worrying about sticking to the script, it encourages us to broaden our thinking and look for clues to other paths that might arise.

This is a state of thinking where you must suspend judgment, take in a broad range of information, and generate a large quantity of ideas, much like we did when we worked through our Venn diagrams and constructed our portfolios. It's not about evaluating your options; that's what focusing is for. Instead, it's about going wide to uncover non-obvious ideas that just might inspire your next move.

Entrepreneur Leslie Bradshaw had always had a pretty clear vision for her life. She had a set of goals for her career, a sense of the type of living environment she would thrive in, and a deep desire to be surrounded by friends and community. She also knew she wanted a family.

Over the course of her twenties and early thirties, she built an exciting and fulfilling life that in many ways lined up with her dreams and in many more ways far exceeded what she had imagined in college and early adulthood. But the family piece eluded her. It wasn't that she had put partnerships on the back burner while building her career; far from it! She had invested deeply in several significant relationships, but none of them were right for her in the long-term. So as she approached the second half of her thirties, she decided to think more broadly about what a future family might look like for her.

She set off in "flare" mode, investigating the alternative avenues of building a family that many of her friends and close colleagues had pursued. From same-sex partners to single mothers by choice to those who cultivated a "found family" rather than a nuclear one, she realized she had at least eight options, seven of which she hadn't yet considered:

1. Conceiving naturally
2. IVF with her own eggs and sperm from her future partner
3. IVF with her own eggs and sperm from a donor
4. Surrogacy with her eggs inseminated by a future partner's sperm, carried by another woman
5. Surrogacy with her eggs inseminated by sperm from a donor, carried by another woman
6. Partnering up with someone who already has kids
7. Adopting or fostering kids, with or without a partner
8. Choosing not to have kids, but continuing to participate in the lives of young people through mentoring and being an aunt

By looking to those in her life who didn't have the option of conceiving naturally—the starting point for most people when thinking about a family—she was able to uncover a host of alternative models. And while the odds of any one of those paths working out for her may seem low, "when I look at all of these options together, I cannot help but feel more empowered and hopeful that at least one could pan out," Leslie told me.

Eugene YK Chung looked to a different source of inspiration when he kept an eye on outside forces. The son of an accountant and an opera singer, he had taken to both technology and storytelling from an early age. But throughout his formal education, as well as the first decade of his career, these interests had to run on parallel paths. He could be an artist and filmmaker, or he could be a tech entrepreneur and venture capital investor. But as to whether they would ever intersect? That was unclear.

Virtual reality had been hovering in the wings since the 1980s, with tons of promise but never reaching a tipping point. "We've had theater for thousands of years, opera for hundreds of years, and the moving picture for a little over a century. I never thought I'd live to see the emergence of a categorically new medium of storytelling. But I did."

Suddenly in the mid-2010s, the technology adoption curve clicked into place, and all of the R&D behind smartphones and processing chips, as well as video rendering software, collided with the wearable hardware movement. Eugene realized that these outside forces would make the metaverse (powered by both augmented and virtual reality technology) the new artistic medium he'd been waiting for. So he left his job in venture capital and went all in as the founder and CEO of Penrose Studios. While he's been flattered to have Penrose compared to the "Pixar of VR," Eugene believes immersive storytelling is the medium of the future, sitting in a category all its own.

"You can find signals of change in the news and on social media, in scientific journals and in TEDx talks, in podcast interviews and at protests,"[5] writes future forecaster and game designer Jane McGonigal in her book *Imaginable: How to See the Future Coming and Be Ready for Anything*. "They pop up wherever new ideas are shared and wherever surprising events are documented."

FOCUS: BUILD SCENARIOS FROM
PROBABLE ⟶ PLAUSIBLE ⟶ POSSIBLE

Once you've broadened your aperture and brainstormed a wide range of potential futures, it's time to shift gears and start to focus. The goal here is *not* to pick just one future that you will drive toward, but rather to construct scenarios that range from *probable* (with likely outcomes assuming no major changes in circumstances) to *plausible* (believable outcomes if several facets of life change dramatically) to *possible* (potential outcomes if life as we know it looks radically different than it does today).

This is execution mode, not creative meandering. Become systematic, seek data, and ask for feedback as you evaluate the range of scenarios you might face and the resulting plans you want in place.

Why are we spending time creating scenarios of a future that might be probable, plausible, or possible? Because by constructing these stories we are creating what some futurists call "future memories." These can be incredibly powerful in dealing with futures that are upsetting, unwanted, or traumatic. When we've created future memories, "the very first emotion we feel isn't shock but recognition," according to McGonigal. "We recognize this strange new world because we've spent time there, in our imagination, before. Recognition communicates to us: *You know this. You've got this.* It's a powerful antidote to feelings of helplessness and fear."

Probable scenarios are likely the ones you are already considering. They are, for the most part, what you imagine will happen next. Yet even though they are probable, they are not guaranteed. So we want to pressure test the underlying assumptions that *must be true* for this version of the future to play out. How certain or precarious are those assumptions? If they turn out to be false, what do we want to be prepared to do differently?

CASE STUDY: THERE'S NO PLACE LIKE HOME

Lizzie* was still in her "giddy newlywed" phase when she and her husband started talking about buying a house in the Denver suburbs. They had been college sweethearts, and after almost a decade of long-distance dating while each pursued their careers, they were elated to finally put down roots and think about their next chapter of building a family. The Denver housing market had started to boom over the last few years and they were anxious to get in while their savings would still cover a down payment. But every offer they put in kept losing out to a higher bid, a faster close, or an all-cash deal. So they increased their budget to the top of what felt comfortable, but they still weren't winning.

---

* At her request, some identifying details have been changed.

Lizzie's husband wanted to raise their budget again. They were both employed and had reasonable job security with a track record of salary growth and strong bonuses. If they tapped out their savings, it felt probable that they could rebuild their cushion quickly. They didn't yet have children and there were no other considerable liabilities on their plate in the near future. Why not stretch their budget a bit further so they could finally be homeowners?

But Lizzie wasn't sure she was comfortable with those assumptions. What if one of their companies went under? They were both working at fast-growing startups, which meant the odds were decent that at least one would implode at some point. And their parents were aging. Lizzie was an only child and wasn't confident her parents were in the strongest financial position should something happen on their end. Before she would consider emptying their savings to buy a house, she wanted to sit down with her parents and understand how they were doing.

Two weeks later, Lizzie and her husband were seated in her parents' family room in New Jersey ready to talk about retirement savings and long-term plans when her mom dropped a bombshell: Lizzie's dad had been diagnosed with Alzheimer's and it was progressing pretty rapidly. It was highly likely he would need to move into some kind of care facility, and while she didn't know what that would cost exactly, she did know that there was no way they'd be able to afford it on their own. Her mom wasn't asking for money (yet), but she was asking Lizzie to help with the research and the forms to figure out how he could get the care he would need.

Over the next eighteen months, Lizzie took a leave of absence from her job and split her time between Denver and New Jersey, helping her parents navigate the complex processes and paperwork of elder care in America. She and her husband decided not to buy a house in order to have the financial flexibility to live off of one income for a while. "The only thing worse than the last year and a half would have been if we had bought a house we couldn't afford and I had felt trapped to stay in my job and deal with this situation from afar."

When Lizzie and her husband were house hunting, they were planning for a future based on the assumption that her parents were healthy and financially stable. But, given their age, it was probable that they would need Lizzie's help at some point. The big unknown was *when*? Before Lizzie and her husband moved ahead with their real estate plans, they wisely looked into that unknown and were able to pivot accordingly.

The second kind of scenarios—plausible scenarios—are ones where you can see how an outcome *could* happen, but a series of choices or changes would need to occur for those futures to come to pass. The opportunity here is to assess those choices and changes and determine if there is anything you can do to make them more or less likely, depending on whether or not you want them to transpire.

Let's go back to Leslie for a moment: While assessing the portfolio of eight options for a future family, Leslie realized that freezing her eggs was an important step for half of the plausible paths she was considering. So she decided to dive into that process and invest in several cycles of egg retrieval to increase the likelihood that one of those scenarios could work out. It was an expensive decision and took a meaningful toll on many other parts of her life. But it was an easy one to make once she realized that *not* freezing her eggs would prevent her from having those options later. She opted to take the necessary steps to make the plausible scenarios for having a family a little more probable.

The final set of scenarios—possible scenarios—are, for the most part, ones you likely don't spend much time considering. These are futures that depend on either cascading miracles or a series of unfortunate events that seem both unlikely and improbable. Yet they have a non-zero chance of happening and so are, by definition, possible. And to ignore them entirely is to ensure you are unprepared if they do happen.

For example, most people don't choose to sit around and ponder how and when they might die. It's an unpleasant way to spend your time and there are usually far too many unknowns to even start to formulate a possible scenario. But when I was pregnant with my first child I chose to face down the possibility that I could die in childbirth. As a healthy, educated white woman in a major metropolitan region with access to excellent medical providers, my odds for surviving labor were better than those of many other American women, but a positive outcome was far from guaranteed. The United States has the highest rate of maternal mortality in the developed world and it has *more than doubled* in the three-ish decades since my mother had me.[6]

So instead of ignoring this possible future, I took steps to take care of my family in the unlikely event it did transpire: I wrote up a will and documented my final health directives; I increased my life insurance coverage; and I left behind letters for my unborn child, my husband, and a few close friends with everything they'd need to know, from passwords and financial accounts to how much I loved them and what they had meant to me. When I made it through labor and recovery, I briefly considered destroying those letters and returning things to "normal" but then realized I'd rather keep the plan in place to be prepared for other unlikely, yet possible, futures where I might die unexpectedly. It's not my favorite thing to think about, but I do feel relief in knowing I've addressed this outcome.

WHAT IS FEASIBLE? MODELING FUTURE GROWTH, OPPORTUNITY, AND RISK

Once you've considered the range of probable, plausible, and possible scenarios, the final step is to consider what is feasible—that is, what resources (time, money, team) do you need to execute on those scenarios and how realistic are those resources in your current situation? This is where you have leverage with your Portfolio Life: As you look at your assessment of the future, you're not locked into a simple yes or a no in response to the question "Is this feasible?" You are looking for ways to rebalance your portfolio to *make* your desired scenario (more) feasible.

Stephanie Pereira was three months into a job that made her cry every day when she finally admitted her path wasn't working. It was New Year's Eve and the twenty-eight-year-old was in a loft in NYC surrounded by "fascinating people who did fascinating things" and she was miserable. Her degrees were in photography and arts administration, but she hadn't quite figured out where she fit or what she wanted to do with her life. She also didn't have a financial safety net that would allow her to just walk away from her job.

So she gave herself three weeks to figure out how to reduce her expenses and earn enough money to buy her the time she needed to explore different scenarios. "I spent the next eighteen months doing the most random things," she recalled with a laugh. She volunteered with a festival, was an educator at an arts museum, worked in public schools, wrote grants for nonprofits, was a researcher—all in service of figuring out what she wanted to be and how she wanted to show up.

After a year and a half of eating "really cheap tacos—not those fancy five-dollar tacos, mind you, but homemade, bare-bones tacos"—she landed at Eyebeam Art and Technology Center, a nonprofit that helps artists engage with technology and society. From there she has built an incredible career at the crossroads of art, technology, and community, with leadership roles at Kickstarter, the New Museum, crypto startup Rally, and creator platform Tellie. But to find her path she first needed to explore, and to do that she needed a feasible financial plan.

Take your future into your own hands by charting a feasible course through the uncertainty ahead.

FORECASTING WITH A PARTNER

I've been using financial modeling and sensitivity analysis to forecast potential futures for more than fifteen years. Together, they are tools that have served me well as I've sought to understand the implications of different decisions or test the riskiness of various assumptions. But until I met my husband, these tools only had to serve me. Once I was considering building a life with a partner, I realized how valuable it could be to apply this approach to our potential future together *before* we started building that future.

Discussions of money came up fairly early on in our relationship. I knew from past experience that widely divergent attitudes about earning, spending, saving, and donating money could have a huge impact on a partnership, and when we both went through big career shifts in the first six months of dating, it was a natural opportunity to start the conversation. While I moved from a nonprofit leadership role to an executive position at a fast-growing startup, Chas left his private law firm job to return to the public sector and join the leadership of a small New York City agency. Within the span of a few months, I got a large raise while he took a substantial pay cut. And given our various interests and potential portfolios, we knew this wouldn't be the last time such a dramatic shift might occur.

So as we were starting to discuss marriage, I asked Chas to sit down and build a financial model with me to forecast the next ten years of our life together. We had already discussed basic finances when we moved in together and had to jointly apply for a lease—our credit scores, debt, assets, and regular spending habits were already out in the open. And we had talked in broad strokes about our ambitions and values and dreams for the future. But I wanted us to dig into the reality of choices around career paths, children, housing, childcare, discretionary spending, savings goals, and other financial obligations we might see popping up. More than wanting to know that our dreams were plausible, I wanted to know that Chas would put in the hard work to map them out, surfacing the tensions and trade-offs we might have to conquer to make our future feasible.

One Saturday morning, after he made bacon and eggs and I had had enough coffee to be a reasonable human being, we spent three hours at our kitchen table building out a financial forecast for our life together. It wasn't a road map for what *would* happen, but rather was simply an exercise to map out how our lives *could* fit together, and the twists and turns that might be challenging as we became a family. We built the model monthly for the first three years, then annually for seven more, noting how tight money would be in the years we had young children, before public school would lessen the burden of childcare costs. We also could see how important it was to keep our housing and discretionary costs modest for far longer than we might have liked if we wanted the flexibility in our career to toggle between the public, private, and non-profit sectors. And we could see how other investments, from additional graduate degrees to sabbaticals to world travel, would need to be carefully planned and prioritized as our responsibilities grew.

By the end of the exercise, I knew without a doubt that he would be an incredible life partner for me, sharing in the mental load of our dual Portfolio Lives along with the joys. So I wasn't too surprised when he casually asked, "Should we pick a date?" while I put away my laptop. I grinned as I replied, "I've been holding these two weekends in October. Do either of them work for you?" And that was how we got engaged. (A few weeks later we designed a ring and he got down on one knee for the fun of it, but I still think of our financial model as the totem of our commitment to a future together.)

CREATE THE FUTURE YOU WANT

Futurists flare to look for bread crumbs, identifying signals of change, hacks from extreme users, and the tipping point of outside forces. Then they focus, testing those diverse inputs to see how they could inform a range of future scenarios. Determining the feasibility of those future scenarios requires modeling out resources and testing the sensitivity of the assumptions in that model. Combined, this is the art and science of forecasting: recognizing patterns in the present, thinking about how those changes will impact the future, and charting a feasible path to be actively engaged in building what happens next, rather than waiting to let the future surprise you. In the end, that's what the Portfolio Life is all about: owning your agency to craft the life you deserve.

Build a Life Worthy of You

In December 2021, just a few days before the end of the year, Carla Stickler, the actor-turned-engineer from Chapter 2, got the text message she had been anticipating. Carla and her husband, Adam, were driving from Chicago to a cabin in northern Michigan to recharge for a week after a particularly hectic fall. But as COVID raged through the Northeast, recently restarted Broadway shows were struggling to stay open. The omicron variant was proving to be less virulent than earlier variants, but was far more transmissible, and onstage performers were uniquely at risk of contracting the virus because they couldn't wear masks at work.

As Carla wrote code in her new life as a junior software developer at a tech startup, she watched her former castmates of *Wicked* cycle through actors in the role of Elphaba. After the lead got sick, they put in understudies, then backup understudies, then swings. (And *Wicked* wasn't the only show suffering; at one point in December, so many theater workers were out sick that nearly half of the plays and musicals on Broadway were canceled.[1] Those that did manage to stay open had to get creative with casting. One night, *The Lion King* had the child actor who normally played Simba step into the role of Nala, while his understudy went on as Simba, because both actors who normally played Nala were sick.)

Soon, out of options, the producers of *Wicked* started reaching out to former cast members who had left the show, which is when Carla's phone lit up. Despite leaving her acting career more than a year earlier, and having not performed the role of Elphaba in nearly seven years, Carla was being asked to fly to New York and help out. So instead of heading to the Upper Peninsula, she hopped on a flight to the Big Apple. After just one brush-up rehearsal, she stepped into the hardest role on Broadway, belting iconic songs while literally defying gravity, flying forty feet in the air thanks to a hydraulic lift and some epic stage magic.

For Carla, it was a "full circle" moment. "Having the opportunity to perform [Elphaba] again after having left the biz is giving me the closure I have been missing. If I never performed again, I could rest easy knowing that something out of this world happened last night," she reflected on Instagram the next day. And as her story went viral, it was also a wake-up call that she didn't have to shelve her identity as an artist to be taken seriously as a software engineer. Hundreds of people reached out to tell her they were inspired by her example of excellence in multiple worlds at once. Seeing her made them feel they had permission to be exactly who they were: vibrant, talented, uniquely shaped puzzle pieces. So as she washed off her green stage makeup and returned to her new life in Chicago, Carla decided to rewrite her story one more time:

~~Carla Stickler is a Broadway actor and voice teacher.~~
~~Carla Stickler is a software engineer working in tech startups.~~
Carla Stickler is a professional multihyphenate advocating for the inclusion of artists in STEM.

The world is changing faster than ever before. In the midst of that change, it can feel daunting to aim for a life that is fulfilling, financially stable, and flexible enough to accommodate all of the dimensions of your Venn diagram. It can also feel like a personal shortcoming when the playbook our parents and grandparents set out for us looks utterly impossible to follow. Yet you are entitled to build a life filled with joy, growth, love, adventure, beauty, and rest. And that's what a Portfolio Life aspires to be.

Over the last 200 or so pages, we've learned how to embrace all of our dimensions, separating our worth from our work. We've uncovered our priorities and developed the vocabulary ("no") and commitment to protect them. And we've stepped into the roles of the CEO, CMO, COO, CFO, CSO—the whole C-suite, really—as we put in place the right people, systems, and tools to make our Portfolio Lives possible.

It takes more work to chart an uncharted course; there's no doubt about that. But that extra work offers you something in return, something your parents and grandparents didn't have: the combination of stability and flexibility that allows you to be as unique and multidimensional as you are. It unlocks the opportunity to forge a future outside of a narrowly defined path, and instead embrace the richness of a life truly worthy of you. And honestly, you should demand nothing less. Because, it's true: You *do* only live once.

Acknowledgments

Hannah Robinson is the type of editor every author dreams of working with. She is somehow a magician, a surgeon, and a therapist who saw what this book could be and coaxed it out, one chapter at a time. Hannah, thank you for your partnership, your pep talks, and your flexibility when I had a baby two months before this manuscript was due. (Let's not do that again, yes?) My thanks as well to the editorial, production, and publicity teams at Grand Central Balance who have been an absolute joy to work with.

Joy Tutela is as much a book doula as an agent, and her team at the David Black Literary Agency is the best of the best. For more than a year she worked with me to find the right way to share these ideas, cycling through seven or eight (truly terrible) versions of the proposal before we landed the plane. Thank you for helping me find the scaffolding to bring this book to life and for our long, meandering talks as I circled Prospect Park mid-pandemic. You kept this book alive even when I insisted it was dead. Thank you.

I had an incredible team of early readers who provided feedback, pushed my research, and questioned how many egregious puns I really needed. My sincere thanks to Sally McGraw, Rene Paula, Alex Cavoulacos, Kathleen Carey, Carla Stickler, and Katie Orenstein for your detailed notes. Thanks as well to the kind humans who allowed me to share their stories in this book. Your inspiring case studies helped make these ideas three dimensional and show the unbelievable range of experiences that can exist in this model. And thank you to my colleagues at Harvard Business School who answered my research questions, provided encouragement, and offered critical feedback on the manuscript. Any errors that remain are mine alone.

The peppy illustrations throughout the book and the templates you can download from the book website are the work of the talented designer Giovanna Castro, who I am grateful to partner up with for the third time. Similarly, I'm delighted to work with Elan Morgan again for the book website and my personal website. They are both incredible human beings and gifted creatives and you'd be wise to reach out to both if you are ever looking for collaborators. My immense thanks as well to Ashley Sandberg and the entire team at Triple7 PR for supporting the publication of this book. It has been an absolute pleasure to work with you.

I owe a debt of gratitude to Cate Scott Campbell for breathing life into three seasons of *The Limit Does Not Exist*. Without you I would have never seen just how many listeners were in search of inspiration and guidance as they built lives outside the status quo. Thank you for taking the podcasting leap with me at SXSW in 2016.

Thank you to my coaches, negotiators, connectors, cheerleaders and truth tellers: Catherine Jennings; Melissa Plamann; Alexandra Silber; Rachel Beider; Carla Stickler; Kathryn Minshew; Alex Cavoulacos; Alex Tryon; Margaret Eby; Glynnis MacNicol; Rachel Sklar; Ann Shoket; Esi Sogah; Megan Lemley; TheLi.st; my sister, Stephanie Alderman; my mom, Beverly Wallace; my in-laws, Kathleen and Charles Carey; and the extended Moron Family clan. Thank you to my Quincy co-founder, Alex Nelson, and our professor, advisor, and investor Tom Eisenmann for being the catalysts for my entrepreneurial journey. I also want to extend my deepest thanks and appreciation to my late mentor, Clayton Christensen.

Finally, I must call out the emotional and logistical support, creative feedback, and enthusiastic childcare from my husband, Chas Carey, that made this book possible. I started it when we had one kid and finished it when we had two, and in between we moved states, he finished an MFA and started a new job, and I taught MBA students up until five days before giving birth. None of this would be possible without the partnership we co-created over the last seven years, and I am so utterly grateful for you and how you show up every day for our family. And to Arden and Sebastian, thank you for turning my life upside down in all of the best ways.

Notes

Introduction: Life, Disrupted

1. Cramer, Reid, Fenaba Addo, Colleen Campbell, J. Choi, B. Cohen, C. Cohen, W. R. Emmons et al., "The Emerging Millennial Wealth Gap," *New America* (October, 2019).
2. Hobbes, Michael, "Generation Screwed," Huffington Post, December 14, 2017, https://highline.huffingtonpost.com/articles/en/poor-millennials/.
3. Baum, Sandy, Diane Cardenas Elliott, Jennifer Ma, and D'Wayne Bell, "Trends in Student Aid, 2013. Trends in Higher Education Series," *College Board* (2013). Calculations based on average per-student borrowing in 1980 and 2010.
4. US Census Bureau, Current Population Survey/Housing Vacancy Survey, March 15, 2022.
5. Projection for the class of 2015 based on a NerdWallet analysis of federal data.
6. Chang, Clio, "The Generation Shaped by Layoffs," GEN x Medium, December 16, 2020, https://gen.medium.com/the-generation-shaped-by-layoffs-e735ef79aa1f.
7. Petersen, Anne Helen, "How Millennials Became the Burnout Generation," Buzz-Feed News, September 14, 2021. https://www.buzzfeednews.com/article/annehelen petersen/millennials-burnout-generation-debt-work.
8. Bialik, Kristen, and Richard Fry, "Millennial Life: How Young Adulthood Today Compares with Prior Generations," Pew Research Center's Social & Demographic Trends Project. Pew Research Center, April 1, 2022. https://www.pewresearch .org/social-trends/2019/02/14/millennial-life-how-young-adulthood-today -compares-with-prior-generations-2/.
9. Gelles, David, *Man Who Broke Capitalism: How Jack Welch Gutted the Heartland and Crushed the Soul of Corporate America—and How to Undo His Legacy* (New York: Simon & Schuster, 2022).

Chapter 1: The New Normal

1. Burke, Peter, *The Polymath: A Cultural History from Leonardo da Vinci to Susan Sontag* (New Haven, CT: Yale University Press, 2021).
2. "Industrialization, Labor, and Life," National Geographic Society, accessed June 26, 2022, https://www.nationalgeographic.org/article/industrialization-labor-and-life/.
3. Rafferty, John P, "The Rise of the Machines: Pros and Cons of the Industrial Revolution," Encyclopedia Britannica, accessed June 26, 2022, https://www.britannica .com/story/the-rise-of-the-machines-pros-and-cons-of-the-industrial-revolution.

4. Niiler, Eric, "How the Second Industrial Revolution Changed Americans' Lives," History.com, January 25, 2019, https://www.history.com/news/second-industrial-revolution-advances.

5. Martin, Roger, "The Age of Customer Capitalism," *Harvard Business Review* 88, no. 1 (2010).

6. "Carbons to Computers," Smithsonian Learning Lab, 1998, http://www.smithsonianeducation.org/educators/lesson_plans/carbons/text/birth.html.

7. Allen, Tammy D., John P. Rafferty, and Grace Young, "State-Organized Farming," Encyclopedia Britannica, November 7, 2014, https://www.britannica.com/topic/history-of-work-organization-648000/State-organized-farming.

8. Pearlstein, Steven, "How the Cult of Shareholder Value Wrecked American Business," *Washington Post*, November 25, 2021, https://www.washingtonpost.com/news/wonk/wp/2013/09/09/how-the-cult-of-shareholder-value-wrecked-american-business.

9. Laura, Robert, "Saying Goodbye to Retirement Traditions," *Forbes*, June 30, 2021, https://www.forbes.com/sites/robertlaura/2013/01/26/saying-goodbye-to-retirement-traditions/.

10. Martin, "The Age of Customer Capitalism."

11. EPI analysis of unpublished Total Economy Productivity data from Bureau of Labor Statistics (BLS) Labor Productivity and Costs program, wage data from the BLS Current Employment Statistics, BLS Employment Cost Trends, BLS Consumer Price Index, and Bureau of Economic Analysis National Income and Product Accounts.

12. "Digest of Education Statistics, 2020," National Center for Education Statistics (NCES), US Department of Education, 2020, https://nces.ed.gov/programs/digest/d20/tables/dt20_330.10.asp.

13. "The State of the Nation's Housing," Joint Center for Housing Studies at Harvard University, 2018.

14. Statistics, US Bureau of Labor, "Consumer Expenditures in 2019," 2020.

15. Statistics, US Bureau of Labor, "Consumer Expenditures in 2021," 2022.

16. Gelles, David, "How Freelancing Is Changing Work," *New York Times*, August 13, 2021, https://www.nytimes.com/2021/08/13/business/hayden-brown-upwork-corner-office.html.

17. Newport, Cal, "Why Are so Many Knowledge Workers Quitting?" *New Yorker*, August 16, 2021, https://www.newyorker.com/culture/office-space/why-are-so-many-knowledge-workers-quitting.

18. Roose, Kevin, "Welcome to the YOLO Economy," *New York Times*, April 21, 2021, https://www.nytimes.com/2021/04/21/technology/welcome-to-the-yolo-economy.html.

19. Kreizman, Maris, "Where Did My Ambition Go?" GEN x Medium, June 26, 2020, https://gen.medium.com/where-did-my-ambition-go-c800ab4ad01d.

20. Thompson, Derek, "Workism Is Making Americans Miserable," *Atlantic*, August 13, 2019, https://www.theatlantic.com/ideas/archive/2019/02/religion-workism-making-americans-miserable/583441.

21. Jai Chakrabarti, "Embracing the Whole You: You Are More than Your Job," Fast

Company, July 6, 2021, https://www.fastcompany.com/90651651/embracing-the -whole-you-you-are-more-than-your-job.

Chapter 2: The Four Pillars of a Portfolio Life

1. Nielsen, Jared A., Brandon A Zielinski, Michael A Ferguson, Janet E. Lainhart, and Jeffrey S. Anderson, "An Evaluation of the Left-Brain vs. Right-Brain Hypothesis with Resting State Functional Connectivity Magnetic Resonance Imaging," *PLoS One* 8, no. 8 (2013): e71275.

2. Gazzaniga, Michael S, "The Split Brain in Man," *Scientific American* 217, no. 2 (1967): 24–29.

3. Pines, Maya, "We Are Left-Brained or Right-Brained," *New York Times Magazine*, September 9, 1973, 32–33.

4. Knoblauch, Max, "Icebreakers with...Mathematician and Former NFL Player John Urschel," Morning Brew, December 10, 2021, https://www.morningbrew .com/daily/stories/2021/12/10/icebreakers-with-mathematician-and-former -nfl-player-john-urschel.

5. Jaschik, Scott, "Age, Experience and Bias," Inside Higher Ed, June 6, 2008, https:// www.insidehighered.com/news/2008/06/06/age-experience-and-bias.

6. Azoulay, Pierre, Benjamin F. Jones, J. Daniel Kim, and Javier Miranda, "Age and High-Growth Entrepreneurship," *American Economic Review: Insights* 2, no. 1 (2020): 65–82.

7. McBride, Sarah, "The Typical Unicorn Founder Started Their Business at 34," Bloomberg, May 21, 2021, https://www.bloomberg.com/news/articles/2021-05-21/what -s-the-average-age-of-a-startup-founder-it-s-34-study-says.

8. Franses, Philip Hans, "When Did Nobel Prize Laureates in Literature Make Their Best Work?" *Creativity Research Journal* 26, no. 3 (2014): 372–374.

9. The actual text is "The only true voyage of discovery, the only fountain of Eternal Youth, would be not to visit strange lands but to possess other eyes, to behold the universe through the eyes of another, of a hundred others, to behold the hundred universes that each of them beholds, that each of them is; and this we can contrive with an Elstir, with a Vinteuil; with men like these we do really fly from star to star." Proust, M, "The Captive (La Prisonnière)," Vol. 5 of *Remembrance of Things Past* (À la Recherche du temps perdu). Translated from the French by CK Scott Moncrieff. A Project Gutenberg of Australia eBook (2018).

10. Dyer, Jeffrey H., Hal Gregersen, and Clayton M. Christensen, "The Innovator's DNA," *Harvard Business Review* 87 (2009).

11. After the HBR article, they published their findings in a book, also worth reading if you're interested: Dyer, Jeff, Hal Gregersen, and Clayton M. Christensen. *Innovator's DNA, Updated, with a New Preface: Mastering the Five Skills of Disruptive Innovators* (Boston, Harvard Business Press, 2019).

12. Handy, Charles, *The Age of Unreason*, Harvard Business Press, 1991.

13. 2019 Layoff Anxiety Study conducted by the Harris Poll on behalf of CareerArc. August 15, 2019. https://resources.intoo.com/guides/layoff-anxiety-study.

14. Lashbrook, Angela, "The Overwhelming Anxiety of Corporate Millennial Tik-Tok," GEN x Medium, April 6, 2021, https://gen.medium.com/the-overwhelming -anxiety-of-corporate-millennial-tiktok-d391b76c2722.

15. Lee, Caroline, "The Power of the Extreme User and Designing (In)correctly," Accomplice, December 19, 2018, https://accpl.co/power-extreme-user-designing-incorrectly/.

16. Aurand, Andrew, Dan Emmanuel, Dan Threet, and Diane Yentel, "Out of Reach," Washington, DC: The National Low Income Housing Coalition, 2021.

17. Novello, Amanda, "The Cost of Inaction: How a Lack of Family Care Policies Burdens the U.S. Economy and Families," National Partnership for Women and Families, July 2021. https://www.nationalpartnership.org/our-work/resources/economic-justice/other/cost-of-inaction-lack-of-family-care-burdens-families.pdf.

Chapter 3: A Caveat: Failure

1. Ramirez, Jeffery, Janalee Isaacson, Deborah Smith, and Brenda Senger, "Teaching Life Lessons: When Millennials Fail," *Building Healthy Academic Communities Journal* 2, no. 1 (2018): 50–59.

2. Sagar, Sam S., David Lavallee, and Christopher M. Spray, "Why Young Elite Athletes Fear Failure: Consequences of Failure," *Journal of Sports Sciences* 25, no. 11 (2007): 1171–1184.

3. Blackburn, Amy C., and Deborah B. Erickson, "Predictable Crises of the Gifted Student," *Journal of Counseling and Development* 64, no. 9 (1986): 552–554.

4. Blackburn, Amy C., and Deborah B. Erickson, "Predictable Crises of the Gifted Student."

5. Seibert, Scott Ed, Maria L. Kraimer, and Peter A. Heslin, "Developing Career Resilience and Adaptability," *Organizational Dynamics* 45, no. 3 (2016): 245–257.

6. Seligman, Martin EP, "Building Resilience," *Harvard Business Review* 89, no. 4 (2011): 100–106.

7. Nathoo, Zulekha, "'Failing Up': Why Some Climb the Ladder Despite Mediocrity," BBC, March 3, 2021, https://www.bbc.com/worklife/article/20210226-failing-up-why-some-climb-the-ladder-despite-mediocrity.

8. Glass, Christy, and Alison Cook, "Performative Contortions: How White Women and People of Colour Navigate Elite Leadership Roles," *Gender, Work & Organization* 27, no. 6 (2020): 1232–1252.

9. Malesic, Jonathan, "The Future of Work Should Mean Working Less," *New York Times*, September 23, 2021, https://www.nytimes.com/interactive/2021/09/23/opinion/covid-return-to-work-rto.html.

10. Ucbasaran, Deniz, Dean A. Shepherd, Andy Lockett, and S. John Lyon, "Life After Business Failure: The Process and Consequences of Business Failure for Entrepreneurs," *Journal of Management* 39, no. 1 (2013): 163–202.

11. Nobel, Carmen, "Why Companies Fail—and How Their Founders Can Bounce Back," HBS Working Knowledge, March 7, 2011, https://hbswk.hbs.edu/item/why-companies-failand-how-their-founders-can-bounce-back.

12. Block, Jeanne H., "Differential Premises Arising from Differential Socialization of the Sexes: Some Conjectures," *Child Development* 54, no. 6 (1983): 1335–1354.

Chapter 4: What's In Your Venn Diagram?

1. Griffin, Abbie, and John R. Hauser, "The Voice of the Customer," *Marketing Science* 12, no. 1 (1993): 1–27.

2. Guest, Greg, Emily Namey, and Mario Chen, "A Simple Method to Assess and Report Thematic Saturation in Qualitative Research," *PLoS One* 15, no. 5 (2020): e0232076.

3. Petanjek, Zdravko, et al. "Extraordinary Neoteny of Synaptic Spines in the Human Prefrontal Cortex," *Proceedings of the National Academy of Sciences* 108, no. 32 (2011): 13281–13286.

4. Steimer, Andreas, and André Mata, "Motivated Implicit Theories of Personality: My Weaknesses Will Go Away, but My Strengths Are Here to Stay," *Personality and Social Psychology Bulletin* 42, no. 4 (2016): 415–429.

Chapter 5: Design the Business Model for Your Life

1. Rosario, Isabella, "When the 'Hustle' Isn't Enough," NPR, April 3, 2020, https://www.npr.org/sections/codeswitch/2020/04/03/826015780/when-the-hustle-isnt-enough.

2. Carter, Niambi M., "Why Black People Should Be Rethinking the 'Hustle' Mentality," TheGrio, July 3, 2020, https://thegrio.com/2020/07/03/black-hustle-mentality/.

3. Baptiste, Bethany, "The Tragedies of Trying to Get Agented," Bethany Baptiste, October 25, 2020, https://www.bethanybaptiste.com/blog/the-tragedies-of-trying-to-get-agented.

4. "Seven Years a 'Cobbler.'" Einstein at the patent office. Swiss Federal Institute of Intellectual Property, accessed June 26, 2022, https://www.ige.ch/en/about-us/the-history-of-the-ipi/einstein/einstein-at-the-patent-office.

5. Sessions, Hudson, Jennifer D. Nahrgang, Manuel J. Vaulont, Raseana Williams, and Amy L. Bartels, "Do the Hustle! Empowerment from Side-Hustles and Its Effects on Full-Time Work Performance," *Academy of Management Journal* 64, no. 1 (2021): 235–264.

6. Blint-Welsh, Tyler, "Stacey Abrams on Her New Book and Why Publishers Passed Twice," *Wall Street Journal*, April 26, 2021, https://www.wsj.com/articles/stacey-abrams-interview-book-justice-sleeps-11619440116.

Chapter 6: Craft Your Portfolio

1. Gagne, Yasmin, "Prince Harry Says Quitting Can Be Good for Your Mental Health," *Fast Company*, December 6, 2021, https://www.fastcompany.com/90702784/prince-harry-says-quitting-can-be-good-for-your-mental-health.

Chapter 7: Define Your Personal Balanced Scorecard

1. Raja, Siva, and Sharon L. Stein, "Work–Life Balance: History, Costs, and Budgeting for Balance," *Clinics in Colon and Rectal Surgery* 27, no. 2 (2014): 71.

2. Moss Kanter, Rosabeth, "The Imperfect Balance between Work and Life," *Harvard Business Review*, August 7, 2014, https://hbr.org/2012/08/the-imperfect-balance-between.

3. Wynn, Alison T., and Aliya Hamid Rao. "Failures of Flexibility: How Perceived Control Motivates the Individualization of Work–Life Conflict," *ILR Review* 73, no. 1 (2020): 61–90.

4. Mazmanian, Melissa, Wanda J. Orlikowski, JoAnne Yates, "The Autonomy Paradox:

The Implications of Mobile Email Devices for Knowledge Professionals," *Organization Science* 24, no. 5 (2013): V1337–1357.

5.   Wynn, "Failures of Flexibility."

Chapter 8: Build Your Team

1.   Taussig, Alex, "3 Ways to Land a VC Job," *Fortune*, February 16, 2012, https://fortune.com/2012/02/16/3-ways-to-land-a-vc-job/.

2.   Feeney, Brooke C., et al., "Predicting the Pursuit and Support of Challenging Life Opportunities," *Personality and Social Psychology Bulletin* 43, no.8 (2017): 1171–1187.

Chapter 9: Tell Your Story

1.   Gee, Laura K., Jason Jones, and Moira Burke, "Social Networks and Labor Markets: How Strong Ties Relate to Job Finding on Facebook's Social Network," *Journal of Labor Economics* 35, no. 2 (2017): 485–518.

2.   Granovetter, Mark S., "The Strength of Weak Ties," *American Journal of Sociology* 78, no. 6 (1973): 1360–1380.

Chapter 10: Manage Your Time

1.   Edwards, Jim, "Reddit's Alexis Ohanian Says 'Hustle Porn' Is 'One of the Most Toxic, Dangerous Things in Tech Right Now,'" Business Insider, November 6, 2018, https://www.businessinsider.com/reddit-alexis-ohanian-hustle-porn-toxic-dangerous-thing-in-tech-2018-11.

2.   Goh, Joel, Jeffrey Pfeffer, and Stefanos A. Zenios, "The Relationship between Workplace Stressors and Mortality and Health Costs in the United States," *Management Science* 62, no. 2 (2016): 608–628.

3.   Schulte, Brigid, "Working Ourselves to Death: What Is American Karoshi?" New America, April 11, 2022, https://www.newamerica.org/better-life-lab/blog/working-ourselves-to-death-what-is-american-karoshi/.

4.   Nakajima, Seiichi, *Introduction to TPM: Total Productive Maintenance* (New York: Productivity Press, 1988): 129.

5.   Lu, Jingyi, Quingwen Fang, and Tian Qiu, "Rejectors Overestimate the Negative Consequences They Will Face from Refusal," *Journal of Experimental Psychology*; Applied (2022).

6.   "[Infographic] Cost of Industrial Downtime: 20 Mind-Boggling Stats," BehrTech, May 11, 2021, https://behrtech.com/blog/infographic-20-mind-boggling-stats-on-cost-of-industrial-downtime.

7.   Pinsker, Joe, "What Is Life Like When We Subtract Work from It?" *Atlantic*, May 23, 2022, https://www.theatlantic.com/family/archive/2022/05/us-sabbatical-helps-work-burnout/629956/.

8.   DiDonna, DJ, "The Urgent Case for Sabbaticals for All," Time, November 17, 2021, https://time.com/charter/6120287/sabbaticals-time-off-great-resignation/.

9. "2019 Employee Benefits Survey," Society for Human Resource Management, April 24, 2020, https://www.shrm.org/hr-today/trends-and-forecasting/research-and -surveys/pages/benefits19.aspx.

Chapter 11: Crunch the Numbers

1. Bennett, Jessica, "I'll Share My Salary Information If You Share Yours," *New York Times*, January 9, 2020, https://www.nytimes.com/2020/01/09/style/women-salary -transparency.html.
2. Bullock, Maggie, "Aminatou Sow on Making $300,000 and Sending Money to Her Family," The Cut, March 1, 2019, https://www.thecut.com/2019/03/aminatou-sow -interview-money-spending.html.
3. Perhach, Paulette, "A Story of a Fuck Off Fund," The Billfold, January 20, 2016, https://www.thebillfold.com/2016/01/a-story-of-a-fuck-off-fund/.

Chapter 12: Forecast the Future

1. Schwab, Klaus, Thierry Malleret, and Amy Webb, "Futurist Amy Webb on Why Scenario Planning Is Key to Creating a More Resilient World," World Economic Forum, January 19, 2022, https://www.weforum.org/agenda/2022/01/futurist-amy -webb-on-the-importance-of-scenario-planning/.
2. MIT Sloan Management Review, "6 The Flare and Focus of Successful Futurists," in *When Innovation Moves at Digital Speed: Strategies and Tactics to Provoke, Sustain, and Defend Innovation in Today's Unsettled Markets* (Cambridge, MA: MIT Press, 2018): 101–110.
3. MIT Sloan Management Review, "6 The Flare and Focus of Successful Futurists."
4. MIT Sloan Management Review, "6 The Flare and Focus of Successful Futurists."
5. McGonigal, Jane, *Imaginable: How to See the Future Coming and Feel Ready for Anything—Even Things That Seem Impossible Today* (New York: Spiegel & Grau, 2022).
6. Division of Reproductive Health, National Center for Chronic Disease Prevention and Health Promotion, "Pregnancy Mortality Surveillance System," Centers for Disease Control and Prevention, accessed June 26, 2022, https://www.cdc.gov /reproductivehealth/maternal-mortality/pregnancy-mortality-surveillance-system .htm.

Conclusion: Build a Life Worthy of You

1. Paulson, Michael, "Now Is the Winter of Broadway's Discontent," *New York Times* January 16, 2022, https://www.nytimes.com/2022/01/16/theater/broadway-omicron -closings.html.

About the Author

A self-described "human Venn diagram," **Christina Wallace** has built a career at the intersection of business, technology, and the arts. She is currently a Senior Lecturer of Entrepreneurial Management at Harvard Business School and is an active startup mentor and angel investor. She was previously co-host of *The Limit Does Not Exist*, a podcast about the intersection of STEM and the arts, and co-authored *New to Big: How Companies Can Create Like Entrepreneurs, Invest Like VCs, and Install a Permanent Operating System for Growth* (April 2019, Currency).

A serial entrepreneur, Christina spent a decade building businesses in fashion, media, and edtech, including a venture inside the American Museum of Natural History focused on getting more girls into coding and technology. She was also, very briefly, a management consultant with the Boston Consulting Group and began her career at the Metropolitan Opera. Christina studied piano and cello at Interlochen Arts Academy, graduated magna cum laude from Emory University with degrees in mathematics and theater studies, and earned an MBA from Harvard Business School.

In her free time, she sings with various chamber choirs; embarks on adventure travel, including summiting Mount Kilimanjaro and trekking to Everest Base Camp; and is a mediocre endurance athlete, with twenty-two half marathons, three triathlons, and three (slow) marathons under her belt. She lives in Cambridge with her husband, Chas Carey, and their two children, Arden and Sebastian.